SONDERKOMMANDO ELBE

SONDERKOMMANDO ELBE

The Luftwaffe's Kamikaze Force

Walter S. Zapotoczny Jr.

First published in Great Britain in 2026 by
Fonthill
An imprint of
Pen & Sword Books Ltd
Yorkshire – Philadelphia

Copyright © Walter S. Zapotoczny Jr. 2026

ISBN 978-1-78155-941-3

The right of Walter S. Zapotoczny Jr. to be identified as Author of this work has been asserted by him in accordance with the Copyright, Designs and Patents Act 1988.

A CIP catalogue record for this book is available from the British Library.

All rights reserved. No part of this book may be reproduced, transmitted, downloaded, decompiled or reverse engineered in any form or by any means, electronic or mechanical including photocopying, recording or by any information storage and retrieval system, without permission from the Publisher in writing. NO AI TRAINING: Without in any way limiting the Author's and Publisher's exclusive rights under copyright, any use of this publication to "train" generative artificial intelligence (AI) technologies to generate text is expressly prohibited. The Author and Publisher reserve all rights to license uses of this work for generative AI training and development of machine learning language models.

Typeset by Simon and Sons ITES Services Pvt. Ltd., Chennai, India.
Printed and bound in the UK by CPI Group (UK) Ltd, Croydon, CR0 4YY

The Publisher's authorised representative in the EU for product safety is Authorised Rep Compliance Ltd., Ground Floor, 71 Lower Baggot Street, Dublin D02 P593, Ireland.
www.arccompliance.com

For a complete list of Pen & Sword titles please contact
PEN & SWORD BOOKS LIMITED
47 Church Street, Barnsley, South Yorkshire, S70 2AS, England
E-mail: enquiries@pen-and-sword.co.uk
Website: www.pen-and-sword.co.uk
Or
PEN AND SWORD BOOKS
1950 Lawrence Rd, Havertown, PA 19083, USA
E-mail: Uspen-and-sword@casematepublishers.com

For those who fought in the skies over Europe

Foreword

In full disclosure, I was Dr. Walter Zapotoczny's professor at American Military University, where I taught hundreds of students with varying degrees of interest in history, and likewise varying levels of intellectual, writing, and research skills. Most of my courses required me to spend a lot of my time teaching academic writing as much as teaching history.

Many students took a lot of cultivating to get them up to the accepted level required to complete these courses. Others started out already prepared for the rigors they would endure. Walter was one of the latter, and he became one of only thirteen students I recommended for the Great Papers forum to graduate with honors. He was one of my best.

We remained in contact over the years, and his interest in World War II was equal to mine, and as he wrote books and conducted research we would speak from time to time. I knew about his project on Sonderkommando Elbe, and he reached out to me, knowing that I was a Luftwaffe expert, with hundreds of interviews with former German pilots and a few TV documentaries, films, and books to my credit.

I knew after I read the rough draft that he had a winner with this subject, and I had great first-person information from some of the participants who planned and commanded this unit. I gladly shared this information with Walter, as I have done with other up-and-coming historians, such as Adam Makos. I found it gratifying to see a former student reach the highest levels of academia and start publishing books of this nature as well as teaching. Both are very demanding.

Walter's approach to the subject is nothing less than what I had expected; detailed, poignant, and informative, but most important historically accurate. Writing military history is difficult enough due to the research that is involved, but to write about a group of young men who were ideologically driven or simply desperate enough to volunteer to throw their lives away in such a lost cause demands a different intellectual approach.

What you will read will be how this amazing and insane concept became an operational reality, which is probably difficult for most readers to comprehend. However, it did happen; young men (some being mere boys) on both sides did die, a few survived, and the rest as they say is "history," and Walter has prepared it for you. I am proud of him.

Prof. Colin D. Heaton
Gloucester, NC

Acknowledgments

Thank you Rene Scheer for providing all the German books and materials. They helped immensely. A special thanks to Colin Heaton, professor, author and old friend, for sharing his interviews and pictures, for editing and writing the Foreword.

Adolf Galland in his bomber jacket, 1945. (*Luftwaffe Archives*)

Contents

Foreword		7
Acknowledgments		9
Introduction		13
1	The Bombing of Germany	17
2	The Strategic Situation in Late 1944/Early 1945	34
3	Defending the Skies of the Reich	44
4	The State of the Luftwaffe in Late 1944/Early 1945	59
5	Special Aviation Units Before Sonderkommando Elbe	68
6	Creation of Sonderkommando Elbe	92
7	Use of Pervitin by Sonderkommando Elbe Pilots	108
8	Eighth Air Force Target List for April 7, 1945	111
9	The Attack on April 7, 1945	119
10	Sonderkommando Pilots	146
11	Allied Reports	163
12	Damage to Allied Bombers	171
13	The Aftermath of the Sonderkommando Elbe Mission	175
14	Epilogue	181
Appendix A: Abbreviations and Definitions		184
Appendix B: U.S. Eighth Air Force Aircraft Types Used on April 7, 1945		188
Appendix C: Aircraft Used by Sonderkommando Elbe on April 7, 1945		194
Appendix D: Aircraft Used by the Wilde Sau		198
Appendix E: United States Airborne Weapons		200
Appendix F: German Airborne Weapons		201
Appendix G: Selected Biographies		204
Endnotes		207
Bibliography		219

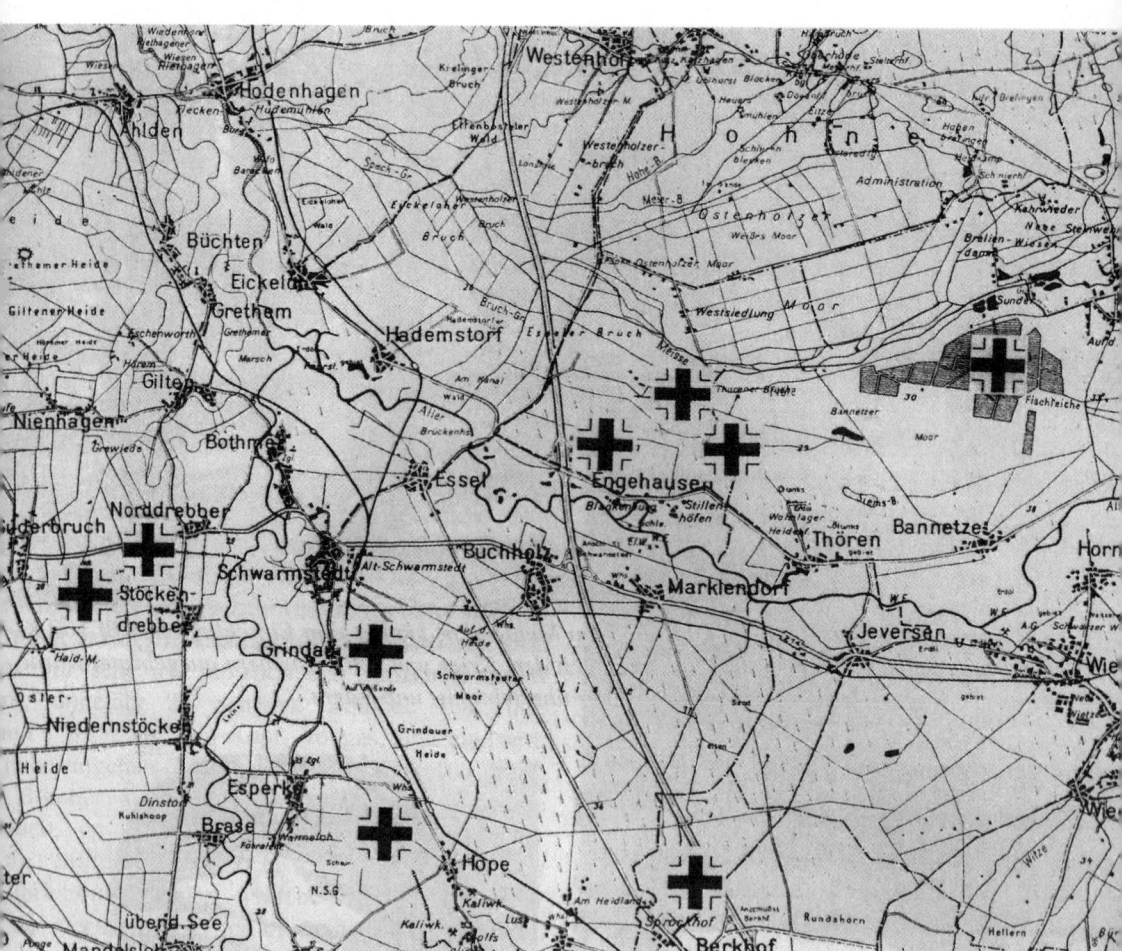

Locations of crashed German fighters, April 7, 1945. (*Bundesarchiv*)

Introduction

The Sonderkommando Elbe was a terrifying example of the depths to which desperation can drive men.
—Winston Churchill

One of the lengthiest and most brutal campaigns during World War II unfolded in the open skies of Western Europe between 1943 and 1945, constituting an unparalleled aerial clash that remains etched in history. The stage was set for this epic confrontation between the United States Army Air Forces (USAAF) and the Luftwaffe (German Air Force), marking a pivotal chapter in the annals of warfare. The USAAF embarked on an ambitious offensive, aiming to cripple Germany's industrial prowess through precise bombing. Their overarching objective was to showcase the supremacy of air power as a solitary force capable of securing victory. The Luftwaffe, on the defensive, valiantly resisted the relentless onslaught of American bombers, employing seasoned pilots and a formidable array of fighter aircraft, including the battle-tested Messerschmitt Bf 109 and the exceptional Focke-Wulf Fw 190. The protracted conflict gradually tilted in favor of the United States, prompting Germany to unleash a series of cutting-edge jet and rocket aircraft. Among these, the Me 262 jet fighter and Me 163 Komet rocket fighter emerged as lethal adversaries, surpassing anything the Americans had in their arsenal. Notwithstanding Germany's technological advancements that outpaced Allied research during this period, the resultant weapons faced challenges in development. Despite their potential, Adolf Hitler and other leaders within the Third Reich squandered any strategic advantage that these innovations might have conferred upon the Germans. The war in the skies over Western Europe thus became a testament to the intricate interplay between technological progress, strategic decisions, and the ultimate outcomes of one of the most monumental conflicts in human history.

In the twilight of World War II, as the Nazi regime grappled with the relentless advance of the Allied forces, a last-ditch effort emerged from the depths of desperation. Germany, beset by a series of significant setbacks and faced with the encroaching tide of the Allies, found itself in dire need of a game-changing strategy. It was in this crucible of desperation that the concept of Sonderkommando Elbe was born—a unit that drew inspiration from the harrowing exploits of Japanese *Kamikaze* pilots wreaking havoc in the Pacific theater. Sonderkommando, meaning "special command" in German, was an apt moniker for this audacious undertaking, and Elbe, a tribute to the prominent river coursing through Germany, reflected the Nazi High Command's determination to stymie the Western Allies' progress at all costs.

The Zeppelin Company in Germany, named after Count Ferdinand von Zeppelin, was working on a rocket plane when the war ended. It was called the Zeppelin Rammer. The Rammer was to be towed aloft by another fighter (probably an Me 109 or Me 110) and then released at the desired altitude. After being released, it would ignite a solid-fuel rocket and accelerate to 600mph. The small plane had fourteen small rockets housed in its nose, which could be fired at an enemy aircraft. The fighter could then make a second pass to ram the target if needed. The designers were convinced that the Rammer would be able to slice through a bomber's tail section with little or no damage to itself due to the heavily reinforced leading edges on the wings. After an attack, the Rammer would glide to the ground and land on its retractable skid. The Rammer was proposed in the last six months of the war, but its progress never went beyond the design stage.

The notion of Sonderkommando Elbe was more than a mere tactical maneuver; it was a manifestation of unwavering fanaticism and fervent allegiance to the Nazi cause. The pilots chosen for this unit were not mere volunteers; they were zealots, driven by an unshakable belief in the righteousness of their mission. These aviators viewed themselves as sacrificial martyrs, prepared to forfeit their lives to safeguard their homeland from the encroaching tide of the Allies. While the similarity to the Japanese *Kamikaze* ethos might seem apparent, a fundamental distinction set the German approach apart. Japanese pilots embarking on suicide missions were committed to remaining at the helm of their planes until impact, often with the unfortunate outcome of missing their intended targets. In stark contrast, the German pilots were directed to ram their aircraft into enemy planes and jettison the canopy before impact, and if they survived, to jump out. Most would jump just before impact—a tactical directive that afforded them the slim chance of survival.

Sonderkommando Elbe's combat debut occurred during the war's waning days, a testament to the depth of the Nazi regime's desperation. The unit's pilots engaged in daring sorties, successfully downing several enemy aircraft through their audacious maneuvers. Yet these triumphs were purchased at an exorbitant price—the lives of many young pilots who perished in the throes of combat. The unit's short-lived existence, born of dire necessity and fervent loyalty, was ultimately dissolved as the war's end became inevitable.

The saga of Sonderkommando Elbe unfolds as a haunting testament to the concluding chapters of the Nazi regime, unraveling a narrative that delves into the profound desperation and unyielding determination of its adherents. In the closing days of World War II the aviators of Sonderkommando Elbe emerged as a striking embodiment of allegiance, standing poised to endure any extremity for the sake of their country's cause.

As the Nazi regime faced imminent collapse, the Sonderkommando Elbe pilots were tasked with a desperate and perilous mission—to ram their fighter planes into Allied bombers. This unconventional tactic aimed to disrupt the formidable air power of the Allies and buy precious time for the crumbling German war effort. The aviators willingly embraced this *Kamikaze*-like strategy, illustrating the extreme lengths individuals can go to when fueled by ideological fervor. Their sacrifice, however, did not alter the course of history. Instead, it remains a poignant chapter in the annals of warfare, highlighting the complexities of human allegiance and the harrowing choices individuals make in the throes of desperation.

This book investigates the period leading up to and after the constituting of Sonderkommando Elbe and delves deep into the lives and experiences of the audacious pilots involved. The narratives unearthed offer a glimpse into their diverse backgrounds, the motivations that propelled them, and the trials they faced as members of this unconventional unit. Through meticulous analysis of previously undisclosed documents and firsthand accounts, this book provides a comprehensive chronicle of one of the most extraordinary and enigmatic military formations in history. This endeavor is not solely a recollection of the pilots; it is also an excavation of the driving ideology that steered these individuals toward their selfless acts. Embedded within their stories is an exploration of the tenacity of nationalism and a stark portrayal of the consequences wrought by unswerving devotion to a cause.

Sonderkommando Elbe's mission was more than a strategic gambit; it was a desperate gamble to alter the course of history in the dying embers of World War II. The endeavor rallied a cohort of highly skilled and committed pilots who stood ready to relinquish their lives, propelling their aircraft into Allied bombers with the aim of disrupting the enemy's relentless bombing campaign. For the pilots, the risks were insurmountable, but their resolve was unshakeable. Driven by an unwavering sense of duty and an unbreakable loyalty to their nation, they embraced a perilous path with the fervent hope of turning the tide of battle and safeguarding Germany from its impending doom.

USAAF 8th AIR FORCE BOMBER BASES (HEAVY) IN ENGLAND DURING WWII
TAIL FIN & WING IDENTIFICATION LETTERS

1st AIR DIVISION B17s

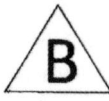

(SAMPLE LETTER)

2nd AIR DIVISION B24s

(SAMPLE LETTER)

3rd AIR DIVISION B17s

(SAMPLE LETTER)

GROUP LETTER	BOMB GROUP	LOCATION	GROUP LETTER	BOMB GROUP	LOCATION	GROUP LETTER	BOMB GROUP	LOCATION
A	91st	BASSINGBOURN	A	44th	SHIPDHAM	A	94th	BURY ST EDMUNDS (ROUGHAM)
B	92nd	PODINGTON	B	93rd	HARDWICK	B	95th	HORHAM
C	303rd	MOLESWORTH	C	389th	HETHEL	C	96th	SNETTERTON HEATH
G	305th	CHELVESTON	D	392nd	WENDLING	D	100th	THORPE ABBOTTS
H	306th	THURLEIGH	F	445th	TIBENHAM	G	385th	GREAT ASHFIELD
J	351st	POLEBROOK	H	446th	BUNGAY (FLIXTON)	H	388th	KNETTISHALL/FERSFIELD
K	379th	KIMBOLTON	I	448th	SEETHING	J	390th	FRAMLINGHAM (PARHAM)
L	381st	RIDGEWELL	J	453rd	OLD BUCKENHAM	K	447th	RATTLESDEN
P	384th	GRAFTON UNDERWOOD	K	458th	HORSHAM ST FAITH	L	452nd	DEOPHAM GREEN
S	401st	DEENETHORPE	L	466th	ATTLEBRIDGE	P	487th	LAVENHAM
U	457th	GLATTON	P	467th	RACKHEATH	S	34th	MENDLESHAM
W	398th	NUTHAMPSTEAD	U	492nd	NORTH PICKENHAM	T	490th	EYE
No Letter	482nd	ALCONBURY	W	489th	HALESWORTH	W	486th	SUDBURY
			Z	491st	METFIELD/NORTH PICKENHAM	X	493rd	DEBACH

Eighth Air Force bomber bases in England. (*Eighth Air Force Archives*)

1
The Bombing of Germany

During the Battle of Britain (July 10 to October 31, 1940) and the London Blitz (September 1940 until May 1941), the British populace was eager to demonstrate its resilience and sought retribution for the destruction of the nation's cities. In response, the RAF's (Royal Air Force) Bomber Command initiated a series of retaliatory nuisance raids, initially targeting Berlin and German military installations. As the campaign progressed, the focus shifted towards German cities in an attempt to undermine the morale of the German population. Daytime missions resulted in significant British losses, prompting a switch to nighttime bombing. However, precision bombing under the cover of darkness proved challenging, with many bombers struggling to locate and hit their targets. Only a third of the bombs landed within 5 miles of their intended destinations, making the RAF attacks more perilous for livestock than for Germans. Additionally, the lack of fighter escort for the RAF bombers led to increased losses to German night fighters.[1]

Realizing the inadequacy of their bomber force, British Prime Minister Winston Churchill made the decision in November 1941 to scale-up the bombing offensive against Germany, obtaining cabinet approval to bolster Bomber Command to 4,000 aircraft. In February 1942, Air Chief Marshal Arthur Harris assumed leadership of Bomber Command, earning the nickname "Bomber" Harris.[2] Harris diverged from the strategy of precision bombing, dismissing it as a panacea that allowed easy repairs to pinpoint targets. Instead, he advocated for large-scale area-bombing assaults on population centers, aiming to render inhabitants homeless and diminish civilian morale, particularly among industrial workers. Harris firmly believed that this form of bombing alone could secure victory in the war against Germany.[3]

Fortunately for Harris, the British aircraft industry was in the early stages of producing a significant quantity of four-engine, long-range bombers such as the Avro Lancaster and Handley Page Halifax. These aircraft were capable of carrying the heavy bombloads and massive bombs that Harris had envisioned for his strategy. To validate his theory of area bombing, Harris opted to target several

German cities based on their vulnerability and proximity to England, rather than their military significance. The initial city chosen was Lubeck, a German port, which the RAF bombed on the night of March 28, 1942. Over half of the city, with buildings primarily constructed from wood, was engulfed in flames.

Subsequently, the German city of Rostock-Warnemünde, housing a Heinkel aircraft factory, was subjected to bombing over four nights, yielding even more favorable results. Encouraged by these accomplishments, Harris authorized Operation Millennium, a thousand-plane raid on Cologne scheduled for the night of May 27, 1942. This monumental bomber force, the largest aerial armada ever assembled, flattened 600 acres of the city, demolishing 250 factories, resulting in 469 casualties, and igniting a fire visible for 200 miles. Remarkably, only forty-one bombers were lost in the mission.[4]

The success of the Cologne raid provided a significant morale boost for Bomber Command, and the newly knighted Sir Arthur Harris authorized similar raids in June on the German cities of Essen, housing the massive Krupp armaments works, and Bremen, where the Focke-Wulf factory was situated. Unfortunately, these raids yielded limited success, with many RAF bombers lost to flak and enemy fighters. The challenges of organizing such huge numbers of aircraft ruled out further large-scale attacks until Bomber Command could regain its full strength. More concerning was the observation that Cologne and the other targeted cities were gradually recovering, with German war materiel production remaining relatively unaffected. Intelligence reports even indicated that the morale of German civilians was surprisingly high, contrary to the British belief that only they could endure such spirits amidst bombing attacks, as seen during the Blitz of London.

Harris required support for Bomber Command to achieve victory according to his strategy. He harbored hopes that the U.S. Eighth Air Force, gradually forming in England, could provide precisely what he needed.[5]

On February 20, 1942, Brigadier General Ira C. Eaker of the USAAF arrived in London, with the immediate task of identifying suitable locations for U.S. bomber bases. His superior, General Henry H. "Hap" Arnold, the head of the USAAF, had instructed Eaker to both assess Bomber Command and eventually lead the U.S. bombing offensive once a sufficient number of bombers had been transported from the United States.[6]

Eaker and Arnold were proponents of the theories of former U.S. general 'Billy' Mitchell, who, after World War I, advocated that the upcoming conflict would be determined in the skies. Mitchell believed that targeting crucial military production sites through bombing would cripple the enemy's ability to wage war and break their will to fight. This perspective aligned with the ideas of Italian air power theorist General Giulio Douhet and the first air chief marshal of the RAF, Hugh Trenchard, in the 1920s. Trenchard specifically argued that a devastating aerial assault would lead to a breakdown in civilian morale and potentially spark a revolution.

Mitchell, Douhet, and Trenchard all envisioned the bomber as the primary weapon in future wars, considering it invincible.[7] Despite the challenges faced by Luftwaffe bombers in the Battle of Britain, American generals insisted that their more heavily armed bombers would ultimately triumph against the Germans. Former British Prime Minister Stanley Baldwin, a supporter of this belief, famously stated, "The bomber will always get through,"[8] emphasizing the perceived superiority of heavily armed bombers against enemy pursuit planes.

The strategic perspective of American generals also drew from theories developed at the Air Corps Tactical School in Maxwell Field, Alabama. According to these ideas, every industrialized nation had vulnerable economic sectors, the destruction of which would lead to the collapse of the entire national economy. These critical bottleneck industries encompassed ball bearing manufacturing plants, petroleum production facilities, and transportation systems. This conceptual framework ultimately influenced the selection of numerous military targets by the American military.

After his arrival in London, Eaker held discussions with his British counterpart, Harris, and they quickly discerned significant disparities in their approaches to conducting the bombing offensive. One major point of contention was the choice between day and night bombing. The British had endured substantial casualties during daytime operations and found that night missions were more successful, resulting in fewer losses. Harris attempted to persuade Eaker to collaborate with the RAF on their night bombing missions. However, Eaker argued that the American bomber crews en route to England were exclusively trained for daylight missions, and retraining would necessitate several months.[9] Furthermore, the involvement of the emerging U.S. bomber force in the RAF's nighttime missions would impede the commencement of the Eighth Air Force's independent operations, scheduled to begin later that year.

Another point of contention revolved around the choice between precision and area bombing. Although less precise, area bombing demonstrated its devastating potential, as evidenced by the RAF raid on Cologne, particularly in the context of night missions. On the other hand, pinpoint precision bombing offered the advantage of crippling crucial German installations, such as factories and oil plants, while minimizing civilian casualties. The American bombers possessed an impressive tool enabling precision bombing—the Norden bombsight. This device was integrated with the bomber's automatic pilot, allowing the bombardier, when focusing on the bombsight, to position the aircraft more accurately over the target. The Norden bombsight was renowned for its precision, with claims that it could "drop a bomb in a pickle barrel from 20,000 feet."[10]

However, Harris argued that frequent cloudy weather, which covered Europe 60 to 70 percent of the time, combined with the smoke generated by German industry, could render the bombsight ineffective. He contended that to hit a barrel from 20,000 feet, one must first be able to see the barrel, highlighting the potential limitations of precision bombing under certain weather and environmental conditions.

Ultimately, the Allies disagreed on the choice of bombers. In 1942, the primary heavy bomber for the USAAF was the Boeing B-17, known as the Flying Fortress. This aircraft was heavily armed with ten .50-caliber machine guns, providing more firepower than the main British heavy bomber, the Lancaster. Eaker, adhering to the doctrine of the heavy bomber, asserted that the B-17's firepower would enable it to withstand daylight attacks by Luftwaffe fighters, even without protective fighter escort. General Arnold later rejected the British request for the United States to build Lancasters, as he believed they were inadequately armed.[11]

The British, however, were skeptical about the B-17's performance. Its bombload, approximately 4,000lb, was significantly smaller than that of the Lancaster, which, when modified, could carry up to 10,000lb of bombs. The Lancaster would later carry the 22,000lb "Big Boy" bomb against the German battleship *Tirpitz*. Additionally, several Flying Fortresses used by Bomber Command in a few 1941 raids had been heavily damaged by German fighters. Eaker countered that the British had misused the B-17, emphasizing its effectiveness in large formations where its collective firepower would be formidable. He acknowledged that for added protection, the Fortresses should ideally have fighter escort as far as the fighters' range permitted.[12]

Eaker believed that if the Americans conducted daylight bombing while the British continued their nighttime raids, it would exhaust the German defenses by maintaining round-the-clock alertness. This strategy would compel the Luftwaffe to divert some of its aircraft from the Russian offensive, alleviating pressure on the Soviets, who were urging Britain and the United States to establish a second front. Harris, however, remained doubtful about the U.S. capability to conduct successful daylight bombing. Consequently, persistent debates between the two resolute commanders ensued throughout the initial months of Eaker's tenure in England.[13]

In the spring of 1942, Harris handed over some old RAF bases to Eaker and the Eighth Air Force, assisting the Americans in acquiring land for constructing additional airfields. The majority of these bases were situated northeast of London in East Anglia, strategically positioned for easy access to Europe and, eventually, Germany. By June of the same year, the final preparations were completed for the first among the 127 bases that the Eighth Air Force would occupy. Soon after, the initial B-17s and their crews arrived, having flown 2,119 miles from the United States through Newfoundland, Greenland, and Scotland. The RAF contributed by providing crucial gunnery training to the American crews. During this period, Major General Carl Spaatz, the new commander of the Eighth Air Force, also arrived. Gradually, the Eighth Air Force was coming together as a formidable fighting force.

On August 17, the 97th Bomb Group of the Eighth Air Force conducted the first USAAF daylight bombing mission over Europe. Twelve B-17s, escorted by RAF Spitfires to the French coast, targeted the railroad marshaling yards and repair shops at Rouen, 65 miles northwest of Paris. Approximately half of the bombs hit the intended target, and all the bombers returned to base safely, encountering minimal resistance from some Luftwaffe Fw 190 fighters. Eaker, who participated as an observer, expressed satisfaction with the outcome of this initial American test of daylight bombing.[14]

Two days later, twenty-four B-17s targeted a Luftwaffe fighter base at Abbeville in northeast France, achieving high bombing accuracy without any aircraft losses. On September 5, the Eighth Air Force experienced its first heavy bomber losses when two B-17s were shot down during a raid on an aircraft factory near Rouen. Due to a missed rendezvous, nine Flying Fortresses without fighter escort confronted twenty attacking Bf 109s and Fw 190s. Despite the losses, Eaker believed that the B-17 had demonstrated its ability to defend itself against enemy fighter attacks if necessary.

A more significant test occurred on October 9, when the largest U.S. attacking force to date, comprising 108 bombers, targeted the French steelworks at Lille. Among these aircraft was the other main U.S. heavy bomber, the Consolidated B-24. While the B-24 could fly faster and carry a larger bombload than the B-17, it was believed that the Flying Fortress could endure more battle damage. Both bombers faced heavy opposition from Luftwaffe fighters during the raid. Only nine bombs hit the target, and the force lost three B-17s and one B-24. Despite these losses, the Americans were jubilant after the raid because gunners reported shooting down fifty-six Luftwaffe fighters. However, this claim was later revealed to be a significant exaggeration, as only one German fighter was confirmed lost.[15]

By the autumn of 1942, the Eighth Air Force was filled with confidence. In its initial missions, it had incurred minimal losses, thereby validating U.S. confidence in daylight precision bombing. The British were also starting to ease their demands for the Americans to shift to night bombing. Even with fighter escort only until the French coast, the Americans believed their bombers could withstand any challenges posed by the Luftwaffe. However, it is important to note that the conditions during these early missions had worked in favor of the United States. The weather had been excellent, and the severity of antiaircraft fire and fighter attacks had been relatively low. Furthermore, while the British were conducting raids deep into German airspace, the early U.S. missions had targeted sites in France, Belgium, and the Netherlands, which were relatively close to their home bases. Crucially, they had yet to encounter the full strength of the Luftwaffe.[16]

The initial jubilation following the Eighth Air Force's successful bombing raids on France was short-lived as the final months of 1942 brought setbacks. Unfavorable weather conditions led to the cancellation of numerous missions, with only twelve being carried out in November and December. The situation worsened when the Eighth received orders to transfer almost one hundred bombers and crews to support Operation Torch, the Allied invasion of North Africa. This move also elevated General Eaker to the head of the Eighth, replacing General Spaatz, who now led the air offensive in North Africa.[17]

During this period, most of the Eighth's bombing raids targeted U-boat yards in France in response to the growing U-boat threat in the Atlantic. However, these raids inflicted limited damage on the U-boat pens, as their robust concrete walls and roofs could withstand direct hits from 1-ton bombs. The pens were also heavily fortified with antiaircraft guns and fighters, resulting in substantial losses for the U.S. forces.[18]

As 1943 began, Winston Churchill grew increasingly critical of U.S. bombing operations. No U.S. missions had been conducted over Germany, unlike the nightly bombing campaigns carried out by the RAF. Churchill believed that American generals were hesitant to subject their daylight bombing theory to its most challenging test. Additionally, the United States lacked a long-range escort fighter capable of protecting bombers over Germany. The latest U.S. fighter, the P-47B Thunderbolt, had a range of only 550 miles, leaving the bombers unescorted and vulnerable to Luftwaffe fighters for over half the distance to German targets.[19] When retrofitted with drop tanks, the range could be extended to 1,100 miles, meaning targets deep within Germany could receive fighter cover.

During an Allied strategy meeting on January 14, 1943, in Casablanca, Churchill discussed with President Franklin Roosevelt the idea of having the Eighth Air Force join the RAF in night bombing. In the run-up to the Casablanca Conference, RAF Air Chief Marshal Charles A. Portal wanted the USAAF to join the RAF in night bombing, since during daytime, the B-17 bomber would be vulnerable to Luftwaffe fighters. Because the RAF's Bomber Command had suffered heavy losses during daylight raids, Portal thought nighttime bombing was the right approach. Harris, commander of RAF Bomber Command, concurred and said that area bombing or "city-busting" could wreck the German economy and war machine, making an Allied invasion of Northwest Europe unnecessary. However, one RAF official who had met with USAAF leaders during 1941 discussions in Washington, D.C., knew they wanted to conduct daytime bombing over Germany. Air Vice Marshal John C. Slessor, Assistant Chief Plans, sent a note to the British secretary of state for air, Archibald S. M. Sinclair, explaining that the U.S. was deeply committed to daylight precision bombing. Although Roosevelt was unlikely to side with Churchill against his generals, General Arnold, upon learning of Churchill's intentions, promptly directed Eaker to London to address the prime minister. Eaker, armed with a single sheet of paper outlining his arguments, met with Churchill and, after expressing his support for daylight bombing, handed over the document. Churchill read through the arguments, pausing at a statement by Eaker that emphasized, "By bombing the devils around the clock, we can prevent the German defenses from getting any rest."[20]

He repeated this sentence twice, then turned to Eaker and acknowledged, "You've made a strong case here. While you have not convinced me that you are right, you have convinced me that you should have further opportunity to prove your case."[21] Churchill assured Eaker that he would meet with Roosevelt and retract his suggestion that the United States should collaborate with the British in night bombing.

Elated that the U.S. daylight bombing strategy had successfully endured and convinced that this agreement would stand as one of the pivotal decisions of the war, Eaker promptly departed for London. On January 21, 1943, the U.S. and British leaders issued the Casablanca Directive, articulating their stance on various aspects, including the bombing of Germany. Crafted with consideration for the aircrews undertaking the missions, the directive emphasized that the primary objective would be the progressive destruction and dislocation of the German military, industrial, and economic system, and the undermining of the morale of the German people to a point where their capacity for armed resistance was fatally weakened. It also granted the Eighth Air Force the authority to take every opportunity to attack Germany by day, to destroy objectives that were unsuitable for night attack, to sustain continuous pressure on German morale, to impose heavy losses on the German day fighter force, and to contain German fighter strength away from the Russian and Mediterranean theatres of war. Just two days after Eaker's return to London, he sanctioned the first Eighth Air Force bombing mission against Germany.[22]

On January 27, 1943, two Bomb Wings, the 1st and 2nd, with ninety-one aircraft, set out for the submarine factories at Vegesack near Bremen, in northern Germany. Fifty-five of them reached the target; seven bombers were B-24s, the rest were B-17Fs. Two B-17s bombed Emden instead. When it became evident that the target was obscured by clouds, the bombers altered their course for Wilhelmshaven, on Germany's North Sea coast, where they released their bombs on the U-boat facilities. The unaccompanied force encountered minimal losses, with only three bombers downed by enemy fighters, while managing to shoot down seven of the German attackers. Although bombing accuracy was not optimal, the day marked a significant event as the U.S. Eighth Air Force had finally executed a mission targeting an objective within Germany.[23]

In a subsequent bombing of Wilhelmshaven a month later, resistance increased, resulting in the loss of seven U.S. bombers. On March 18, a fleet of ninety-seven U.S. bombers decimated two-thirds of the U-boat shipyards at Vegesack. Only two bombers were lost, and American gunners claimed an impressive tally of fifty-two downed German fighters. Later analysis showed that there were no losses of German fighters on this mission.

Nearly a week after the Vegesack raid, General Eaker disclosed the Eighth's achievements over the past thirteen months to a gathering of war correspondents: fifty-one missions, ninety bombers lost, and 356 German fighters shot down. Eaker acknowledged that the reported totals against German aircraft were likely inflated, as multiple gunners often claimed credit for shooting down the same plane, and some German fighter pilots pretended to be shot down. Despite the exaggerations, the early success of the Eighth affirmed the U.S. generals' confidence that their heavy bombers could conduct unescorted daylight raids over Germany without incurring substantial losses. Their faith in the doctrine that the bomber will always get through remained unshaken.[24]

However, a lingering concern among the generals was whether the Luftwaffe had the capacity to shoot down enough American bombers to make daylight bombing economically untenable. Despite German fighter force chief Adolf Galland's appeals to strengthen fighter defenses in the West, his superiors did not perceive the Allied air attacks as an imminent threat. Consequently, most of the Luftwaffe's fighters were engaged in the failing Mediterranean campaign, resulting in weaker resistance to the U.S. and British bombers over Western Europe than could have been anticipated.

As they planned more unescorted raids into Germany, Arnold and Eaker were actively urging Washington to strengthen the Eighth with additional bombers and fighters. In a single day in May 1943, the number of Eighth Air Force bombers surged from 100 to 215. Concurrently, in that same month, the Allies approved the Combined Bomber Offensive (CBO) Plan, outlining that the Eighth was slated to receive nearly 3,000 more heavy bombers by the year's end.[25]

Despite the generals' conviction that unescorted bombers could withstand missions without fighter escort, a crucial challenge persisted—the absence of a long-range, maneuverable escort fighter capable of penetrating deep into Germany and returning. During engagements over the English Channel and France, the P-47 Thunderbolt, while more robust and faster in descent than the Luftwaffe's Fw 190, had limitations in climbing speed. In mid-1943, the P-47C, and later the D variant with the better engine and four-bladed prop and supercharger, were introduced; they could now outclimb both German fighters, except the Fw 190D9 in 1944.

Another U.S. fighter, the P-38 Lightning, was considered a potential long-range escort due to its twin-engine durability and distinctive twin-boom design that was easily recognized by American bomber gunners. However, the P-38 proved less agile than the Bf 109 and Fw 190, facing engine issues at high altitudes.[26] Prior to evaluating the P-47 or P-38 as long-range escorts, the development of a satisfactory external drop tank—whose priority had been low until 1938, as assigned by USSAF brass—was imperative. Consequently, the bombers would continue operating independently once the fighter escort turned back over northern France and the Low Countries.[27]

The decision to continue unescorted bomber missions would ultimately lead to tragedy for the bomber crews, exacerbated by the USAAF's decision to halt the production of an outstanding long-range escort fighter, citing a lack of immediate necessity. This fighter, the P-51 Mustang, at first developed for the British in 1941, initially had an underpowered Allison engine at high altitudes.

However, when the British outfitted it with the Rolls-Royce Merlin engine, the Mustang's performance improved significantly. Additionally, the Mustang surpassed the Thunderbolt in range, boasting an extra internal fuel tank behind the pilot, and its Merlin engine consumed roughly half the fuel used by the P-47.

Regrettably, the USAAF's material division deemed the Merlin engine too susceptible to gunfire because it was liquid-cooled. This decision was reached despite the fact that the successful fighters of the early war period, such as the RAF's Supermarine Spitfire and the Luftwaffe's Messerschmitt Bf 109, were both powered by liquid-cooled engines. Furthermore, as the North American P-51 Mustang was originally designed for the British and featured a British-made engine, there was less enthusiasm for the fighter than if it had been exclusively American. This misjudgment significantly delayed the production of the P-51. However, events would demonstrate that the United States was not alone in making ill-advised decisions regarding its aircraft.[28]

While the Eighth Air Force initiated its opening raids on Germany, the RAF's Bomber Command launched the night offensive into the Ruhr Valley, Germany's industrial center. On May 16, 1943, the RAF deviated from its usual area bombing strategy when a squadron of Lancasters performed a precision bombing mission. They dropped specially designed bouncing bombs on three reservoirs in the Ruhr, successfully breaching two dams. Despite the daring Dam Busters raid, it failed to halt industrial production in Germany's Ruhr district in North Rhine-Westphalia. The RAF continued with its area bombing strategy, inflicting significant damage on the Ruhr and planning a large-scale attack on Hamburg, Germany's largest port, the first instance of coordinated American daylight bombing and RAF night bombing on a single target, named Operation Gomorrah.[29]

Simultaneously, the Eighth Air Force encountered the escalating effectiveness of Luftwaffe fighter attacks and antiaircraft fire against their B-17s and B-24s. While a May 7 raid on Antwerp saw all bombers return safely, a subsequent mission over Saint-Nazaire on France's Atlantic coast resulted in the loss of seven out of thirty-one bombers. Two raids on the Baltic port of Kiel in mid-May incurred fourteen losses for the Eighth, but a return raid on June 13 saw a staggering twenty-six out of 182 bombers shot down. Nine days later, the Eighth attacked the Ruhr region, with 182 B-17s and B-24s facing intense fighter opposition to bomb the synthetic rubber plant at Huls, effectively disrupting production for months.[30]

July witnessed a lull in Allied bombing raids, mainly targeting coastal France. However, on the evening of July 24, nearly 800 RAF bombers launched Operation Gomorrah on Hamburg. Employing strips of tinfoil to confuse the Kammhuber Line radar, the force successfully dropped almost 3,000 tons of bombs on Hamburg. The next day, U.S. bombers, avoiding the city itself, targeted Hamburg's shipyards and docks, losing nineteen B-17s out of sixty-nine.[31] That night, the returning RAF bombers released incendiary bombs on the already burning city, where the water mains had burst due to previous attacks.

With more fires erupting across Hamburg, the air above the city became intensely heated. As the hot air ascended, cool air rushed in to fill the void. This phenomenon led to the creation of tornadoes of fire throughout the city, merging into one enormous whirling inferno measuring 2½ miles high and 1½ miles in diameter. Nothing could halt this horrifying firestorm as it swept through Hamburg, consuming or melting everything in its path.

Thousands of people were drawn into the inferno or instantly incinerated in the intense 1,800°F heat, with many trapped in air raid shelters. Those who were not burned suffered from suffocation, carbon monoxide poisoning, or were crushed by collapsing buildings. The German government's reaction to the initial bombing of Hamburg was marked by a combination of attempts to manage public perception, maintain morale, and address the practical challenges posed by the extensive destruction caused by the air raids. The Nazi regime sought to control the narrative surrounding the bombings. Propaganda efforts were employed to downplay the extent of the damage, exaggerate Germany's resilience, and portray the Allied bombing campaign as ineffective. Following the destruction caused by the bombings, the German authorities organized evacuation efforts to relocate civilians from heavily damaged areas to safer locations. Additionally, plans for the reconstruction of the city were developed, focusing on rebuilding essential infrastructure and housing. The Luftwaffe responded by increasing defensive measures over German cities. Antiaircraft defenses, including flak cannons and searchlights, were intensified to protect urban areas from aerial attacks. Tactics to disrupt the Allied bombing raids, including night-fighting strategies and the use of radar, were considered. Hans-Joachim "Hajo" Herrmann, who later commanded Sonderkommando Elbe, commented:

> I was given the green light to operate "*Wilde Sau*" [Wild Boar, a tactic whereby German fighters attacked Allied night bombers caught in the glare of searchlights] at my own discretion after August [1943], since we were still not truly organized into a unit, although Goering knew that I would not be ready and fully operational until September, when all of [our] allocations and provisions had been secured. During the night of the Hamburg raid he called me, and asked; "How soon can you be ready?" I told him at least six more weeks, and he told me I had less than two hours to get my "unit" airborne and prove my theory. This was part of the insanity I had to deal with.[32]

The bombing of Hamburg, in which the Eighth Air Force played a minimal role, unleashed a nightmarish spectacle of death and destruction, unparalleled in the history of city bombings. It was not until 1957 that it was conclusively determined that around 50,000 inhabitants perished in the raids. The final bombs fell on Hamburg on August 2, and news of the catastrophe quickly spread throughout Germany. Albert Speer, the German minister of armaments, warned Hitler that if the Allies continued such bombing, the war would be lost rapidly.

Luftwaffe leaders pledged that the devastation suffered by Hamburg would never be repeated in another German city. From Hermann Göring downwards, they prioritized strengthening the fighter force at the expense of bombers, transforming the Luftwaffe into a defensive force to repel U.S. and British bombers and regain air superiority for Germany.

Göring, chief of the Luftwaffe, sought Hitler's approval for these strategic shifts, but the infuriated Führer dismissed any discussion of a defensive war, especially from Göring. Instead, Hitler sought vengeance for the bombing of Hamburg through a renewed Luftwaffe bombing offensive against London. Göring, deeply disturbed, left the meeting, and Adolf Galland later discovered him in uncontrollable sobs. (The aerial bombing of London did not commence until January 1944 and was notably ineffective, earning the nickname "baby blitz" from the British.)[33]

While the destruction of Hamburg had minimal impact on Hitler, it did bring about a unifying effect among Luftwaffe leaders. For the first time, they all concurred with Galland that the Allied bombing offensive posed a serious threat, necessitating drastic measures.

On August 1, 1943, the same day Speer was cautioning Hitler about the Allied bombing threat, the U.S. Ninth Air Force, featuring three bomber groups temporarily transferred from the Eighth, conducted an extensive raid on the oil refineries in Ploesti, Romania. Departing from their base in Benghazi, Libya, for Operation Tidal Wave, approximately 177 B-24s flew at low altitudes towards the heavily fortified refineries, which provided Germany with more than one-third of its oil. Eleven bombers dropped out due to mechanical issues, and navigational mistakes directed the remaining aircraft over the most heavily defended approach to Ploesti.[34]

The B-24s faced devastating, close-range antiaircraft fire during their bombing run, with one Liberator after another being shot down at treetop level. Maneuvering through chimneys and explosions from refinery storage tanks, many surviving bombers were singed by flames from the Ploesti inferno. Those that managed to complete the bombing run were swiftly attacked by a *Schwarm* of Luftwaffe fighters. Only half of the attacking force returned to Benghazi; fifty-three were lost, while many surviving bombers diverted to other Allied bases or landed in neutral Turkey.

The raid on Ploesti proved disastrous for the Ninth Air Force, resulting in 579 men killed, wounded, or captured, the loss of 53 B-24s, and another 55 severely damaged. Despite destroying 40 percent of Ploesti's refinery capacity, the production was promptly increased in the remaining refinery units, ensuring an uninterrupted oil supply to the German military. The mission was considered a failure, with no immediate follow-up raid was ordered.[35]

Due to the setback from the Ploesti raid and a delay in receiving 200 bombers from the United States, the Eighth Air Force was not operating at full capacity in August. Additionally, challenges persisted in developing drop tanks for escort fighters. The P-47s were unable to accompany the bombers for the entirety of missions deep into Germany, and the first P-51s were not expected until late autumn.[36] However, despite the absence of a long-range escort fighter, Eaker believed that waiting until all issues were resolved would be detrimental, as German industry continued to produce weapons and materials.

Plans had long been in place for the Eighth to bomb Schweinfurt, a Bavarian town housing five plants responsible for approximately 52 percent of Germany's ball bearing production. Disrupting these factories would significantly impede the German war effort, given the critical role of ball bearings in the manufacturing of precision machinery for airplanes, tanks, ships, and artillery guns. Schweinfurt, considered too small for the night bombers of the RAF, became an ideal target for the Eighth's precision daylight bombing strategy and a test of the belief that heavily armed B-17s could endure without fighter escort. The August 17 raid on Schweinfurt would mark the deepest penetration into German airspace by U.S. aircraft at that point.[37]

Another target was the Messerschmitt aircraft factory at Regensburg, producing nearly 200 fighters monthly. It was thought that if Regensburg was attacked first, it would divert Luftwaffe fighters away from Schweinfurt, the more critical target. The Fourth Bombardment Wing, led by Colonel Curtis LeMay, was assigned to bomb Regensburg and then land in Algeria, while the First Bombardment Wing, under Brigadier General Robert B. Williams, was to attack Schweinfurt and return to bases in England.[38]

On the morning of August 17, thick fog enveloped the Eighth's airfields in England. Despite a delay of a few minutes due to the weather, LeMay's B-17s took off for Regensburg. However, Williams' aircraft, scheduled to depart ten minutes later, were grounded for over three hours. Although the initial tactical advantage of the two-pronged raid was thus lost, the decision was made to proceed, considering the risks of landing with a full bomb load. When the fog lifted, the First Bombardment Wing took off, significantly behind schedule.

Encountering antiaircraft fire but minimal fighter opposition as they crossed into German-occupied Holland, LeMay's B-17s experienced relatively low resistance. Most Luftwaffe fighters avoided engaging with the P-47 escort fighters, aware that the Thunderbolts would soon return to their bases in England. Despite issues with the P-47's paper drop tanks, which leaked and were unusable at high altitudes, LeMay's Thunderbolt escorts could reach Aachen, just inside the German border, with this extended range.

As LeMay's fleet entered German airspace, the U.S. escort fighters, depleted of fuel, had to return to England. Immediately, Luftwaffe Fw 190s and Bf 109s engaged the B-17s, using machine guns and cannon fire. Some twin-engine Bf 110 fighters, positioned outside the range of American machine guns, launched 4-foot-long rockets into the bomber formations. Certain German fighters even released 500lb time-fused bombs on the Fortresses. Numerous B-17s succumbed to the relentless attacks, falling out of formation in flames, and the sky became cluttered with debris and parachutes from numerous damaged aircraft. Due to the dispersed nature of German fighter bases, with replacements rising as others exhausted their fuel and ammunition, the American bombers faced a continuous assault in a formidable display of Luftwaffe firepower, leaving the surviving U.S. crews awestruck. According to John Curatola, "This staggered wave of German fighter units rotating the attacking, landing, refueling, re-engaging was Galland's personal plan, all coordinated by a central command authority for each sector."[39]

As the Fourth Bombardment Wing reached Regensburg, fifteen B-17s had been shot down. Nevertheless, the remaining 131 Fortresses, many of which were damaged, successfully made it to their targets, hitting the Messerschmitt buildings with high-explosive and incendiary bombs. Satisfied with the destruction of their target, LeMay's bombers turned south toward Algeria. Three more B-17s were lost before the last of the Luftwaffe fighters ceased pursuit near the Alps.

Simultaneously, General Williams' First Bombardment Wing, consisting of 230 B-17s, entered German airspace and confronted the reinvigorated Luftwaffe. Avoiding direct attacks on the bombers until the P-47 escort had departed, 200 Fw 190s and 100 Bf 109s shot down thirty-six B-17s, more than in the morning raid. Despite this, the bombers pressed on and eventually found the target factories in Schweinfurt. Over 420 tons of bombs were dropped, causing significant damage to the ball-bearing works. However, the Fortresses still had to face enemy fighters on their return journey to England. Once again, Luftwaffe firepower inflicted losses on the bomber formations, bringing down one B-17 after another until the P-47s arrived near the German border to escort the battered survivors home across the English Channel.[40]

Soon after the surviving crews had landed, the toll of the Schweinfurt and Regensburg raids on the Eighth Air Force became apparent, with sixty B-17s shot down and the loss of 600 crewmen. Among the bombers that safely landed in England and North Africa, 122 were damaged, and twenty-seven of those were beyond repair. Many Americans began questioning whether the damage inflicted by these raids justified the horrendous losses. For Adolf Galland, whose Luftwaffe fighter arm had suffered the loss of thirty-six aircraft out of approximately 300 scrambled, with an additional twelve written off, this was convincing evidence that the American heavy bomber offensive could be rendered too costly by a strong German fighter defense. Nevertheless, his own forces could ill afford the losses they had suffered.

Crews of the Eighth were disappointed to learn that, instead of conducting a follow-up night raid on Schweinfurt, the RAF had bombed the German secret weapons facility at Peenemünde on Germany's Baltic coast on the night of August 17. The island was now the test site for two vengeance weapons, the V-1 jet-powered flying bomb and V-2 liquid-fueled rocket. The raid resulted in the deaths of many top German scientists and delayed the V-1 and V-2 programs for months. Hajo Herrman commented:

> My phone rang, it was Göring. He ordered my group to take off to intercept the British going to Berlin. I took 12 of my pilots including "Nose" Mueller

and we took off. But after a while we were redirected northeast. I pushed my fighter hard only to be told that I was not allowed to enter that airspace around Peenemünde, "I did not have clearance", so we listened into ground control to locate the bombers, as our single seat fighters did not have radar. Peenemünde was that top secret, not even I knew what was going on.[41]

The RAF's bombing of Peenemünde following the U.S. attack on Schweinfurt exemplified the lack of cooperation between the two air forces in what was mistakenly called the Combined Bomber Offensive. In subsequent weeks, the battered Eighth continued to bomb targets in northern France, well within the range of fighter escorts. Additional bomber reinforcements were flown in from the States, including the new B-17G, equipped with a nose gun turret to fend off frontal attacks. Despite the challenges, General Arnold persisted in calling for attacks on Germany, leading to several unescorted raids on targets in East Prussia and occupied Poland.

The devastating cost of the Schweinfurt raid shocked Americans, including President Roosevelt, who expressed concern over the loss of sixty bombers and raised questions about the viability of the daylight bombing offensive. Eaker, whose initial optimism had waned, cease planning unescorted missions into Germany, realizing that without long-range fighter escorts, the Eighth Air Force faced imminent obliteration. Two weeks after the Schweinfurt raid, Eaker received positive news: Arnold had ordered increased production of the P-51, and the first Mustangs were designated for the Eighth Air Force.[42]

Over the following weeks, only a few raids, mostly on occupied France and with fighter escorts, were conducted. In mid-November, the first P-51B Mustangs arrived in England by ship. By the month's end, the newly formed 354th Fighter Group, equipped with twenty-four P-51s, was undergoing training. On December 1, the 354th's commander, Lieutenant Colonel Don Blakeslee, led the Mustangs across the Channel for their debut mission to Emden in northwestern Germany, claiming their first Luftwaffe "kill" on December 16.[43]

The P-51 quickly established itself as the premier active fighter in the Western theater. Outperforming the Bf 109 and Fw 190 in maneuverability and speed, with a top speed of 440mph at 30,000 feet, it definitively solved the challenge of long-range escort. With its fuel-efficient engine and internal fuel tank, the P-51 had the range to escort B-17s and B-24s deep into Germany and back. Bomber crews were optimistic that they would no longer face missions as costly as the two Schweinfurt and Regensburg raids. The development of a 150-gallon drop tank further extended the P-47's range into German airspace. The Eighth Air Force received a consistent supply of trained crews and replacement bombers, with around 500 B-17s and B-24s available by the end of October.[44]

As the Eighth regained strength, RAF Bomber Command continued night attacks on German targets. Kassel in central Germany was hit with 1,800 tons of bombs on October 22, resulting in a firestorm akin to the one in Hamburg. Subsequently,

Bomber Command shifted focus to Berlin, with Harris believing that destroying the German capital would end the war. Despite disagreement from U.S. generals, Harris persisted in conducting raids on Berlin through to the spring of 1944, later redirecting his forces to support the preparations for the invasion of France.

In addition to altering fighter tactics, Allied commanders devised Operation Argument,[45] intending to strategically bomb enemy factories producing fighter aircraft and components. The operation—a joint effort involving the Eighth Air Force, the Fifteenth Air Force based in Italy, and the RAF—was scheduled to begin during a period of favorable weather, a rarity in Europe during January and February. The first Eighth Air Force raid in 1944 involved 633 B-17s and B-24s attacking targets in Germany, including the Focke-Wulf factory at Oschersleben.[46] This marked the successful introduction of the P-51 as an escort fighter, with fifteen German fighters downed by Mustangs. Despite most bombers turning back due to bad weather, the remaining aircraft inflicted significant damage on the Focke-Wulf factory at a cost of thirty-four bombers lost.

Further raids on Frankfurt and other targets faced weather-related challenges, prompting Spaatz to expedite Operation Argument for completion by March 1. On February 20, despite unfavorable weather in England, Spaatz ordered heavy bombers from the Eighth and Fifteenth air forces to hammer aircraft, engine, and ball-bearing plants by day, and RAF bombers attacked by night. Codenamed Operation Argument, it became known as "Big Week." Over 1,000 bombers, escorted by 700 fighters, targeted central Germany and Poland, leading to twenty-one bombers being shot down by the Luftwaffe. The Eighth and Fifteenth air forces attacked German aircraft production centers during this period, with a focus on Bf 109 factories.[47]

Schweinfurt was hit on February 24, along with RAF bombings in the evening. The Gotha factory, producing Bf 110s, suffered damage. Bad weather ended Big Week on February 25, which resulted in the loss of sixty-four bombers.[48] Despite claiming success, the impact of Big Week was limited, as German aircraft production capabilities were not completely destroyed. Albert Speer's ministry of armaments took charge of fighter production and increased output. Galland found hope in the undamaged jet-powered Me 262 prototypes at Augsburg.

With D-Day approaching, Allied leaders debated the direction of the bombing offensive. Eisenhower favored attacking oil centers, while Spaatz and Harris advocated continuing the bombing of key German industries. The Transportation Plan—focusing on roads, bridges, and rail lines in France—faced opposition due to concerns about civilian casualties. The RAF, however, successfully tested precision attacks on rail centers.

While RAF attacks persisted on Berlin, the Eighth joined in daylight bombings on March 4 and 6. The Battle of Berlin saw heavy losses on both sides. On March 30, a disastrous RAF mission over Nuremberg, illuminated by a full moon, resulted in 108 bombers being shot down by Luftwaffe night fighters, leading to a reduction in deep raids by the RAF.

U.S. long-range escort fighters, particularly P-51s and P-47s, demonstrated their effectiveness against Luftwaffe fighters during the spring of 1944. Aggressive American pilots, with diminishing opposition from German fighters, engaged in strafing sweeps over Luftwaffe airfields, destroying numerous enemy aircraft on the ground. The Luftwaffe's dwindling resources became a growing concern.

By the summer of 1944, Allied bombers cruised above the remnants of the Third Reich with minimal opposition, facing occasional jet attacks. The collapse of the German army on both the Western and Eastern fronts was largely attributed to the impact of Allied bombing, especially on transportation systems. These attacks virtually halted wartime production by disrupting the movement of raw materials and finished goods. Further bombardments ensued, and by February 1945, almost every German city with a population exceeding 100,000 had suffered severe damage.

One notable exception to the Allied bombing was Dresden, situated 100 miles south of Berlin in eastern Germany. It had a major marshaling yard nearby and was a transit area. Except for its rail yards, Dresden lacked militarily significant targets, possessing no antiaircraft guns and just one bomb shelter. The Casablanca Directive, issued as a result of the Casablanca Conference of January 21, 1943, was a generalized targeting strategy for the Combined Bomber Offensive. It had established the top priority as the destruction of German submarine construction yards, with the German aircraft industry second on the priority list. However, the Pointblank Directive of June 1943 put the German aircraft industry, and particularly that portion of which was dedicated to the production of single-engine fighters, at the top of the priority list. Pointblank identified nineteen vital German industries (and the number of targets associated to them) which if destroyed would stagnate the German war machine. Rail, barge, and surface roads were included in the list.

Regarding the bombing of Dresden, Lieutenant General James Doolittle, who commanded the Eighth Air Force from January 1944, commented: "Dresden was just one of several cities bombed to prevent German reinforcements' arrival at the front. The Soviets wanted Dresden bombed, and I ordered the strikes. The British had already been busy there."[48]

Recognized as the Florence of Germany, Dresden boasted splendid architecture dating back to the thirteenth century. While its normal population was 633,000, the figure had doubled in early 1945 due to an influx of refugees escaping the advancing Russian armies. On the night of February 13, a force of 244 RAF Lancasters unleashed incendiary and high-explosive bombs on Dresden. The ensuing firestorm, reminiscent of Hamburg, ravaged 8 square miles of the old city, tearing apart buildings, uprooting trees, and consuming hundreds in its fiery vortex. A second wave of 550 RAF bombers intensified the onslaught with additional bombs, and the city's intense heat was palpable from 20,000 feet above. On the following day, Ash Wednesday, 450 U.S. bombers aimed to target the rail yards, but obscured by clouds and smoke, they inadvertently bombed the city, compounding the devastation.[49]

Dresden burned for seven days and eight nights, its flames visible for 200 miles. The scale of destruction overwhelmed the limited number of survivors, with initial estimates suggesting 135,000 casualties.[50] As the war neared its conclusion, appalled Americans and Britons questioned why Dresden had been subjected to such devastation. Even Winston Churchill, facing public outcry, began to reassess the strategy of bombing German cities solely for terror purposes. He expressed a need for more precise targeting of military objectives such as oil and communications rather than engaging in acts of terror and wanton destruction.[51] This was the situation in Germany in late 1944 and early 1945 as its leaders struggled to come up with plans to halt the relentless Allied bombing campaign.

2

The Strategic Situation in Late 1944/Early 1945

In late 1944 and early 1945, Germany found itself in a dire strategic situation. The country was under attack on multiple fronts and was struggling to maintain its military and economic resources. One of the key factors that contributed to Germany's difficult situation was the loss of its air superiority and the relentless Allied bombing. As noted by historian David Irving in his book *The War Between the Generals*, the Luftwaffe had suffered significant losses following the Normandy landings in the summer of 1944. This was compounded by the Allied bombing campaign, which had destroyed much of Germany's industrial infrastructure and made it difficult for the Luftwaffe to repair its planes and maintain its operations.[1]

Germany's situation was also impacted by the fact that it was fighting a multi-front war. In the east, Germany was facing a strong and determined Soviet Union that was advancing towards Berlin. In the west, the Allies had landed in Normandy and were pushing eastwards towards Germany. According to historian James Holland in his book *The Rise of Germany, 1939–1941*, this created a difficult strategic situation for Germany, as it was forced to fight on two fronts simultaneously.[2] The situation was further complicated by the fact that Germany's military and economic resources were severely depleted. The war had taken a heavy toll on Germany's population and infrastructure, with millions of people dead or wounded, and much of the country's industrial capacity destroyed. This made it difficult for Germany to continue fighting a war on multiple fronts, particularly as the Allies had access to greater resources and manpower.[3]

Another key factor that contributed to Germany's difficult strategic situation was the leadership of Adolf Hitler. The Führer had become increasingly isolated and erratic during this period, and his decisions often went against the advice of his military commanders. According to historian Ian Kershaw in his book *Hitler: 1936–1945*, Hitler's decision to focus on developing wonder weapons such as the V-1 and V-2 rockets, rather than building up the country's conventional military forces, was a major strategic mistake that weakened Germany's position.[4]

The Strategic Situation in Late 1944/Early 1945

Despite these challenges, Germany continued to fight, even attempting to launch a series of offensives in late 1944 and early 1945. One of the most significant of these was the Battle of the Bulge, which began in the Ardennes in December 1944. According to historian Antony Beevor in his book *The Second World War*, the battle was intended to split the Allied forces in two and capture the port of Antwerp, which would have given Germany access to much-needed supplies.[5] However, the Battle of the Bulge ultimately proved unsuccessful for Germany, as Allied forces were able to regroup and push back against the Ardennes offensive. The battle had also resulted in heavy losses for Germany, depleting the country's military and economic resources even further.[6]

As the war entered its final stages, Germany's strategic situation continued to deteriorate. The country was running out of resources and its military forces were being pushed back on all fronts. Hitler's leadership had become increasingly erratic, and he was refusing to consider surrender, despite the fact that Germany was clearly losing the war. This led to a breakdown in communication and coordination between the various branches of the military, with different commanders making decisions based on their own interpretations of Hitler's wishes.[7] At the same time, the Allies were closing in on Germany from both the east and the west, with Soviet troops advancing steadily towards Berlin and Allied forces pushing through Holland and Belgium.[8] The German armies were stretched thin, with soldiers and resources being pulled in multiple directions. Many German soldiers were exhausted and demoralized, having already suffered heavy losses on multiple fronts.[9]

In addition to military setbacks, Germany was experiencing severe economic and logistical difficulties. The Allied bombing campaign had badly disrupted German industry and transportation networks, making it difficult to move troops and supplies.[10] The country was also facing severe shortages of food and fuel, leading to widespread hunger and suffering among the civilian population.[11] Despite these challenges, Hitler refused to consider capitulation and instead doubled down on his commitment to continue fighting. He ordered the mobilization of all available resources and the implementation of a scorched-earth policy, with German troops destroying anything that could be of use to the advancing Allies.[12] This further eroded morale among German soldiers and civilians, who could see the futility of continuing the fight.

The landscape that unfolded in Germany during the fateful period of late 1944 and early 1945 was marked by an unprecedented sense of desperation and all-encompassing chaos. The nation found itself ensnared in the vice-like grip of a multifaceted crisis—military, economic, and logistical tribulations converging with an acute leadership vacuum. As the Allies bore down from all sides, Nazi Germany's leadership teetered on the precipice of disarray, struggling to rally coherent strategies amid the tumultuous torrent of events.

The Allied bombing campaign on Germany up to April 1945 left an indelible mark on the country, profoundly shaping the course of World War II and leaving lasting scars on its infrastructure, economy, and civilian population. This relentless aerial onslaught, predominantly carried out by British and American air forces, had far-reaching and multifaceted consequences that extended beyond mere physical destruction.

Industrial Devastation

The relentless bombing campaign unleashed during World War II stands as a testament to the unprecedented intensity of aerial warfare, leaving an indelible mark on Germany's landscape and war effort. Targeting vital industrial hubs, manufacturing centers, and intricate transportation networks, cities such as Berlin, Hamburg, Dresden, and Cologne found themselves at the epicenter of unparalleled destruction.

The aftermath of these continual bombings was characterized by a nation marred by ruins and debris. Pivotal factories, refineries, and production facilities lay in ruins, rendering them impotent and unable to contribute to Germany's war machinery. The cumulative impact of the bombings was staggering, thrusting the Nazi war industry into a relentless struggle to maintain production rates amid mounting challenges.

The disruption caused by the bombings had a far-reaching ripple effect, exacerbating the scarcity of vital resources essential for the continuation of Germany's war endeavor. The once-thriving industrial heartlands were transformed into scenes of devastation. The relentless onslaught of aerial attacks not only physically dismantled cities and industries, but imposed a psychological toll, serving as a constant reminder of the Allies' resolve to bring an end to the war.

In the face of such destruction, Germany found itself compelled to divert valuable resources to repair and rebuild its war-damaged infrastructure. The bombing campaign shaped the strategic landscape of the conflict. The war machine that once operated seamlessly now faced the arduous task of reconstruction amid the chaos left in the wake of aerial bombardment.

The legacy of these relentless and devastating aerial assaults endures as a powerful chapter in history, etched in the annals of wartime resilience. The scars left on the German landscape serve as a poignant reminder of the human cost by those who endured the day and night bombings during one of the darkest periods of the twentieth century.[13]

Infrastructure Disruption

The extensive and unyielding bombing sorties unleashed upon Germany during World War II marked a chapter of unprecedented destruction, leaving behind a shattered infrastructure. Among the primary targets were the vital arteries that facilitated the movement of troops, equipment, and essential supplies—the railways, bridges, and roads that formed the lifelines of military logistics. This strategic targeting manifested as a systematic assault designed to paralyze the German war machine by hampering its capacity to maneuver swiftly and respond effectively to the ever-encroaching Allied advances.

Railways, often likened to the circulatory system of any military operation, bore the brunt of meticulous and relentless bombardment. The result was a network left in tatters, strewn with twisted metal and debris, rendering rail transportation virtually impossible. Bridges, those vital connectors spanning rivers and valleys, were reduced to skeletal remnants. Their destruction impeded the flow of reinforcements and resources, stifling the flexibility that Germany so desperately needed to counter the multi-front challenges posed by the Allies.

Roadways, too, fell victim to this orchestrated campaign of destruction. The intricate web of roads that once crisscrossed the German landscape, teeming with military convoys and supplies, lay in disarray. Potholes, craters, and debris imposed lengthy delays, impeded communication, and disrupted the fluidity of the German war effort.

The cumulative impact of this orchestrated infrastructure assault was profound. The mobility of German forces, once a hallmark of their military prowess, was severely constrained. Swift coordinated counterattacks became near impossible as the logistical backbone of the German war machine crumbled. The inability to reinforce embattled fronts or to shift resources to where they were most needed eroded Germany's strategic advantage of interior lines. As the Allies pressed on everywhere, the German military found itself hamstrung by logistical hurdles, resulting in fragmented and disjointed efforts to stave off the tide of advance.

A strategic paralysis was inflicted upon the nation, eroding the German military's capacity to withstand the Allied onslaught on multiple fronts. The targeted destruction of railways, bridges, and roads created a landscape of impediments, hindering the Nazi war machine's ability to adapt and respond, creating impassable bottlenecks which curtailed the flow of supplies and reinforcements to the hard-pressed and outnumbered defenders of the Reich, and contributing significantly to the unraveling of Hitler's regime as the Allies closed in on ultimate victory.[14]

Loss of Skilled Workforce

The unforgiving bombing campaign waged during World War II exacted a grievous toll on Germany's civilian populace, creating a haunting landscape scarred by profound loss, dislocation, and enduring suffering. The relentless aerial onslaught led to a massive loss of life, shattering families and decimating communities. Once-vibrant neighborhoods, bustling with the rhythms of daily life, were reduced to nothing but rubble and ashes, serving as a stark testament to the destruction wrought from above.

The aftermath of these devastating air raids extended far beyond the immediate loss of life; it permeated the very fabric of German society, resulting in the upheaval of families and communities. Faced with the constant danger of bombings, families were compelled to seek refuge far from their homes, resulting in widespread displacement. The social fabric that once bound communities together was torn asunder, disrupting the delicate equilibrium of labor and production. The skilled workforce, integral to the maintenance and repair of the industrial infrastructure, found itself dispersed as individuals grappled with the dire challenges of survival, evacuation, and the exigencies of war.

This cascading effect had profound and far-reaching implications for Germany's war effort. The absence of skilled workers presented a formidable obstacle, impeding the nation's ability to restore and rejuvenate its industrial machinery. The intricate dance of production and repair, so vital for the maintenance of the war machine, was disrupted as the labor force found itself fragmented and dispersed across the war-torn Reich. The human resources necessary for the critical task of rebuilding and maintaining the war-damaged infrastructure were siphoned away, leaving the nation grappling with a vacuum that proved difficult to fill.

The bombing campaign, while strategically targeting military and industrial installations, inadvertently dealt a severe blow to the human infrastructure that formed the backbone of Germany's war effort. The disruption of communities and dislocation of skilled workers exacerbated the challenges faced by a nation already teetering on the brink of collapse. The ability to mobilize resources, both human and industrial, became increasingly compromised as the bombings continued to wreak havoc on the home front.

The impact of the air raids went beyond physical destruction; it left an enduring psychological scar on the German populace. The constant threat of bombings and the sight of once-thriving cities reduced to ruins created a climate of fear and despair. The resilience of the civilian population was tested as they confronted the enormity of loss and destruction, grappling with the challenges of rebuilding their lives amid the chaos of war.

The scars left by the devastating air raids would endure long after the war, serving as a poignant reminder of the profound and lasting impact of aerial warfare on civilian populations.[15]

Fuel and Resources Shortages

The extensive bombing campaign transcended military and urban targets, extending its reach to critical nodes of Germany's economic infrastructure, particularly oil refineries and storage facilities. These strategic strikes had dire consequences that rippled far beyond the immediate theaters of conflict, precipitating an acute shortage of petroleum products with profound implications for both military endeavors and the daily lives of civilians.[16.]

The consequences of the disruption of vital fuel-related installations first reverberated in Germany's military operations. Mobility, recognized as the lifeblood of warfare, was hamstrung as the scarcity of fuel constrained the German military's ability to mobilize and deploy forces efficiently. Tanks, aircraft, and mechanized units that relied on petroleum-based fuels found their operations hindered, eroding the strategic maneuverability essential for countering the advances of the Allies.

Beyond the realm of warfare, the fuel shortages permeated into civilian existence, leaving an indelible mark on everyday life. Transportation networks, both public and private, were severely compromised, inhibiting the movement of people and goods across the nation, constricting trade and commerce, indeed all economic activity. Agricultural productivity suffered a significant blow, with machinery that relied on fuel-driven engines rendered all but useless, jeopardizing food production at a time of crisis.

The scarcity of fuel reached even into the most quotidian aspects of life, creating a pervasive and enduring impact on the civilian population. Everyday necessities became harder to procure as distribution networks struggled to cope with limited resources. Public services and essential industries found themselves grappling with reduced capabilities, exacerbating the challenges posed by wartime conditions. The bombings that targeted oil-related facilities thus set in motion a chain of events with ramifications that extended well beyond military strategy.[17]

In the face of acute fuel shortages, the German populace was forced to contend with a new reality. The scarcity not only affected the availability of basic necessities but also disrupted the rhythm of daily life, imposing hardships on families and communities already grappling with the devastating consequences of war. The interdependence of various sectors became glaringly evident as the fuel shortage underscored the vulnerability of a nation caught in the throes of conflict.

The multifaceted impact of the bombings on oil-related facilities highlighted the interconnectedness of wartime dynamics. Strategic targeting had repercussions that reached far beyond military objectives, shaping the contours of conflict and everyday life alike. The acute fuel shortages were a stark reminder of the intricate web of dependencies that defined the wartime experience, where disruptions in one sector sent shockwaves through the entire socio-economic fabric of a nation. The scarcity of fuel became not just a logistical challenge but a profound and enduring facet of the collective wartime experience, leaving an indelible mark on both the military and civilian struggle.[18]

Psychological Impact

The unrelenting bombing campaign on Germany exacted a heavy toll not only in terms of physical destruction but also the psychological trauma of the German population. As the skies became battlegrounds, civilians were thrust into a ceaseless cycle of fear and anxiety, their lives disrupted by the ominous drone of incoming aircraft and the harrowing crescendo of approaching danger.

Air raids plunged neighborhoods and entire cities into a state of perpetual alarm. Families were jolted from their routines, forced to abandon daily activities at a moment's notice as warning sirens wailed, a chilling herald of imminent peril. Seeking refuge in hastily constructed shelters or any semblance of protective cover became an agonizing routine. The omnipresent specter of death from above cast a giant shadow, stripping away any sense of security and enveloping the population in a pervasive atmosphere of uncertainty.[19]

The psychological impact of bombing extended far beyond immediate moments of danger. The cumulative toll on mental well-being was profound, as civilians grappled with persistent dread and the mental toll of a prolonged state of crisis. Children grew up amidst the cacophony of air raid alarms, while adults were perpetually haunted by the specter of their homes reduced to rubble and their lives snuffed out by the indiscriminate rain of explosives. The bombings became a crucible for shifting sentiments and attitudes towards the Nazi regime. As the populace bore witness to the apparent inability of their leaders to shield them from bombardment, skepticism began to gnaw at the foundations of allegiance. Resentment burgeoned as civilians questioned the competence and priorities of a leadership that seemed incapable of safeguarding the lives and well-being of its own citizens.[20]

The dissonance between the rhetoric of Nazi propaganda and the grim reality on the ground was stark. The juxtaposition of Hitler's grandiose promises of invincibility and the devastation wrought by enemy bombs was an affront to the population's faith. As the bombings inflicted tangible hardships and emotional trauma, the populace's confidence in the regime was eroded, sowing seeds of doubt and disillusion.

The ordeal of enduring air raids, the constant threat to life and limb, and the stark dissonance between rhetoric and reality engendered a profound impact that reverberated long after the last bomb fell. The scars borne by the civilian population were not solely external; they were etched into the collective consciousness, ultimately contributing to the unraveling of the once-unwavering bond between the people and their leaders.[21]

Strategic Redirection

As Germany found itself ensnared in the clutches of mounting devastation during the latter stages of World War II, a harrowing juggling act ensued—one that demanded the delicate allocation of increasingly scarce resources between the imperatives of the military and the exigencies of the domestic front. The unremitting raids, coupled with the need to tend to the wounded, rebuild shattered cities, and provide for the displaced, shifted the focus away from the war machine that had once seemed all-consuming.[22]

The acute needs of the civilian population exacted an unforeseen toll, demanding not only tangible resources but also the time and attention of key personnel who were pivotal to the strategic command structure. The scarcity of basic necessities forced a recalibration of priorities as the nation's leaders scrambled to ensure the survival of the populace amidst the havoc wrought by the Allied aerial onslaught. This diversion of resources, both material and human, came at a significant cost—one that reverberated across the military landscape. With each resource redirected toward rebuilding and provisioning, the efficacy of the war effort dwindled. As the frontlines bore the brunt of dwindling supplies and diminishing reinforcements, Germany's ability to mount a robust and effective resistance against the advancing Allies was fatally undermined. The once-mighty military machine, whose thundering advances had struck fear into the hearts of adversaries, now found itself hampered by the scarcity of essentials and a compromised strategic focus.[23]

This complex balancing act between military necessity and domestic urgency became a delicate dance of priorities, revealing the stark reality of a nation teetering on the brink of collapse. The dichotomy between the imperative to defend against external threats and the urgent need to address internal crises became increasingly pronounced.

As resources—both human and material—were stretched thin, the resilience of the German war effort collapsed. The meticulous planning and execution that had characterized Germany's military strategies in the early years of the war were replaced by a sense of desperation and improvisation. The repercussions of this diversion reverberated through the final chapters of World War II, casting a shadow over Germany's capacity to fight on. The logistical strain became particularly evident in the diminished capabilities of the German military. Strategic reserves, once a linchpin of the Reich's military flexibility, dwindled. The scarcity of fuel and essential supplies hampered the mobility of troops and the operational readiness of military equipment. The ability to launch swift and coordinated counterattacks, once a hallmark of Germany martial success, was increasingly eroded.

The diversion of key personnel to address the needs of the domestic front further weakened the military's command structure. Skilled individuals who were essential to strategic planning and execution found themselves grappling with the challenges of managing civilian crises. The erosion of military effectiveness was not solely due to material shortages; it was compounded by a depletion of the human capital that had been instrumental in Germany's military prowess.[24]

As the war dragged on, the delicate dance between military necessity and domestic needs became more precarious. The Nazi war machine struggled to function amidst the ruins of bombed cities and the myriad challenges of sustaining a beleaguered civilian population. The relationship between the home front and the frontlines became a critical factor, the needs of one intrinsically linked to the fortunes of the other.[25]

Preparation for Invasion

The bombing campaign, raining destruction from the skies, emerged as a pivotal stratagem in the broader tapestry of World War II. Its impact extended beyond the immediate devastation it wrought. In the grand theater of military strategy, the bombings played from the start a crucial role in the orchestration of a meticulously choreographed symphony that had aimed to soften Germany's defenses, paving the way for the crescendo of Allied ground invasions.

The systematic weakening of Germany's capacity to resist became the linchpin of this strategy. The bombings—targeting key industrial, logistical, and strategic assets—rendered the German war machine increasingly vulnerable. The relentless bombardment exacted a toll that reverberated far beyond the immediate sites of impact, sowing chaos, disruption, and uncertainty into the very fabric of German military operations. This deliberate erosion of Germany's ability to mount an effective defense proved an instrumental prelude to the Normandy landings and the subsequent offensives. As the Allies stood poised to launch their ground invasions, the cumulative effects of the bombings had strategically enfeebled the Reich's resilience. The once-vaunted defense mechanisms, reeling from the aerial onslaught, found themselves grappling with a diminished capacity to counter the impending threat.[26]

The Normandy landings, executed with meticulous precision on the beaches of northwestern France, were enabled by the strategic groundwork laid by bombing. The bombing campaign had induced a state of disarray and confusion, leaving the German military in disarray as it grappled to regain equilibrium amid the chaos. The subsequent offensives that unfolded were, in essence, built upon the foundation of strategic vulnerability that the bombings had wrought. The disoriented defenses struggled to coordinate, the eroded logistical backbone strained to support comprehensive counterattacks, and the once-impregnable fortifications faltered under the weight of unyielding assault.

The bombings were not merely an act of destruction; they were a calculated overture to a grand symphony of warfare. Their role in softening Germany's defenses was pivotal, setting the stage for the invasions that reshaped the trajectory of World War II. The strategic weakening inflicted by the bombings was integral to the Allies' ultimate triumph over the forces that had held Europe captive.[28]

Cultural and Architectural Loss

The bombing raids, while primarily aimed at strategic and military targets, unleashed a wave of destruction that rippled through Germany's cultural fabric. Cities steeped in historical significance, custodians of centuries-old architectural marvels, were not spared from the maelstrom. Among these venerable urban centers, Dresden, with its storied past and architectural grandeur, emerged as a poignant symbol of the devastation exacted by the bombing campaign.

The aerial onslaught inflicted substantial damage upon Dresden's landmarks and cultural treasures. Iconic structures that had borne witness to centuries of human history were reduced to rubble and ash, erasing irreplaceable vestiges of the past. The resplendent baroque spires and ornate edifices that had adorned the city's skyline for generations succumbed to the inferno.

The loss extended beyond mere physical structures; it encapsulated the very essence of cultural heritage and shared history.[29] Priceless artworks, manuscripts, and artifacts that had been lovingly preserved for posterity were consumed by the flames. The toll exacted upon Dresden's cultural heritage was a painful testament to the unintended consequences of conflict, a reminder of the impermanence of human achievements in the face of the ravages of war.[30]

An indelible scar was left upon Germany's architectural and artistic legacy. The loss of cities like Dresden stood as a solemn reminder of the fragility of mankind's shared cultural inheritance. As the ashes settled over once-proud landmarks, the toll on cultural treasures stood as a stark testament to the cost of conflict.

The Allied bombing campaign on Germany up to April 1945 contributed significantly to the weakening of the Reich's military, industrial, and logistical capabilities. The relentless assault not only reshaped the strategic landscape of World War II but also left an enduring imprint on the nation's psyche, infrastructure, and socio-economic fabric.

Yet, amid this maelstrom, one figure was unmoved by the impending cataclysm: Adolf Hitler. His dogged determination to defy the mounting odds defied reason, his commitment to the war never wavering. However, his steadfastness was mirrored by an erosion of clarity within the echelons of command. Hitler's intentions became enigmatic, a riddle that his subordinates grappled to decipher amidst the confusion, this lack of coordinated direction only exacerbating the turmoil around them.

In these desperate circumstances, Germany's beleaguered struggle was no match for the Allies' formidable arsenal of resources. The scales had tipped decisively as the Allies asserted their superior might, Germany tumbling inexorably towards defeat.[31]

3
Defending the Skies of the Reich

The Beginning of the Luftwaffe

In February 1936, the French Chamber of Deputies had endorsed a Franco-Soviet Pact, with a vote of 353 in favor and 164 against. Exploiting this development as a pretext, Hitler proceeded to reoccupy the demilitarized zone of the Rhineland, including Aachen, Trier, and Saarbrucken. The Luftwaffe, its limited resources comprising a mix of old and new aircraft, was ill-prepared for this relatively minor military action. To divert attention and create a false impression of strength, the only existing flying school that was training fighter pilots had to be disbanded, redirecting aircraft elsewhere. With a shortage of pilots, mechanics were outfitted in pilot uniforms and photographed alongside planes they were unable to fly. The available aircraft across Germany were showcased at different airfields, painted in various color schemes to exaggerate their numbers. This deceptive strategy proved highly successful, leading the global community to accept the charade as evidence of the Third Reich's newfound air power.[1]

Before these incidents unfolded, Mussolini had been waging a relatively modern war against Emperor Haile Selassie's tribesmen in Ethiopia, the major powers in Europe were consumed with futile efforts to stop this unjust aggression. Capitalizing on the turmoil, Hitler strengthened his control over the Rhineland by dissolving the Reichstag and orchestrating a re-election, which he won with an overwhelming popular vote of 99 percent of the German electorate.

In July 1936, civil war erupted in Spain. This development was viewed as a prime opportunity by several influential European nations to use Spain as a testing ground for evaluating military equipment and tactics in real operational conditions, gaining valuable experience. Russia dispatched I-15 and I-16 fighters—the Polikarpov I-15, nicknamed *Chaika* (Seagull), was a Soviet biplane, and the Polikarpov I-16, or *Rata* (Rat), a Soviet monoplane—as well as SB-2 bombers to support the communist government forces in Spain. France primarily sent Potez 540 bombers, Dewoitine D371 fighters, and other French types. Meanwhile, Mussolini and Hitler chose to assist General Francisco Franco, the leader of the revolutionary forces, sending thousands of men and hundreds of tons of equipment over the next three years. If the Spanish had been left to resolve their own issues, it is conceivable that much bloodshed could have been avoided, given the initial even match between the two sides, especially in the air. However, both factions began receiving powerful support from foreign nations. The Luftwaffe's involvement in this theater included a volunteer corps officially designated as "188," but widely known as the Condor Legion. Among the elite members of this group was Adolf Galland, who would later emerge as the leader of the German fighter force.[2] In his book *The German Aces Speak*, Colin Heaton give us a view of the kind of person Galland was:

> Galland, well known and admired by his enemies across the English Channel as an honorable and chivalrous foe, had found an enemy he could not vanquish: his own leadership. The consummate warrior was constantly engaged in heated battle with absolutist politicians, intellectual inferiors, and demagogues, who considered honor and chivalry a weakness and unnecessary in the modern age of warfare.[3]

Luftwaffe personnel selected for service in Spain were provided with civilian attire, various forms of identification, and Spanish currency, all supplied by a clandestine office in Berlin established to conceal the operation's identity. Many of those chosen were enthusiastic about this assignment, as it meant promotion to a rank one level higher than their existing status, accompanied by an increase in pay. In the end, most found that the rewards justified their initial enthusiasm. The next phase of the journey to Spain began when groups of volunteers were relocated to Doberitz, a central assembly point. Disguised in civilian clothing and posing as *Kraft Durch Freude* (Strength Through Joy) tourists, a diverse array of maintenance and support personnel traveled to Hamburg for embarkation, ostensibly bound for Genoa in Italy, but actually en route to Spain.

Communication challenges between the "tourists" and their loved ones were addressed by creating a mail drop under the care of Max Winkler in Berlin, SW 6811. Anyone desiring to correspond with members of the Condor Legion could send their mail through this intermediary. The initial teams set out from Hamburg on the SS *Usaramo*, accompanied by He 51 fighters and additional components for Ju 52 bombers. These bombers had previously been dispatched to Spanish bases with the assistance of Hisma Air Transport units. The Spanish and German Spanish–Moroccan Transport Company (HISMA) and the entirely German Raw Materials and Goods Purchasing Company (ROWAK), were established. The planes were actively transporting French Moorish troops from Morocco to Spain, with an estimated 14,000 soldiers being conveyed using this method.

In the autumn of 1936, substantial aircraft support from France and Russia reached Spain. Faced with this situation, General Franco sought help from Hitler and Mussolini, leading to the dispatch of the primary contingent of the Condor Legion. Upon their arrival in Cadiz, a parade celebrated their presence. While initial bombing raids on government-held facilities proved somewhat ineffective, they did lay the groundwork for subsequent military actions in Poland and other locations.[4]

The Condor fighter forces comprised Fighter Group J 88, which included three squadrons, each equipped with twelve aircraft. The bomber force K 88 comprised four squadrons of Dornier Do 17 bombers and Junkers Ju 52 transports, known for their slow speed and vulnerability. These aircraft were only really effective in daylight when accompanied by a significant number of fighters. The inclusion of Junkers Ju 86D bombers, which were nearly as ineffective as the Ju 52s, further supplemented the fleet. Surprisingly, the air battles unfolded with much greater intensity than expected. At the peak of the Spanish Civil War, the German aviation industry was in the initial stages of manufacturing modern, high-performance aircraft meant to be deployed as primary unit equipment. Notably, in bomber production, the Heinkel He 111 and the Do 17 received high praise during testing and evaluation. The Messerschmitt Bf 109, a single-seat fighter, demonstrated superior capabilities across the board for its era. The Ju 87, commonly known as the Stuka (short for *Sturzkampfflugzeug*, "dive-bomber" in German), gained a stellar reputation, largely due to the support from General Ernst Udet, a distinguished air ace and hero of World War I. Regrettably for the Luftwaffe's later performance in World War II, this backing led to the premature abandonment of the development of four-engine strategic bombers. A tragic accident involving a He 70, resulting in the death of General Walther Wever, a highly regarded mind in the Luftwaffe, extinguished any prospects for the creation of a long-range bomber. Consequently, efforts toward four-engine aircraft were redirected primarily for future naval attacks.

In 1938, the Condor Legion started to be equipped with Do 17s, which proved highly effective and resulted in the formation of a dedicated Do 17 unit within the legion. These were supplemented by a significant number of Ju 87s, always deployed alongside fighter aircraft for protection. The Stuka was notably slow and lacked maneuverability. It was also quite susceptible to attacks, although its slow speed and the capability to pull out of a dive at low altitudes allowed pilots to execute precise dive-bombing assaults. The replacement of the Henschel Hs 123 biplanes with the Ju 87 contributed to its favorable perception by the German high command. Each Stuka was equipped with a siren that emitted a piercing scream, unbearable during the dive phase of each attack. This feature further enhanced the reputation of the Ju 87, one that persisted well into the early stages of World War II.[5]

In 1935 and 1936, when fighter units were established, they fell under the jurisdiction of *Luftgaue* for administration, supply, and operations. This arrangement meant that they were under the authority of a province (*Gau*) within

Germany, with the province's governor effectively serving as the commander of the fighter forces. Primarily, *Luftgaue* (air districts) organizations focused on defense, akin to the role played by the Air National Guard in the United States during the same period. This emphasis on defense stemmed from Germany's concerns that other nations might take military action to disrupt its armament programs, which had been prohibited by treaties at the end of World War I. As there were no actual hostilities, assessing the effectiveness of having fighter aircraft units controlled by geographical commands, such as the *Luftgaue* organization, proved challenging. *Luftgaue* refers to the administrative and territorial divisions within the Luftwaffe during the pre-World War II period. The concept of *Luftgaue* was part of the broader organizational structure of the German air force during a time when defense considerations, particularly in the context of potential interference with armament programs, were prominent.

During peacetime maneuvers, bomber formations were commonly deployed without fighter escorts because the range of single-engine fighters did not align with strategic bombing plans. Sometime between 1937 and 1938, a decision was made to establish twin-engine fighter units specifically for escort purposes, known as *Zerstörer* (Destroyer) units.

In the Spanish conflict, it became evident that providing fighter escorts during daylight hours was essential whenever there was a potential for enemy fighter engagement. Despite the introduction of swift bombers like the Do 17 and He 111, the practice of using fighter escorts persisted, as all involved parties recognized their necessity. Both the Russian and Republican air forces consistently employed fighter-escorted bomber missions during daylight operations. In Germany, there arose a discrepancy in operational planning as the Do 17 and He 111 were employed in maneuvers, while the operational fighters at that time included the Arado 65 and 68, as well as the Heinkel 51, all of which were outdated and sluggish. This created a perception that future bombers would consistently outpace the available fighters.[6]

The firsthand experience with the Bf 109 in Spain swiftly dispelled the notion that bombers would always outpace fighters. Surprisingly, this experience should have prompted an extension of the range of fighter aircraft to match that of bombers, potentially paving the way for the development of strategic forces. However, this crucial step was never undertaken. Instead, the belief persisted that twin-engine fighter destroyers could rival or even outperform single-engine fighters, a perspective that ultimately led to serious consequences.

In Spain, low-level ground-attack missions were consistently carried out without the presence of fighter escorts. In the event of opposition from enemy fighter aircraft, the Heinkel 51 formations had the capability to defend themselves. Simultaneously, the Condor Legion provided indirect cover by conducting fighter sweeps in the vicinity during these missions. When operations targeted enemy airfields situated farther behind the front lines, both fighter and ground-attack units were assigned a coordinated time over the target. It is important to note that there was never direct protection provided to the ground-attack or tactical units during these operations.

A pivotal moment in the evolution of the future Luftwaffe occurred during what can be described as nothing more than a weaponry test on an unprotected Spanish town devoid of any military significance and lacking defenses. On April 26, 1937, Guernica, a community of 10,000 residents in the Basque region of Spain, was chosen for a German experiment aimed at evaluating the effectiveness of mass aerial bombing. In the mid-afternoon of that day, the Condor Legion deployed all available aircraft to target Guernica. The assault commenced with He 51 fighters, which bombed and strafed anything in motion both within and outside the town, before departing in impeccable formation. After this unwarranted assault, He 111 medium bombers executed precise bombing from medium altitude, causing extensive devastation to the already crumbling town. Following numerous bomber formations that flew over the target, releasing their destructive payloads, heavy explosive bombs were succeeded by a multitude of incendiaries. These devices, released from clustered containers, transformed the shattered town into an inferno. The bombs disrupted all communications, obliterated transportation infrastructure, and entirely overwhelmed any potential firefighting or rescue efforts that might have been undertaken.[7]

The assault continued for around three hours, resulting in the total obliteration of Guernica and the death of 1,600 men, women, and children. While such casualties might seem small compared with what was to come between 1939 and 1945, at the time the raid on Guernica stood unparalleled in military history due to its method of execution and the destruction it caused. The global response was so overwhelming that it even surprised Franco and his supporters, yet it did little to alter the perceived necessity of the bombardment. The German propaganda machine countered criticism directed at the Condor Legion by denying the participation of any German aircraft in the bombing. Galland, who was not present in Spain at the time, believed the bombing of Guernica resulted from errors due to primitive bomb sights and inexperienced aircrews. However, he acknowledged the reluctance of Legion members to discuss the matter. During the Nuremberg Trials in 1946, Reichsmarschall Hermann Göring had the final say on the subject, confirming that Guernica had been a testing ground for the Luftwaffe and adding that while it was a pity, they could not do otherwise as Germany had nowhere else to try out its aircraft.

It is undeniable that the Luftwaffe amassed invaluable experience in Spain. Actual combat proved irreplaceable, allowing numerous members of the Condor Legion to increase their experience as they ascended to high-ranking positions within the Luftwaffe when Germany initiated its own military campaigns. A fighter pilot truly discovers their capabilities only when faced with a genuine adversary. Emerging unscathed from the first encounter instills a confidence that cannot be acquired through any other means, enabling them to confront subsequent challenges with increased assurance.[8]

During the Spanish Civil War, the Germans conducted trials on their organization, operations, and equipment, refining techniques that would prove invaluable at the outset of World War II. As an example, they departed from the prevailing wing tip-to-wing tip formations, employed by every other air force globally, in favor of the more flexible pair or "finger four" formations, invented by Werner Mölders, which the United States Army Air Corps later adopted. This consists of four aircraft flying in a formation that resembles the spread-out fingers of a hand when viewed from above. Each aircraft in the formation is positioned to provide optimal situational awareness, firepower, and defensive coverage. The Spanish conflict allowed the Luftwaffe to evaluate new aircraft that had not yet entered production in Germany under combat conditions, helping to identify and rectify any shortcomings. Additionally, they had the opportunity to develop new aircraft types that would eventually surpass those used by the major powers.

Yet despite their successes, the Luftwaffe overlooked several lessons in Spain. Given the significant inferiority of the enemy in Spain, the Germans were able to wage an air war with minimal opposition. The Russian wood and fabric aircraft proved no match for the high-performance aluminum Bf 109s, and the opposition's bombers fell short of the standards set by modern German bombardment fleets. The perceived weakness of the enemy led the Germans to believe that ground attacks by dive-bombers were unstoppable and invaluable for tactical support. Furthermore, they concluded that large bomber formations could travel to and from targets without the need for fighter escorts. Based on their remarkably low combat losses in Spain, they decided that a relatively low level of pilot training would suffice for the future. They also established exceedingly low aircraft production levels, having been persuaded to do so by analysis of unrealistic information from their Spanish adventure.[9]

World War II

In the buildup to World War II, there existed a divergence in interpretations held by leaders within the Allied air forces and the Luftwaffe regarding the role of bombers in warfare. The Luftwaffe perceived bombers primarily as a tactical instrument, serving to bolster ground operations. Conversely, the RAF and USAAF embraced a more strategic stance, regarding bombers as potent tools for dismantling the enemy's morale and economic infrastructure. This dichotomy was underscored by the influence of strategic bombing visionaries such as Hugh Trenchard (often regarded as the father of the Royal Air Force), Billy Mitchell (American general and aviation pioneer), and Giulio Douhet (Italian general and air power theorist), who shaped the perspectives of the Anglo-American air forces. A subset within the Luftwaffe, including figures like Walther Wever, aligned with this strategic perspective. Wever recognized the importance of strategic bombing as a key element of modern warfare.

Wever's death in 1936 resulted in the abandonment of his strategic vision and the associated development of long-range aircraft that could have underpinned it. Instead, the Luftwaffe shifted its focus to short-range aircraft, a trajectory shaped by the prevailing tactical viewpoint. The trajectory envisaged by Wever and his supporters gave way to a more localized approach, reflecting the broader shift within the German Air Force leadership.

The varying influences of prominent figures and the unfortunate demise of key visionaries ultimately steered the course of interpretations of the role of bombers, significantly impacting their strategic development and deployment in wartime. The Luftwaffe was organized into self-contained *Luftflotten*, or air fleets, each of which covered the air operations for a given geographic area. The following chart shows how aircraft of the Luftwaffe and its *Luftflotten* were organized, as compared to how this was done by the USAAF:

USAAF Number of Aircraft	Luftwaffe Number of Aircraft
Air Force 1,000–3,000	*Luftflotte* 1,000
Wing 140–180	*Geschwader* 80–120
Group 48	*Gruppe* 36
Squadron 16	*Staffel* 12
Flight 4	*Schwarm* 4
Element 2	*Rotte* 2

The composition and contours of the Luftwaffe were not solely shaped by the interplay of strategic and tactical considerations; political and economic factors also exerted their influence. Amidst this intricate tapestry, Adolf Hitler's ambition to wield a formidable and imposing air force loomed large. His vision pivoted on the concept of an expansive air fleet that could wield psychological dominance over adversaries. Hermann Göring vocalized this perspective by emphasizing the magnitude of bomber fleet size, often placing it above their inherent efficacy.[10]

Hitler's prioritization of quantity over quality found a rationale in the resource constraints that defined Germany's circumstances. In a strategic calculus driven by scarcity, the resources required to construct two long-range, four-engine bombers were commensurate with those needed to produce five short-range, twin-engine versions. The scarcity of strategic materials, coupled with the army's preference for swift, concentrated campaigns, directed the trajectory of the Luftwaffe's evolution in the prelude to war. As Germany teetered on the brink of global conflict, the shaping of the Luftwaffe was determined by a complex interplay of strategic objectives, tactical imperatives, and resource constraints. Hitler's fervor for an imposing air force, guided by its size, resonated against the backdrop of a scarcity of resources. The Luftwaffe, conceived with swift and nimble bombers sporting modest payloads and limited range, embodied the synthesis of these multifaceted dynamics. This strategic alignment reflected the prevailing geopolitical and economic realities that would, in the crucible of war, dictate the air force's engagement and performance.

The early moves of the global conflict, as outlined in John Keegan's *The Second World War*, unfolded as a series of Blitzkrieg-type campaigns. These initial military endeavors appeared to lend credence to the notion that a dedicated tactical bomber fleet was needed to provide support for ground operations. Intriguingly, while the Luftwaffe was confident, indeed arrogant, regarding its capabilities, it notably refrained from substantial development of its bomber force. This was in stark contrast to the RAF, which, recognizing the strategic significance of bombers, embarked on a robust enhancement of this arm. By 1942, Bomber Command had undergone a transformative evolution. The command had diligently honed its skills and tactics, coupled with the adoption of advanced aircraft tailored for carrying substantial bomb loads across extensive distances, reaching virtually any city within Greater Germany. This evolution, as chronicled by Keegan,[11] was a decisive departure from the Luftwaffe's strategic approach.

Göring disdainfully dismissed the initial sorties executed by Bomber Command as mere pinpricks. However, as the war unfolded, a discernible shift occurred. By the end of 1942, the nature of these aerial assaults had changed from mere irritants to potent hammer-blows, projecting a prophetic glimpse into the devastation that lay ahead.[12]

The Luftwaffe's misplaced confidence and complacency stood juxtaposed against the RAF's foresighted recognition of the strategic potential of a formidable bomber force. This divergence would ultimately prove a pivotal factor in shaping the course of the war.

Commencing its strategic bombing offensive in January of 1943, the USAAF ushered in an era of profound suffering for German cities and their populace. A dual-fronted aerial assault unfolded, with the RAF orchestrating nocturnal raids, while the USAAF executed daytime missions. This strategic synchronization left scant room for the Luftwaffe to mount retaliatory offensives. When the Luftwaffe attempted to launch raids on the United Kingdom, their efforts often came at the cost of disproportionately heavy losses, exacerbating their precarious position.

The absence of long-range German bombers proved a substantial handicap, impacting not only the theater in the West but also the Eastern Front. The Russians, in a sound strategic move, relocated their industrial hubs—factories, power plants, and steel-producing complexes—beyond the operational range of German aircraft. This posed a dire conundrum for the German bomber force, rendering it impotent. The Luftwaffe thus found itself propelled into innovative improvisation, compelled to devise short-term solutions aimed at augmenting the range and potency of their standard bombers.

As chronicled by Max Hastings in *Bomber Command*, the German response was marked by a resolute determination to transcend their limitations. Ingenious improvisations were set into motion with the aim of bolstering the range and destructive potential of their aerial arsenal. The urgent needs of warfare spurred a creative frenzy, as engineers, tacticians, and pilots converged in their pursuit of solutions that could potentially level the playing field against their technologically superior adversaries.[13] In retrospect, the advent of the USAAF's strategic bombing offensive instigated a chapter of tribulations for Germany's cities and their inhabitants. The asymmetry between the air forces in terms of range and strategic prowess painted a grim picture for the Luftwaffe. It was a period that demanded ingenuity, resilience, and resourcefulness—qualities that Germany's air force endeavored to harness in its quest for parity.

Despite facing critiques directed at its High Command, it is imperative to acknowledge that a limited number of German long-range aircraft did indeed exist. However, these were a scarce commodity, insufficient to coalesce into a comprehensive strategic force. Their deployment was primarily earmarked for extensive reconnaissance or for patrolling the expansive Atlantic. These aircraft, while contributing a measure of long-range capability, were far from constituting a decisive strategic advantage, serving more as specialized tools rather than a cohesive entity.

The challenges confronting the Luftwaffe extended beyond the domain of long-range aircraft. The fighter force, a cornerstone of any air force's defensive and offensive capabilities, encountered its own problems. A prominent point of contention lay in the Führer's steadfast conviction that the air force should be consistently and unequivocally on the offensive. This engendered skepticism toward the defensive role of fighter aircraft. Hitler, entranced by the vision of bombers as instruments of offensive might, discounted the potential of fighter planes to fulfill a defensive role. His ideological stance manifested itself in the continued production of short-range bombers, even in the face of a pressing requirement for fighters to strike at the Allied bomber fleets.

David Irving's *The Rise and Fall of the Luftwaffe* offers a clear perspective on this facet of the Luftwaffe's predicament. It chronicles the paradoxical trajectory shaped by ideological beliefs, where the relentless pursuit of offensive prowess via bombers converged with a neglect of the crucial defensive role of fighter aircraft. This fervent approach bore implications that rippled across the strategic landscape, manifesting in the Luftwaffe's resource allocation and combat capabilities. The presence of limited long-range aircraft provided a glimpse of potential, but the dogged pursuit of offensive dominance by bombers overshadowed the imperative for an adequately supplied fighter force. The Luftwaffe's journey, as elucidated by Irving, epitomizes the intricate decisions, priorities, and beliefs that shaped its trajectory.[14]

At the onset of World War II, the Luftwaffe entered the fray boasting a fleet of high-caliber fighters. A significant proportion of Luftwaffe commanders were drawn from the ranks of former fighter pilots who had honed their skills during World War I. This allegiance to aerial combat instilled an enthusiasm for the fighter branch, compelling these leaders to champion the advancement of cutting-edge technologies, including the pioneering realm of jet propulsion. Indeed, the Luftwaffe deployed jet-powered aircraft in combat before any other air force.

While the Luftwaffe demonstrated a commendable strength in terms of pilot numbers and aircraft resources, the effective deployment of these assets in defense of the Reich proved a formidable challenge. This was hampered by relentless Allied attacks targeting Germany's railway infrastructure, causing disruption to the seamless flow of crucial aircraft components from factories and a consequent lack of essential parts, hampering the Luftwaffe's ability to assemble and maintain their aircraft. The Luftwaffe struggled to piece together individual aircraft components for final assembly, with an obvious knock-on effect on its operational capacity.[15]

Remarkably, Luftwaffe training schools still managed to produce capable pilots to face the rigors of aerial combat. However, severe resource constraints affected the comprehensive training regimen pilots required. The scarcity of fuel and essential resources compromised the depth of training, meaning pilots received too-few hours of flight experience before being thrust into combat against the formidable tide of Allied air forces.

In retrospect, the Luftwaffe's trajectory during World War II emerges as a complex interplay of advancements, challenges, and sacrifices. The early prowess in fighter capabilities, buoyed by the spirit of innovation, is juxtaposed against the logistical quagmire fueled by Allied attacks, the German fighter pilots grappling to maintain their operational tempo under the oppression of enemy air superiority.[16]

By 1943, the Luftwaffe was facing problems with both its fighter and bomber arms that seemed unsolvable. The fighter arm was tasked with countering the Allied raids that were destroying German cities, while the bombers needed to increase their range and bomb-load capacity to compensate for their deficiencies. Hitler continued to rely on the bomber arm to take the war to the enemy. The Luftwaffe had initially performed well in the war, but facing enemies with superior power, technology, and equipment, its performance deteriorated from 1943 until its final defeat in 1945.[17]

The Luftwaffe had been fighting on two fronts since mid-1941, against the Soviets in the East and the Allies over Germany and in the West. However, Luftwaffe commanders believed that they could hold the Red Air Force in check, based on evaluations of battle reports and intelligence appraisals. They had confidence that the German pilots' combat skills could balance out the Soviets' superior numbers of aircraft, and that the situation in the East would remain stable so long as enough German fighters and pilots were sent to the Russian front.[18]

The Luftwaffe's struggle to safeguard the Reich against the relentless tide of the Allied bombing offensive spurred the evolution of specialized forces within its ranks. In confronting this challenge, the Luftwaffe's commanders grappled with distinct modes of attack deployed by the British and American bombers, each marked by its own exigencies and countermeasures.

The British emerged as formidable adversaries, wielding the precision of strategic night bombing. Their bombers navigated through the darkness, guided by the meticulous placement of strategic markers. Pioneering this innovation were the specialized Pathfinder aircraft, entrusted with the pivotal task of marking targets with luminescent flares that guided the bomber formations that followed in their wake. An additional layer of potency was conferred by radar sets, equipping the British bombers with an accuracy that weather conditions failed to curb.

In contrast, American bombers took to the skies by day, with grand formations that disgorged payloads in synchronized unison. This daylight offensive presented an imposing spectacle and a daunting challenge for the Luftwaffe's fighter pilots, tasked with detecting and engaging the American formations.

This situation, as outlined by Max Hastings in *Bomber Command*, shaped the evolution of specialized forces within the Luftwaffe. The contours of battle were manifested not merely in the skies, but also in the tactics, strategies, and technologies that underpinned each aerial engagement. The Luftwaffe's response, replete with specialized forces and innovations, stands as a testament to the adaptability and ingenuity evoked amidst the storms of war.[19]

The German defensive mechanism, when confronted by British night-time raids, revealed a foundational vulnerability, exposing the absence of a dependable electronic apparatus for aircraft detection and interception. This deficiency underscored the shortcomings within the German defenses. The incapacity of German night-fighter units to bring down a significant number of RAF aircraft was a glaring problem, preventing the strategic calculus from tipping towards the realm of uneconomical loss in terms of both aircraft and personnel.

Despite the best efforts of German ground control, the night-fighter pilots of the Luftwaffe struggled to locate their targets, having to rely on visual contact, never easy at nighttime. The progression of the night bombing campaign was marked by the proliferation of bigger and better four-engine RAF bombers with the capability to transport substantial bomb payloads across considerable distances at remarkable speeds.

A symbolic moment in this saga materialized on July 25, 1943, with Bomber Command's assault on Hamburg, culminating in the devastation of the city. The attrition rate for the bombers during this mission stood at a mere 1.5 percent, a notable triumph for the RAF. This remarkable feat was partly attributed to the strategic utilization of a tactical innovation known as "Window." This involved the deployment of slender strips of metallic foil, named Window, into the flight path of the bomber force. These fragments created distorted images on the subpar radar systems employed by the German night-fighters. This interplay of tactics and technology underscored the dynamics at play in the unfolding aerial theater.[20]

Nevertheless, the Luftwaffe night fighters and flak units had a better ratio of kills against RAF bombers than day fighters against the USAAF.[21]

The German defense apparatus was fraught with deficiencies and adversities. The quest to achieve aerial supremacy and operational efficacy was marked by challenges and innovations, with the evolution of the British air assault aided by the ingenious utilization of disruptive tactics.

In the face of the USAAF's formidable aerial presence, the Luftwaffe found itself requiring a recalibration of tactics. The Americans unleashed operations involving hundreds of bombers in tightly choreographed formations, with rows, tiers and lines, that demanded a bespoke response from the German aerial command. The iconic B-17 Flying Fortress and B-24 Liberator bombers were the workhorses that spearheaded the American bombing campaign. The Flying Fortress was a potent emblem of American air power, bristling with a formidable armament of thirteen heavy-caliber machine guns. The remarkable scale of American might became evident within the box formation employed, where no less than 3,900 machine guns converged in an intricate web of interlocking defensive fire zones. This created a deadly deterrent to the Luftwaffe's fighter pilots, rendering attacks on the massive formations fraught with risk.

Central to the American tactical model was the employment of tight formations created by Curtis E. LeMay. Conversely, the Luftwaffe sought to disperse these formidable clusters. The rationale underlying this strategy lay in the recognition that the potency of the American box formation rested on the cohesion of its individual components. The successful scattering of this formation would expose the individual bombers to heightened vulnerability and render them susceptible to the ravages of attack.

As meticulously chronicled by David Brown and Kenneth Macksey in *The History of Air Warfare*, this intricate dance of tactics and countermeasures underscored the dynamic tableau of aerial warfare.[22] The American box formation, a testament to their technological prowess and strategic acumen, posed an imposing challenge to the Luftwaffe. The saga that unfolded in the skies above occupied Europe, encompassing the choreography of formations and their attempted dispersal, bears testament to the complex interplay of strategy, innovation, and adaptability in wartime aviation.

The Luftwaffe encountered two formidable quandaries over the course of the war, both posing distinct operational challenges. The first conundrum revolved around devising effective strategies to counter the nocturnal onslaught of British bombers, while the second pertained to the formidable task of neutralizing the American bombers' audacious daylight raids in imposing formations. A nuanced exploration reveals that the British bombers held a distinct technological edge, one that hinged on the realm of electronics, rendering the task of detection and interception an uphill battle for the German night-fighters. Given the relentless encroachment of British bombers under the shroud of darkness, the Luftwaffe's command directed its energies toward marshaling defenses to thwart them.

However, with the emergence of American bombers executing raids in broad daylight, the German focus shifted precipitously.

A plethora of sometimes audacious solutions were proffered, among these the suggestion to orchestrate monumental explosions to engulf the American planes. An even more daring concept involved the notion of pilots deliberately ramming their own aircraft into the American bombers, a strategy that, while militarily potent, carried the corollary of sacrificing the pilots.

Hitler rejected the notion of suicide missions while endorsing approaches that accorded some prospect of survival for the pilots. Among the strategies proposed, one distinctive scheme involved the deployment of special lightweight aircraft to infiltrate American bomber formations and trigger cataclysmic detonations. A complementary proposition was for towed gliders above the enemy formations, unleashing a flurry of machine-gun fire before culminating in a deliberate ramming maneuver. Max Hastings' comprehensive exploration of the situation lays bare the dynamics that characterized the Luftwaffe's strategic evolution.[23] The distinct challenges posed by British and American bombers had galvanized a wide spectrum of innovative responses, a relentless quest for ingenuity in aerial warfare.

Reich Armaments Minister Albert Speer, entrusted with oversight of the formidable German arms program, embarked upon rigorous analysis and unearthing a trove of objective statistical insights. His deliberations revolved around discerning the thresholds for the successful execution of ramming attacks—an audacious tactical maneuver to stem the American aerial onslaughts. Speer unearthed a paramount revelation, casting the asymmetry in manpower between the Germans and Americans as a critical determinant in the calculus of success. This stark manpower difference, which undeniably favored the Americans, underscored the daunting task facing the Germans. A cardinal principle emerged: for any ramming attack to be deemed effective, it needed a commensurate ratio that tilted the scales toward profitability for the Germans. Speer's estimations underscored that the equilibrium of success could only be attained if a German fighter/rammer succeeded in obliterating three American bombers for every one German aircraft lost in a ramming. Any ratio exceeding the prescribed three-to-one benchmark would render the outcome favorable for the Germans. Hajo Herrman commented on this during a 1999 interview with Colin Heaton:

> I discussed this plan with Göring, Speer and others in a staff meeting, Galland was there, and others. [Note: the others attending included Gordon Gollob, Herbert Ihlefeld, Gustav Roedel, Eduard Neumann, Guenther Lutzow, Hannes Trautloft, Werner Baumbach, and Dietrich Peltz.] I supported the concept as being sound, but I also mentioned that there should be some measure of giving the Kommando pilots a chance of surviving, possibly to fly again. Attacking a

bomber, and then escaping before impact I thought was practical. Still it would be a danger. Galland and the others disagreed strongly.[24]

During a 1984 interview, former colonel Herbert Ihlefeld, *Kommodore* of JG 1, stated:

> This was perhaps the craziest thing I ever heard, and Galland and I both disagreed with this plan. Especially as Goering wanted to take young boys, give them enough training to be airborne, and then waste their lives. I called him [Herrmann] a damned fool, and asked if he would fly such a mission. Ironically, he said "Yes," and I said, "I thought you were smarter than that."[25]

In a 1984 interview, Gustav Roedel, another former colonel and *Geschwaderkommodore* of JG 2, said: "When they asked what our thoughts were, I simply said, 'I think that it is a bad plan, losing an aircraft and a pilot without any guarantee of success.'"[26]

In *Bomber Command* by Max Hastings, this pivotal juncture unfolds as a testament to the intricacies of wartime strategizing.[27] Speer's analytical insights, which meticulously charted the contours of success in ramming attacks, serve as markers within the larger mosaic of aerial combat. The convergence of mathematics, manpower, and military dynamics, as delineated by Hastings, exemplifies the profound interplay of calculated precision and contextual exigency within the Third Reich.

The German army faced a formidable predicament during World War II, one that pivoted on the complex dynamics of the Eastern Front. Hindered by the protracted conflict in this theater, the German army found itself shackled, deprived of the strategic maneuverability essential for launching a decisive summer offensive in 1944. Clashes with the Red Army had exacted a toll on the German army's capabilities, sapping its vitality and compromising its capacity to mount a robust offensive.

The German army grappled not only with the exigencies of the Eastern Front but also with the relentless barrage of the Red Army's unyielding 1943–44 winter offensive. The onslaught of attacks became an enduring trial, demanding the steadfast resolve of the German troops. Against this backdrop, Germany embarked upon the strategic recalibration of withdrawing its forces from the Eastern Front. Simultaneously, a series of diplomatic endeavors unfolded, with European nations allied with Germany against the Soviet Union fervently seeking avenues for peace.

At the same time, the Western Allies were carefully preparing for a cross-Channel invasion. This offered them the prospect of obtaining crucial airfields on the European continent, a strategic advantage that would enhance the effectiveness of Allied fighters, freeing them from the challenges of carrying additional fuel tanks to extend their range. The implications of this strategic advantage went beyond increasing Allied firepower; it meant a substantial increase in the number of adversaries for German fighter pilots to contend with. As expounded within *The Longest Day: The Classic Epic of D-Day* by Cornelius Ryan, the crucible of aerial combat witnessed an ominous confluence of challenges. German fighter pilots, already confronted with the herculean task of penetrating the formidable bomber formations, now faced the specter of United States fighters, poised to unleash their deadly might.[28]

4

The State of the Luftwaffe in Late 1944/Early 1945

The Luftwaffe had emerged as a formidable and crucial component of Nazi Germany's military machinery during the early years of World War II. Playing a pivotal role in supporting ground operations, conducting bombing campaigns, and defending German airspace, the Luftwaffe's dominance was a significant factor in the early successes of the Third Reich. However, as the war progressed into late 1944 and early 1945, the Luftwaffe found itself in a state of crisis.

At the outset of World War II, the Luftwaffe was renowned as one of the world's most powerful air forces. Its prowess was evident in the swift and coordinated air campaigns that accompanied the German invasions of Poland and France, and initially in the Soviet Union. Controlling the skies over much of Europe, the Luftwaffe's early successes were closely tied to its technological advancements and strategic innovations. By late 1944, however, the once-mighty Luftwaffe was grappling with a myriad of challenges. The tide had turned in favor of the Allied air forces, which had gained air superiority. The Luftwaffe's decline was exacerbated by a severe shortage of essential resources—planes, fuel, and experienced pilots—a direct result of the relentless Allied bombing campaigns that targeted German industrial and transportation infrastructure.

One critical aspect of the Luftwaffe's crisis was the depletion of its aircraft and personnel. The attrition rate had taken a toll, the Luftwaffe struggling to replace lost planes and train new pilots at a pace that could match the demands of the conflict. The technological advancements made by the Allies in aircraft design, radar systems, and overall aviation capabilities also posed significant challenges. The Luftwaffe found itself lagging behind in terms of innovation and adaptability, further diminishing its ability to contend with the technologically superior Allied air forces.

Fuel scarcity was another crippling factor for the Luftwaffe in its waning months. Allied bombing campaigns targeting oil refineries and transportation networks had severely hampered Germany's fuel production. The Luftwaffe, like other branches of the German military, faced a dwindling supply of aviation fuel, hindering its operational capacity and reducing the range and duration of its missions.

The crisis of the Luftwaffe was not only a result of material shortages but also reflected a diminishing pool of skilled and experienced pilots. The attrition of seasoned aviators in earlier battles, and the challenges of training new pilots amid wartime constraints, contributed to a decline in the Luftwaffe's combat effectiveness. The state of the Luftwaffe in late 1944 and early 1945 was in stark contrast to its earlier dominance. The Allied air forces had turned the tide, and the Luftwaffe struggled to cope with shortages in every area. This decline, coupled with the constant Allied bombing campaigns and technological advancements, ultimately played a crucial role in the outcome of the air war in Europe during World War II.

Shortage of Planes

The shortage of planes in the Luftwaffe during late 1944 and early 1945 was one of the main factors contributing to the decline of the German air force. Germany's war economy was struggling to keep up with the demands of the conflict, with the production of planes slowing down. This meant that the Luftwaffe was unable to replace the aircraft it was losing in combat, and its overall strength was declining.

One of the key reasons for the shortage of planes in the Luftwaffe was the decline of Germany's war economy. By late 1944, the German economy was in a dire state, with shortages of raw materials and labor. The Nazi regime had prioritized the production of tanks and other military vehicles over planes, in the belief that ground forces would be more important in the war. As a result, the production of planes had slowed significantly. According to historian Richard Overy, by the end of 1944, the Luftwaffe was making just 41 percent of the planes it had produced in 1942. This meant that the Luftwaffe was unable to replace the planes it was losing in combat, meaning its overall strength was declining.[1]

The scarcity of aircraft within the Luftwaffe was aggravated by subpar manufacturing quality. This emanated from the challenges besieging the German war economy, which grappled with the procurement of essential raw materials, chief among them aluminum—a vital component for crafting high-caliber aircraft. This culminated in the production of aircraft constructed from more affordable alternatives like wood and steel, a compromise that had ramifications across the aerial theater.

The aircraft built using such substitutes were inherently endowed with inferior attributes, a stark departure from the benchmark of quality among their Allied enemies. This manifested in aircraft that not only lacked the durability requisite for the rigors of aerial combat but also suffered from impaired maneuverability. These factors cast a long shadow over the Luftwaffe's operational efficacy, rendering them susceptible to destruction during engagement by enemy fighter aircraft.

The State of the Luftwaffe in Late 1944/Early 1945

The scarcity of top-grade materials contributed to the Luftwaffe's deterioration, the compromise in aircraft quality highlighting the challenges that beset the German air force during late 1944 and early 1945.

The shortage of aircraft for the Luftwaffe was accentuated by its rapid attrition in combat. The crucible of late 1944 bore witness to a Luftwaffe ensnared in a desperate struggle for survival. The magnitude of losses sustained burgeoned exponentially, casting a pall over the German air force's operational effectiveness. In the contested skies over occupied Europe, the Allied air forces wielded a palpable dominance. The Luftwaffe was ensnared in a maelstrom of aerial engagements, precipitating the erosion of both planes and pilots at an alarming pace. Historian Williamson Murray's insights underscore the magnitude of this attrition, revealing that a staggering 70 percent of the Luftwaffe's pilots and aircraft were lost in 1944 alone. This jarring statistic underscores the reality that the Luftwaffe was hemorrhaging its operational capacity at a rate that outpaced its ability to replenish.[2] The symbiotic relationship between attrition and scarcity crafted a self-perpetuating cycle of depletion. The mounting losses translated into a strain that far exceeded the Luftwaffe's capacity to produce aircraft. With each fallen pilot and destroyed aircraft, the Luftwaffe's operational prowess eroded further, creating a crippling deficit. The profound implications of this confluence of attrition and scarcity unraveled within the context of a Luftwaffe beleaguered by the unforgiving exigencies of war.

The shortage of planes in the Luftwaffe had a significant impact on the German war effort. The Luftwaffe was unable to provide effective aerial support for ground forces, which often left the army exposed to enemy air attacks. The shortage of planes also meant that the Luftwaffe was unable to engage in offensive operations against Allied targets. The Allied air forces operated with relative impunity, bombing German cities and industrial targets with little opposition from the Luftwaffe. The shortage of planes also had a psychological impact on the German people. The Nazi leadership had portrayed the Luftwaffe as a symbol of German military might, and its decline became a sign of the nation's impending defeat, contributing to a sense of hopelessness and despair among the populace.

The lack of planes during late 1944 and early 1945 was a significant factor contributing to the decline of the German air force. The degradation of the German war economy, the inferior quality of the planes that were being produced, and the high attrition rate of the Luftwaffe all contributed to this shortage, which had a significant impact on the outcome of the war. Without enough planes to defend the Reich, the Allies were able to bomb Germany with relative impunity, causing massive damage to its infrastructure and demoralizing its people. Furthermore, the Luftwaffe was unable to mount an effective defense against the Allied armies advancing towards Germany from both east and west.

Shortage of Fuel

Meanwhile, the Luftwaffe was also facing a critical shortage of fuel in late 1944 and early 1945. This was due to a number of factors, including the Allied bombing campaign, the loss of access to oil-rich territories, and the diversion of fuel resources to other branches of the military. The Allied bombing campaign against German oil facilities was one of the primary causes of the fuel shortage. Beginning in 1942, the Allies launched a sustained aerial campaign against German oil facilities to disrupt the production and distribution of fuel to the German war machine. The campaign intensified in late 1944, with the RAF and USAAF launching large-scale raids against oil facilities in Germany and occupied Europe.

The raids had a devastating impact on German oil production. According to historian Richard Overy, oil production in Germany fell from a prewar level of 44.5 million tons per year to just 12 million tons in 1944.[3] This meant that the Luftwaffe was receiving only a fraction of the fuel it needed to sustain its operations. In addition to the Allied bombing campaign, the loss of access to oil-rich regions also contributed to the shortage. Germany had been heavily reliant on oil imports from the Caucasus region and Romania prior to the war, but the loss of these territories to the Soviets in 1943 and 1944 respectively cut off these vital sources of oil. This forced Germany to rely on synthetic fuels, which were less efficient and more expensive to produce than natural petroleum-based fuels.

The diversion of fuel resources to other branches of the military also contributed to the shortage in the Luftwaffe. As Germany's situation on the Eastern Front deteriorated, the military began to shift its resources to the Western Front, where the Allies were preparing to launch a massive invasion. This meant that the Luftwaffe had to compete with other branches of the military for limited amounts of fuel. The fuel shortage had a number of implications for the Luftwaffe. One of the most significant was that it severely limited the number of operational aircraft that it could field. According to historian James S. Corum, the Luftwaffe was operating at a fraction of its potential strength due to the fuel shortage.[4] This meant that it was unable to mount effective defensive or offensive operations, and its ability to support ground troops was severely curtailed. It also drastically reduced the flight training hours for new pilots, sending underqualified men into combat, and Galland, Ihlefeld, Neumann, Hrabak, Roedel and other *Kommodoren* (wing commanders) told Göring to his face that they would not put those young boys into action.[4]

With limited fuel resources, the Luftwaffe was unable to provide its pilots with the extensive training that was necessary to maintain their proficiency. With many pilots sent into combat with inadequate training, the risk of accidents increased and the effectiveness of operations decreased. The shortage also had implications for aircraft design. With limited fuel resources, the Luftwaffe was forced to design and build planes that were more fuel-efficient. This meant that it had to sacrifice other design features, such as armor and armament, in order to reduce the weight of the aircraft. Luftwaffe planes were thus more vulnerable to enemy fire, while their ability to inflict damage on enemy aircraft and ground targets was lessened.

Corum argues that the Germans' inability to acquire enough fuel was a critical issue for Luftwaffe operations in late 1944 and early 1945. In his book *The Luftwaffe: Creating the Operational Air War, 1918–1940*, he explains that fuel shortages caused by Allied bombing and the lack of domestic oil reserves forced the Luftwaffe to rely heavily on synthetic fuel, which was of lower quality and less dependable.[5] Furthermore, the Luftwaffe's fuel distribution system was inefficient and often disrupted, leading to shortages and delays in refueling planes. In *The Bombers and the Bombed: Allied Air War Over Europe, 1940–1945*, Richard Overy notes that the Luftwaffe fuel allocation system was frequently chaotic, with some units receiving too much fuel while others received too little.[6] This led to a situation where planes were often grounded due to lack of fuel, or pilots were forced to fly shorter missions to conserve supplies.

Another factor contributing to the fuel shortage was the Luftwaffe's heavy reliance on trucks to transport fuel to airfields. The Allied bombing campaign had severely damaged Germany's transportation infrastructure, making it difficult to move fuel supplies from refineries to airfields. Additionally, the constant need to transport troops and supplies to the front lines meant that there were not enough trucks available to transport fuel.[7]

The fuel shortage had a significant impact on the Luftwaffe's ability to conduct operations. It was unable to maintain large numbers of planes in the air for extended periods, limiting the amount of time pilots could spend on combat missions. This was a severe handicap, as it meant the Luftwaffe was unable to establish air superiority or provide adequate air support for ground troops. The shortage of fuel also affected the Luftwaffe's ability to conduct reconnaissance missions, planes often forced to fly for shorter periods to conserve fuel, limiting the amount of territory they could observe.[8]

The fuel shortage thus had a significant impact on the Luftwaffe's ability to defend Germany from the Allied air campaign. With fewer planes available and limited fuel supplies, it was unable to intercept Allied bombers en masse. Instead, it was forced to rely on hit-and-run attacks by small groups of planes, which were often unsuccessful.[9]

Shortage of Experienced Pilots

Another major challenge facing the Luftwaffe in late 1944 and early 1945 was a shortage of experienced pilots. The war had been raging for more than five years by this point, and many of the Luftwaffe's top pilots had been killed or captured. Additionally, the Nazi regime's decision to prioritize the production of fighters over bombers had exacerbated the shortage of pilots, as fighters required more training and skill to operate effectively.[10] As a result, the Luftwaffe was left with a shortage of experienced pilots to fly its remaining planes, which further weakened its overall fighting capability.

One of the Luftwaffe's most experienced fighter pilots was Adolf Galland, who had previously served as the commander of the fighter forces. In his memoir, Galland lamented the shortage of experienced pilots in the Luftwaffe, writing that "the inadequacy of replacement training was becoming increasingly apparent, and with the dwindling supply of experienced pilots, it was impossible to maintain the same standards of efficiency."[11] Galland's observations were echoed by other pilots and commanders, who noted that the shortage of experienced pilots was making it increasingly difficult to defend German airspace. To make matters worse, the regime was also resorting to desperate measures to fill the pilot shortage, such as conscripting teenagers and elderly men into service. These pilots, known as child soldiers and granny pilots, were often given little training and were forced to fly outdated and poorly maintained planes. Unsurprisingly, these pilots were often shot down by the Allies, leading to further losses for the Luftwaffe.

The shortage of experienced pilots also had a significant impact on the Luftwaffe's ability to develop new tactics and strategies. In his book *The German Air Force 1933–1945: An Anatomy of Failure*, Williamson Murray argues that the Luftwaffe's inability to adapt to changing circumstances was partly due to the lack of veteran pilots. Murray writes that "the Luftwaffe was unable to come up with new and effective tactics, primarily because of the loss of experienced pilots and their inability to experiment with new tactics."[12]

Another factor contributing to the shortage of experienced pilots was the increasingly dangerous nature of air combat. As the war progressed, the Allies developed more effective tactics for shooting down German planes, such as the use of radar and the development of new types of ammunition.[13] These advances made it much more difficult for German pilots to survive, even if they were highly skilled.[14] As historian John Keegan notes, "The odds against a German fighter pilot surviving his first sortie in the autumn of 1944 were about three to one."[15] This meant that even if the Luftwaffe was able to train new pilots, they were unlikely to survive long enough to gain significant combat experience.

The shortage of experienced pilots was particularly acute in the fighter units, which were tasked with defending German airspace from Allied bombers. As the war went on, the Allied bombing campaign became more intense, and the Luftwaffe struggled to keep up. According to historian Stephen L. McFarland, the German fighter force had been reduced to a skeleton force by the end of 1944.[16] Many of the pilots who remained were inexperienced, and they were facing an increasingly sophisticated enemy. The Allied bombers were now guarded by long-range fighter escorts, which made it much more difficult for the Luftwaffe to mount effective attacks. As a result, the Luftwaffe was forced to adopt a defensive posture, which further reduced its effectiveness.

The Luftwaffe also struggled with a shortage of ground crew personnel. According to Richard Overy, "The most important deficiency in the Luftwaffe by 1944 was in the supply of ground crew, who were needed to maintain and repair aircraft, service engines, and handle ammunition and fuel."[17] This meant that the Luftwaffe was unable to keep its remaining planes in good condition, which further reduced their effectiveness in combat.

The war had put a great deal of strain on Germany's economy, and the country was struggling to produce the necessary resources to keep the war machine running. This included not just planes and fuel, but also spare parts and skilled mechanics. Consequently, many planes were being sent into battle in a state of disrepair, and there were not enough mechanics to fix them. This led to a situation where many planes were lost due to mechanical failure rather than enemy action.

The shortage of experienced pilots meant the Luftwaffe was losing planes and pilots at an alarming rate. By early 1945, the Luftwaffe was a shadow of its former self. Its planes were outdated, its pilots were inexperienced, and its ground crews were overworked and under-resourced. The Luftwaffe was thus no longer able to mount an effective defense against the Allied air forces, meaning the end of the war was in sight.

Technological Inferiority

In the final years of World War II, the Luftwaffe was faced with an overwhelming technological inferiority when compared to the Allied air forces. The Allied powers had developed advanced aircraft with superior engines, radar, and weaponry, while the Germans were struggling to keep up with the technological advancements due to resource shortages, damaged infrastructure, and poor strategic decisions. This technological disadvantage significantly impacted on the Luftwaffe's ability to compete with the Allies and ultimately contributed to their defeat. In this investigation, we will explore the technological inferiority of the Luftwaffe in late 1944 and early 1945, examining its causes, consequences, and impact on the outcome of the war.

One of the primary reasons for the technological inferiority of the Luftwaffe in the final years of the war was the shortage of resources. By 1944, German industry was struggling to keep up with the demands of the war, with resources and infrastructure severely damaged. This led to a lack of access to raw materials, which impacted the production of advanced aircraft, engines, and weapons. The lack of resources also hindered the development of new technology, as Germany was unable to invest in research and development to keep pace with the Allies. Additionally, the Luftwaffe was unable to maintain and repair existing aircraft, which were rapidly deteriorating due to overuse, lack of proper maintenance, and constant exposure to Allied attacks.

Another factor contributing to the inferiority of the Luftwaffe was its reluctance to embrace new technology. Despite early success in the war, the Germans were hesitant to adopt new technological advancements. One example is the radar technology that was developed by the Allies. The Germans did have a positive evolution in radar technology, especially ground and airborne technology. The overall technological stagnation was a result of a combination of factors, including a lack of resources, bureaucratic infighting, and the arrogance of the German leadership.

The aircraft produced by the Luftwaffe in the final years of the war were vastly inferior to those of the Allies. The Focke-Wulf Fw 190, the primary fighter plane of the Luftwaffe, was a formidable plane when it was introduced in 1941. However, by 1944, it was outdated and unable to compete with the latest Allied fighters. The Messerschmitt Bf 109, which was another mainstay of the Luftwaffe, was also obsolescent and was no match for the Allied planes. Additionally, the Luftwaffe's bombers, such as the Junkers Ju 88 and Heinkel He 111, were outdated and unable to penetrate Allied defenses. The Germans attempted to introduce new planes, such as the Messerschmitt Me 262, the world's first operational jet-powered fighter aircraft, but production was delayed due to a shortage of resources, and only a limited number of planes were produced.

The engines used by the Luftwaffe were another major factor in their technological inferiority. German aircraft were powered by engines that were less efficient and less dependable than those used by the Allies. The Luftwaffe had developed advanced engines early in the war, such as the BMW 801 and the Junkers Jumo 211, but they were unable to keep up with the rapid advancements made by the Allies. The Allies were able to produce more powerful engines that were also more fuel-efficient, giving their planes longer range and greater speed. This meant that the Luftwaffe was at a significant disadvantage when engaging with the Allies in aerial combat.

The weapons used by the Luftwaffe in late 1944 and early 1945 were also outdated and inadequate compared to the advanced weapons of the Allied air forces. German jet fighters, such as the Me 262, were technologically advanced and had the potential to change the course of the war, but production was too slow to make a significant impact. Additionally, the jets required more fuel than conventional aircraft, exacerbating the fuel shortage problem in the Luftwaffe.

In contrast, the Allied air forces had access to the latest technology and were rapidly advancing in their capabilities. The P-51 Mustang, for example, was a highly effective fighter aircraft that was faster and had longer range than comparable German planes. The Allies also had superior electronic countermeasures and radar systems, making it easier for them to detect and intercept enemy aircraft. These technological advantages gave the Allies a significant edge in aerial combat. Furthermore, the Luftwaffe was lacking in other critical areas such as communication and coordination. According to historian Williamson Murray, the Luftwaffe lacked a centralized command structure and

The State of the Luftwaffe in Late 1944/Early 1945

had a fragmented organization that prevented effective communication and coordination between units (Murray, 1983, p. 184). This made it difficult for the Luftwaffe to respond to changing conditions on the battlefield and to mount effective counterattacks.

The Luftwaffe in late 1944 and early 1945 faced significant challenges that contributed to its overall weakness. A shortage of experienced pilots, a lack of fuel and resources, and inferior technology and weapons all contributed to its declining strength. These challenges were compounded by a fragmented command structure and poor communication and coordination between units. Despite the bravery and dedication of individual pilots and ground crew, the Luftwaffe was unable to turn the tide of the war and was ultimately defeated by the Allied air forces.

5

Special Aviation Units Before Sonderkommando Elbe

Leaders of the German aviation units were assessed based on their effectiveness in destroying enemy aircraft, warships, tanks, and transportation, among other targets. However, they also had the opportunity to contribute to their homeland through innovative ideas, garnering personal recognition (Wilfred von Oven, *Finale Furioso; with Goebbels until the end*, Grabert, Tübingen). On August 2, 1943, Major Hans-Joachim "Hajo" Herrmann, having just celebrated his 30th birthday, received the Oak Leaves for the Knight's Cross of the Iron Cross. The German leadership was recognizing the establishment of Jagdgeschwader Wilde Sau (Night Fighter Wing Wild Boar) by Herrmann. The inception of this unit followed the troubling revelation that advanced Allied jamming devices had rendered highly sensitive equipment in German night-fighter aircraft useless. The existing Kammhuber Line night-defense system—complex, costly, and vulnerable—had become virtually obsolete.[1] On June 27, 1943, Göring granted Major Herrmann, a seasoned fighter pilot, permission to implement an old idea against strong opposition from Lieutenant General Josef Kammhuber—developer of the Kammhuber Line—at Hitler's retreat at Obersalzberg, in the presence of Generaloberst Hans Jeschonnek, Chief of the General Staff of the Luftwaffe.

Herrmann's new strategy emerged when the Allies gained the upper hand in radar-controlled interception. Fighters were now instructed to engage British bombers illuminated by searchlights while avoiding their own antiaircraft fire. Despite initial success, increasing losses and unfavorable weather conditions eventually led to the abandonment of this tactic. In Wilde Sau operations, regular fighters like the Bf 109 and Fw 190, flown by experienced pilots, confronted British bombers at night without sophisticated equipment. These volunteer pilots operated in similar fashion to daytime missions, relying on visual cues. Pilots aimed to visually identify and intercept enemy bombers with the assistance of searchlights. Initial tests with former flying instructors skilled in blind-flying techniques suggested that ideal weather conditions involved a specific, not too thick, low-level cloud cover, silhouetting the bomber against backlit clouds for easy spotting by German fighters flying above them.[2]

Coordination with ceasefires by German flak units proved challenging during Wilde Sau operations. To prevent friendly fire, fighters were restricted to specific altitudes. Navigation presented another hurdle, as night-flying aids were rudimentary. A comprehensive system of visual aids—including light beacons, searchlight patterns, flak guns firing tracers through clouds, and parachute flares—was established. Initially, converted bomber pilots were used for their experience in night navigation. The Allied bombing target, an illuminated city, served as an additional navigation aid. As the British increasingly avoided cloudy weather, they soon fell into a new trap: cleverly arranged artificial lighting illuminating the cloud layers from below, so that the bombers now looked like slow-moving marker crosses to the night fighters circling above. Fires on the ground caused by exploding bombs increased this effect.

The Wilde Sau fighters took full advantage of their chances. Colonel General Hubert Weise, Air Force Commander Central, and Field Marshal Erhard Milch were enthusiastic. As the right-hand man to Hermann Göring, Milch was instrumental in building and expanding the Luftwaffe. He and Weise supported Major Herrmann, and Kammhuber suddenly found himself relieved on September 15, 1943. Göring replaced the general of night fighters with the successful Herrmann. Fighter Wing 300 was designated as the core cell of the new night-fighter unit, which consisted of between twelve and fifteen aircraft, and groups in Bonn-Hangelar, Oldenburg, and Rheine immediately began special training. They were quickly joined by the pilots of Fighter Wing 301 in Neubiberg and Fighter Wing 302 in Doberitz—most of whom did not yet have their own aircraft but rather used those of the day fighters based at the airfield.

The three new night fighter groups embodied Herrmann's first special unit, the Wilde Sau, assigned to the newly formed Reich Air Fleet as the 30th Fighter Division.[3] Herrmann was duly promoted to lieutenant colonel as his fame quickly spread. Colonel Viktor von Lößberg's Zahme Sau (Tame Boar) night-fighter interception tactic effectively complemented Herrmann's system. In the Bf 110, the presence of a third man in the cockpit proved to be advantageous for increased observation, recognition, and navigation.

In August 1943, 182 Allied aircraft fell victim to the new tactics of 702 German fighters—96 percent of them four-engine RAF bombers. Over 75 percent of contacts with the enemy were successful. The RAF's Bomber Command was pushed to the brink of failure. Only when the "Corona" disruption method was used did the situation for the British improve a little. Corona involved the use of RAF ground listening and broadcasting stations in England, from which German-speaking RAF men and WAAF (Women's Auxiliary Air Force) women broke into Luftwaffe fighter-controllers' radio frequencies and broadcast false instructions to the enemy fighters.

In the fall of 1943, reorganization within the fighter force led to the expansion of the duties of General der Jagdflieger Adolf Galland (General of Fighters) to include the night-time arena. Galland was told by Göring to give Hermann 500 day fighters for nighttime use. On November 27, Herrmann became commander of all night-fighter units, albeit under Galland. Luftwaffe pilot Wing Commander Wolfgang Falck offered the following opinion of Herrmann:

> One of the most unique events to occur, in which I was somewhat involved, was in June 1943, when Hajo Herrmann entered the picture. He was a bomber pilot, an outstanding airman on all accounts, and he had an idea. He wanted to create a night fighter unit that used day fighters, using searchlights to switch the blacked out cities into brilliantly illuminated locations to hunt British bombers from below, while his pilots flew above them. This way they would be silhouetted against any clouds. At first I was skeptical, but Hajo had some great ideas.[4]

However, after an impressive series of successes, the disadvantages of the Wilde Sau process were becoming increasingly apparent. There were many accidents caused by the fighter planes taking off and landing in the dark. For example, on the night of January 4, 1944, fifteen aircraft were lost without enemy action. Actual fighting time was limited to just thirty minutes due to fuel supply issues. Failure of the only engine meant the total loss of the aircraft; emergency landings at night were impossible. Equipped only with simple navigation instruments, a pilot who became disoriented while flying blind for long periods had to jump out; the aircraft then crashed somewhere. The weather also caused problems for inadequately equipped single-engine night fighters. With 6/10 cloud cover, Wilde Sau tactics became problematic, and with full cloud cover it was impossible.

On January 23, 1944, Reichsmarschall Göring acceded to Galland's request and ordered the cancellation of single-engine night-fighter missions. This was made easier for him by the fact that German industry had now improved operational options for nighttime combat with the introduction of a new on-board device, the SN2. The Lichtenstein SN2 radar was among the earliest airborne radars available to the Luftwaffe in World War II and the first one used exclusively for air interception. Upon realizing that German technology had effectively closed the radar gap, Galland dissolved Herrmann's 30th Fighter Division. However, due to their special qualifications, Herrmann's pilots remained together as part of the bad weather fighter squadrons JG 300 and JG 301.

On March 22, 1944, Herrmann initially took command of the 1st Fighter Division and the protection of Berlin, where the imaginative officer made a name for himself again. In a reversal of his previous views, he advocated a total abandonment of darkening measures in Greater Berlin, which were otherwise scrupulously observed. Whether the city was dark or brightly lit, he said, was irrelevant to technically well-equipped English night bombers. However, enemy fighter aircraft could be attacked much more effectively without blackout.[5]

Probably for psychological reasons and in consideration of a severely tested city population of millions, Herrmann's idea, which was logical in itself, did not take hold.

Herrmann gained popularity for Wilde Sau tactics, which had enabled him to exhibit remarkable inventiveness, with a noteworthy economic consequence. The general opinion was that his approach made excellent use of a war situation where resources were already becoming extremely scarce. This relative economy would be repeated later when setting up ramming units, at least in terms of resources; in the case of single-engine night fighters, these could be inexpensive standard hunting machines. The voluntary principle was no different. The inevitable haste of construction of emergency airfields, defensive installations, and aircraft, along with its effects on the participating pilots, is a recurring feature. Herrmann's Wilde Sau was a unique flying unit whose members stood out for possessing bravery almost to the point of self-sacrifice.

More than a year before the Japanese Admiral Ohnischi orchestrated the first spectacular deployment of organized death planes (*Kamikaze*), the notion emerged in Germany to protect the increasingly threatened homeland through the use of radical air force weaponry. The wounds inflicted by Allied air crews on the unfortunate city of Hamburg during the bloody week of experimental extinction bombings were still fresh. In August 1943, against this backdrop, Flight Captain Hanna Reitsch convened with two associates who shared deep concerns at the Haus der Flieger (House of Aviators) meeting place in Berlin. One of them was Dr. Theo Benzinger, an aviation doctor, and the other was Heinrich Lange, a proven and successful glider pilot. First Lieutenant Lange had achieved success in May 1940 by deploying paratroopers directly at Fort Eben-Emael in Belgium using his DFS-230 cargo glider, a brilliant feat that significantly contributed to the success of the initial phase of the German offensive in the West.

Lange found himself in a state of profound despair. Recently, he had witnessed repeatedly how his fellow glider pilots fell victim to machine-gun fire from British fighters during supply transports in the southern theater of the war. He wasn't alone in deeming this method of deploying cargo gliders as sheer madness. What weighed on him most was the apparent futility of the sacrifice made by his courageous fellow pilots. They were compelled into piloting cumbersome and defenseless cargo gliders, facing almost certain death—without even the rudimentary hope that their sacrifice might inflict harm on their adversary.

Lange derived a somber conclusion from this grim situation: even in the face of inevitable death, he was determined to kill as many enemies as possible. Benzinger and Reitsch shared this perspective, supporting Lange in his conviction and encouraging him to formulate a tactical plan. The core of this plan was a conscious willingness to sacrifice deployed pilots. Lange detailed his view in a seven-page typewritten document, advocating readiness to use a bomb or to pilot a torpedo at the cost of one's own life to either destroy an enemy warship or inflict maximum damage on enemy bombers. Field Marshal Milch, to whom

Lange addressed his letter, presented this unconventional proposal for discussion in a staff and general aircraft meeting on Tuesday, September 14, 1943.

Forty-eight individuals—including general staff officers, Luftwaffe personnel, military staff from the Reich Aviation Ministry, testing specialists, and senior association leaders—were assembled. Notable figures in attendance were Lieutenant Colonel von Lofßberg and Major Hajo Herrmann, who was serving as commander of the Wilde Sau unit. Herrmann, still recovering from a severe injury sustained when his Fieseler Storch (Stork) reconnaissance and liaison aircraft crashed into a high-voltage line at night, stressed the group's mix of inexperienced pilots and veterans. Milch initiated the discussion by highlighting that Lange's proposal for self-sacrifice was just one of several he had recently encountered, all originating from the glider community. He first raised the question of whether suitable aircraft designs could be rapidly developed for such purposes. It was revealed that there were indeed several projects already in development.

One of the proposals already considered envisaged fighter aircraft, each loaded with 250kg of explosives under the wings and 500kg under the fuselage, being flown frontally into enemy bomber groups. Once in a favorable position, pilots would use glow ignition to detonate their charges in order to destroy as many bombers as possible. Another proposal, attributed to General Edgar Peterson, commander of the Luftwaffe test department, which spared the lives of the pilots, involved flying old Ju 88 bombers filled with explosives into the vicinity of enemy groups. The pilots were then to jump out before the ignition triggered the explosive charge. A third possibility reported to the field marshal was to remotely guide unmanned fighter planes filled with explosives into enemy bomber groups. By using such explosive tactics, it was hoped that between four and six heavy bombers from the American air fleet could be destroyed at a time. However, Milch and von Lofßberg were not persuaded by the anticipated explosive impact. Professor Hermann Schardin, a leading German physicist and engineer, indicated that detonations in open airspace only had an effect within a radius of 40 meters, making such an endeavor appear unproductive. After some deliberation, Milch redirected the discussion to its initial focus—Lange's proposal of self-sacrifice. Evidently, this proposal was satisfied with a destruction ratio of one to seven; according to Lange, if he could bring seven enemy aircraft with him, his life would not be in vain.

Petersen found the concept of creating a "death armada" more challenging than resolving navigation or targeting calculations. Eventually, he maintained a strong belief in the feasibility of equipping the Me 410 with the bomber torpedo 2000 for suicide missions against enemy ships in the winter of 1943 or, at the latest, by the spring of 1944. If catapults were employed, there might also be a means of rescuing the individuals involved from a safer glide path or bailout over friendly territory. However, Milch returned to the focus on bombing missions. Lange's proposal for targeting bombers seemed more pragmatic than missions involving self-sacrifice against warships. The notion of ramming heavy bombers' tailplanes, causing destruction through a destroying propeller, garnered approval, especially as there was no need to send pilots to certain death. As Milch pointed out, these pilots could be rescued after escaping by parachute. Disagreements resurfaced regarding the type and specifications of aircraft suitable for this purpose.

Attention was captivated by a Blohm and Voss development—a heavily armored, nearly invulnerable glider designed to engage enemy bomber formations from above, aiming to push, thrust, tilt, and ultimately ram them. This combat glider, designated BV 40, had already been conceptualized. The combat mission for the BV 40 *Glitjager* (glider fighter) involved approaching enemy bomber formations, ascending in a timely manner with the assistance of fast towing aircraft, uncoupling, then executing a steep descent from the front to make the attack as surprising as possible. Deliberately constructed in a rudimentary manner, primarily from wood but fortified with armor on all sides, the driver's compartment constituted 26 percent of the total weight. The BV 40 could withstand impacts of up to 900km/h. When a fighter plane, specifically the Bf 109, towed this type of glider with a rigid drawbar, the landing gear was dropped at the start, reaching an altitude of 7,000 meters in twelve minutes. The maximum permitted towing speed was 550km/h. The pilot, lying prone in the aircraft, presented a relatively small target, and in this position, centrifugal forces exerted weaker effects during the descent.

Experts immediately raised serious concerns regarding the BV 40's lengthy and dangerous towing process. The German Research Institute for Gliding (DFS) in Ainring, near the border to Austria, already had exciting designs for such a glider with rocket propulsion, albeit a sail-reconnaissance aircraft for extremely large lifts. The consensus was that maybe this machine could be considered. When the deliberations had reached this point, Field Marshal Milch suddenly thought of the Me 163 Komet rocket fighter: "What this man [Lange] wants is a simplified Me 163." But upon closer inspection, the effort needed seemed to be too high again, with even a reduced Me 163 being far too expensive for a large-scale operation. Milch mused that what was needed was a "simple, cheap plane ... that's very light." He added: "That could [use] your own propeller to chop off the other's tail."[6]

Milch was already aware at the time that the loss of ramming aircraft had to be acknowledged. However, he insisted that the pilots should at least have the opportunity to save themselves. Milch asserted, "If the man has a good chance of getting away, whether he gets away or not is another question—then he runs no greater risk than any soldier in war. There are many for that."[7] On this matter, Milch's foresight proved correct. Some eighteen months later, the by now Colonel Herrmann—who had silently observed the discussion about self-sacrifice and ramming plans on September 14, 1943—eventually initiated a German ramming unit. All the criteria outlined at that time for such a project were ultimately realized: the assembly of volunteer aircraft pilots, cost-effective ramming aircraft, opportunities for survival, a destroyer propeller, and the intention to shock bomber crews through the audacious ramming of German planes were almost verbatim as envisaged by Erhard Milch. In Milch's perspective, between forty and sixty such "birds" would swoop down on the group, each with a precise target. He believed this approach would destroy up to sixty bombers. "This has a purpose," Milch stated.[8]

At that time, in September 1943, Field Marshal Milch was certainly not aware of his far-sighted words. Before moving on to the next item on the agenda, he demanded consideration of the type discussed "with regard to air combat ... with all emphasis."[9] The design of a BV 40 fighter glider flew for the first time in May 1944—eight months later. Ultimately, seven machines were built; production of twelve others was stopped during the construction process.

The Reich Aviation Ministry was able to accelerate the interrupted work on the glider with an auxiliary rocket and create the DFS 228. The DFS 228 was a rocket-powered reconnaissance aircraft designed by DFS. It was a small, uncrewed aircraft used for high-altitude reconnaissance missions. It was launched from a carrier aircraft, typically a Dornier Do 217 or Heinkel He 111. Once released at high altitude, the DFS 228's rocket engine would propel it even higher, allowing it to take photographs or gather other intelligence over enemy territory. The aircraft was equipped with cameras and other reconnaissance equipment.

Although twelve examples confirmed the expectations, none made it beyond the test areas of the DFS and the Rechlin Institution.[10] Independently of these initially top-secret deliberations and around the same time, SS Sturmbannführer Otto Skorzeny had also secretly discussed similar ideas with the German navy. He envisioned a combined use of small combat weapons from the navy and self-sacrificing men from the Luftwaffe. According to Skorzeny, suicidal dives onto tactical targets as a conscious, heroic act were entirely in keeping with the ideas of a German SS leader. Since its inception, fanatical, tough, almost self-sacrificing behavior in combat had been displayed by the men and leadership of the Waffen-SS, and not just in exceptional cases. Self-sacrifice by individuals in the interests of the German people was considered a heroic act by National Socialist leaders, especially in times of war. However, suicide for selfish reasons was strongly rejected. Both Hitler and Heinrich Himmler, the head of the SS, had expressed thoughts along these lines, and Reichsminister Martin Bormann spelled out corresponding principles in a circular dated July 17, 1944.

Colonel General Robert Ritter von Greim, who had previously endorsed Major von Kornatzki's *Sturm* concept, now also backed initiatives to establish a corps of self-sacrificing Germans. Instead of targeting enemy bombers, the focus shifted to destroying enemy lifelines and industrial centers. Key positions included electricity, power, and waterworks, as well as defense facilities and ships. Volunteer pilots were expected to give up their lives by guiding glide bombs into these designated targets.[11] Experts from the Academy of Aeronautical Research, aviation medicine, and the Ministry of Defense, as well as aircraft designers, naval officers, and representatives of the air force's weapons generals, declared the operational plan sensible and practicable after detailed consultation.[12]

Initially, Hitler vehemently rejected granting his approval when Hanna Reitsch presented the project to him at the Berghof, Hitler's holiday home in the Obersalzberg of the Bavarian Alps near Berchtesgaden, on February 28, 1944, during an informal tea party. Reitsch, recently honored with the Iron Cross, First Class, received permission to proceed with preparations for deploying self-sacrificial weapons. However, Hitler retained the authority to decide when to implement the plan. The witness to this significant conversation was Hitler's air force adjutant, Colonel Nicolaus von Below. To reconcile the apparent contradiction between the accounts presented by Reitsch and Werner Baumbach, commander of a Luftwaffe special operations unit, von Below asserted that Hitler had previously refused self-sacrificing missions. Nevertheless, General Korten, then Chief of the General Staff of the air force, took steps to organize a special corps. Technical preparations were overseen by Heinz Kensche, head of the department at the Reich Aviation Ministry, a qualified engineer with a fervor for flying who had participated in Rhön gliding competitions from 1932 to 1934.

The operational equipment initially considered was an already constructed single-seater of the Me 328 type, with a wingspan of only 5 meters. At a speed of around 750km/h, the glide ratio of this aircraft, which was originally designed as a fighter or destroyer, was 1:5. In the bow it was supposed to carry either a special bomb or a bomb torpedo. Mounted in a piggyback tow on a Do 217 bomber, a self-sacrificing pilot was able to uncouple an Me 328 near the target on his own. The target would then be reached by gliding and destroyed by a targeted fall. Test flights in Horsching near Linz went smoothly. In April 1944, the Reich Aviation Ministry (RLM) awarded a Thuringian company an order to mass-produce Me 328 missiles, but production never began.[13]

After Skorzeny joined the Luftwaffe's project, the focus was on preparing the V-1 retaliatory weapon, an unmanned flying bomb. London suffered the first impact of a V-1 on June 14, 1944. A total of around 8,000 of these guided bombs detonated on English soil over the following three months. However, from September 1, due to the Allied advance across northern France into the Low Countries, V-1s could no longer be launched against England from mainland ramps. Much to Skorzeny's chagrin, Milch's engineers went missing. RLM got to work with their usual thoroughness. In their eyes, a V-1 conversion to a manned aircraft was by no means unproblematic; in any case, they required half a year of development time. That took too long for Skorzeny, who took matters into his own hands.

Using various strategies, Skorzeny, the hero of Mussolini's liberation in September 1943, quickly succeeded in establishing satisfactory production conditions. In the summer of 1944, workers from aircraft companies Heinkel and Junkers initiated the transformation of the V-1. This involved creating three versions: a two-seater instructional aircraft with separate pilot cabins—one in front of the wings and one behind—with dual controls and no engines; a single-seater trainer with skids, landing flaps, and an engine; and a third version, the emergency aircraft, which was a single-seater without an engine and any landing aids. All three models were launched by towing from a He 111 bomber, with the suspension device located under the right wing.[14]

Pilots from the Rechlin Air Force Test Center, along with Flight Captain Hanna Reitsch, conducted test flights using various V 4 aircraft at Lärz airfield in northern Germany. While the Fieseler Fi 103R suicide-guided aircraft (codenamed Reichenberg) demonstrated favorable flight characteristics and posed no significant challenges even for average pilots, not all test flights proceeded without issues. Hanna Reitsch piloted the V 4 at a speed of 850km/h. According to Baumbach, shortly after the completion of testing, an explosion of a glide bomb occurred at the airport hangars at the Prenzlau airfield in Uckermark, where Reichsführer-SS Himmler had established his field quarters. Skorzeny reported a total of twenty-eight delivered missiles, including eight experimental models.

Following an initial period of secrecy, the idea was discussed of establishing an association of suicide aircraft pilots, particularly among the cargo gliders and First Lieutenant Lange's comrades. An advertising campaign was initiated, resulting in the swift receipt of the first volunteer applications. Hanna Reitsch, Heinz Kensche, and even the Minister for Armaments and Ammunition, Albert Speer, spontaneously offered their services. According to Reitsch, a total of seventy ordinary men, mostly fathers, were ultimately selected from the applicants to form a squad.[15] While the Luftwaffe contributed sixty aviators, Skorzeny personally enlisted thirty SS men from his special unit to undergo training with the intention of later deploying them as self-sacrificing pilots. The volunteers had to make the following written declaration: "I hereby report for the SO [meaning self-sacrifice] mission as leader of the manned glide bomb. I am aware that this mission ends in death." The same abbreviation, with apparently the same serious meaning, was later used by the High Command in connection with the first organized ramming operation by German fighter pilots.

General Korten assigned the volunteers to Jagdverband 44 (Kampfgeschwader—Combat Squadron—200), later led by Lieutenant Colonel Baumbach, which had developed as a collection point for special weapons and special combat equipment within the fighter aviation force. KG 200 also included three Ju 290 long-haul aircraft, which, incidentally, had transported special troops to rebellious mountain tribes in Iraq for Skorzeny in the summer of 1943. Zirkus Rosarius (Circus Rosarius), a demonstration unit of captured enemy aircraft, was also part of KG 200. This unit was tasked with testing captured British and American aircraft, all of which were repainted in German markings. The SO men lived in the narrow circle of their military secrecy. Gottlieb Kuschke became their first commander. Generalfeldmarschall Albert Kesselring's former chief quartermaster, Colonel Heigl, who had earned merit as a supply clerk in the summer of 1941, then looked after the group. The group continued to train until the Allied invasion of Normandy, when the day of action seemed to have arrived.

According to the daily report dated June 9, 1944, from the Chief of the Air Force Command in Germany, which mentioned enemy landings in the West, Colonel I. G. Christian informed General Karl Koller about the operational readiness of a KG 200 group, consisting of ten officers and twenty-nine men. The wording used, along with the reference to Colonel Heigl, suggests that this group was characterized as resolute individuals. Koller, who was then in charge of the Luftwaffe command, instructed their deployment on the invasion front. In the end, the lives of the airmen from KG 200 who were willing to sacrifice themselves were saved by the fear of irrevocably sacrificing the unit as well as a rapid advance by the Allied troops. Göring in particular had hesitated to make the final decision. It stayed that way. The enemy landings in the West could no longer be defeated, not even by death-defying self-sacrificing aviators. By August 17, 1944, the Wehrmacht was in full retreat across France.

Originally, ambitious objectives in the realm of operational air warfare had to be adjusted and become more nuanced. Nevertheless, setbacks on the Eastern Front were eventually overcome. As late as June 1943, there were plans for efforts in targeting Soviet industry, extending at least as far as the general line of the Volga. Target documents from the Luftwaffe command staff underwent scrutiny and revisions from Professor Steinmann of the Luftwaffe Administrative Office and President Dr. Karl from the Reich Ministry for Armaments and War Production. These revised targets encompassed comprehensive operations against industrial complexes, including the Kuibyshev industrial combine on the Volga (which served as the temporary seat of the Russian government during the German October offensive in 1941), Chelyabinsk, Sverdlovsk, Magnitogorsk, and other facilities situated on the eastern edge of the Ural Mountains.

Speer, the German minister of arms, faced significant shortages in the Reich. However, he was captivated by the notion of causing substantial harm to the Russian war machine by employing resolute individuals for specific missions against industrial targets. He vigorously supported the project and engaged in frequent discussions with Skorzeny and Himmler about operations targeting electricity plants in Russia.

The only accessible Russian aircraft engine production facilities were the Moscow and Molotov plants in Gorki. The factories in Kuibyshev, Kazan, and Ufa had already become unreachable for the Germans by the beginning of 1944. Hopes of penetrating deeper with He 177 bombers were shattered. General Koller, as the chief of the air force command, cautioned against further delays in his short study "Fight against the Russian Defense Industry," emphasizing that each day of procrastination bolstered Russian offensive capabilities. He advocated for a simultaneous and devastating strike against all energy sources in the Moscow and Upper Volga region but also warned of the heightened defenses of Russian fighters. The greater Moscow area remained a challenging target due to concentrated air defense forces.

Colonel General Ritter von Greim advocated for the reconquering of air supremacy in the East. In written considerations dated February 11, 1944, he identified the Moscow area as a target, a proposition that Koller opposed. As the Eastern Front shifted, the Gorki target area also became out of range. On March 6, Koller identified new targets as the Tula, Aleksin, Ivankova, and Elektroperedatcha power plants. However, with the continued retreat, hopes diminished. Explosive load issues delayed planned operations in KG 200. The release of sufficient fuel by the Ministry of Aviation was a further constraint. Simultaneously, criticism emerged regarding excessive individual attacks. In crucial areas, there was a growing realization that lasting effects were more likely to result from sustained suppression rather than isolated destruction. These insights were gleaned from the use of long-range bombers.[16]

However, the ideological indoctrination of the SO men persisted. Month after month, they remained at Friedenthal, near Altentreptow, anticipating their summons for a final mission, the nature of which was still uncertain. Since late autumn 1944, Heinrich Himmler had been pursuing his own vision of establishing a death squad under his command, utilizing rockets. He had reverted to the initial idea of deploying self-sacrificing men in ramming attacks to destroy large enemy bombers. According to Himmler, these bombers were causing daily suffering to the German people, while the Russian industrial complexes were distant and their effect on the war more ambiguous.

On November 2, 1943, Göring and Milch had already explored options for an aircraft suitable for a self-sacrificing squadron. In 1970, Speer recalled a limited deployment involving a rocket plane, which was tested by Hanna Reitsch, likely referring to the Me 163 rocket fighter. Reitsch was well-known for her contributions to the development of this aircraft. According to Speer, the exceptionally fast rocket fighter was designed to engage in ramming attacks against American daylight bombers, destroying them in the process. Although acknowledging the inevitable destruction of their own aircraft, pilots still had the opportunity to save themselves by parachuting out. In December 1944, a special Me 163 rocket fighter was ready for ramming tests at the JG 400 Fighter Wing in Brandis, in which the leading edges of the wing were reinforced with a steel rail, based on an idea by Heini Dittmar. Dittmar was the only one to advocate that an Me 163 prepared in this way could cut through the wings of enemy aircraft without incurring major damage. His brother, Walter, a former captain and commander of a cargo glider group, who had been severely punished by a court-martial for a disciplinary offense and was now supposed to save himself through special effort, served as the test pilot.

However, there was no rehabilitation or testing of the ram. Major Wolfgang Späte, a fighter ace and Me 163 test pilot, revealed that in January 1945, Walter Dittmar took off in pursuit of a RAF Mosquito fighter-bomber flying at an altitude of 12,000 meters. The wooden structure of the Mosquito offered less resistance to the Me 163 with its steel edges, but it was not destroyed. Me 163 pilots found that since their cannon was ineffective at ranges greater than 2,000 feet, and they needed to take evasive action at 600 feet to avoid collision, they had less than three seconds in which to fire.

Despite contrails almost touching high in the sky, Walter Dittmar did not hit his target at Brandis airfield. He reported engine failure, according to Major Spate. Eventually, it seemed that another missile, designed by Erich Bachem, known for his glider pilot expertise, was more suitable for deploying willing aircraft pilots into enemy bombers as part of an operation on behalf of Himmler. This semi-automatic loss device, named the Bp 20 and referred to as an aircraft rocket projectile, was produced in Bachem's factory in Waldsee, Württemberg, and later designated as Ba 349.

This device provided the Walter liquid rocket HWK 109-509 with a maximum thrust of 1,700hp. Additionally, four Schmidding solid-fuel rockets, each generating 1,200hp thrust, were automatically released. The combined thrust reached 6,500hp, propelling the device with 30,000hp for approximately ten seconds at an average climb speed of 675km/h to a maximum altitude of 16,000 meters. Subsequently, the mission could be accomplished either by utilizing twenty-four or thirty-six bundled 73mm caliber Messerschmitt 33-R4M rockets, housed in a cement block at the front of the bow and covered with a plexiglass hood for improved aerodynamics, or by resorting to ramming. The Natter (Viper), as the device was eventually named, was constructed simply and inexpensively using glued and nailed wood. The separation of the bow, with the seat pulled back by a main parachute, facilitated the recovery of this valuable equipment.[17]

The Bachem Natter, developed in Waldsee and built by Erich Bachem, was a radical design. It was designed as an interceptor for object protection, with the pilot taking off in a vertically positioned Natter when a group of bombers approached. Four lateral booster rockets and the central Walter rocket engine were supposed to "shoot the bird into the middle of the crowd" within a few seconds. After the R4M rockets were fired in the rough direction of the bombers, the aircraft was supposed to split after a short descent period and the pilot returned to earth via parachute.

The four detonable powder rockets were intended to support the Walter-509 engine of the Natter in its vertical ascent into the bombers. There was no time for thorough testing: day after day, city after city was incinerated by heavy U.S. bomber units. Driven by sheer powerlessness, every viable idea was welcome. Lothar Sieber, an excellent pilot who was demoted due to a breach of his watch period, was given the prospect of getting his rank back after a successful first flight. However, one of the four launch rockets did not release as planned on March 1, 1945, and the plane and its pilot crashed to the ground. The imminent end of the war prevented further attempts.

Galland did not support the idea of self-sacrificial missions. Bachem is said to have been impressed by the construction. He wanted to work with Speer for series production in the interceptor role. But then the SS also took over this project, and once again it was all about self-sacrifice. The Bachem company placed the final production order in September 1944.

Following the swift and successful construction of the Natter in just a few weeks, the inaugural unmanned flight occurred on December 22, 1944, employing a vertical takeoff. The test launch was replicated on December 25, this time with a dummy, and it too proved successful. Positioned on its tail, the Natter ascended vertically into the sky with a resounding noise. During horizontal flight, with a maximum duration of seven minutes, the speed approached nearly 1,000km/h. A pilot skillfully guided his Natter at a supposed approaching enemy bomber at operational altitude, launching the rockets. Subsequently, the hull separated from the bow, and the pilot and cockpit descended safely via parachutes. It is noteworthy that these options were not taken into consideration in the event of a ramming impact.

In late February 1945, the SS exerted pressure for manned test flights. The initial flight occurred in Neuberg, near Sigmaringen, and ended in tragedy. First Lieutenant Lothar Siebert, known, among other things, for successfully completing a loop in a cumbersome, three-engine Ju 52, had insisted on being the first person to man the Ba 349. The 23-year-old knew the risk from ten test starts; he had seen failures with his own eyes, including a spectacular total explosion in the gun carriage. Siebert knew that he had to start without automatic control. During takeoff, the canopy flew away and the suction of air jerked the pilot's head up and to the side. At a height of 100 meters, the front part of the aircraft was dismantled, while the remaining part, with the pilot's body, floated 400 meters further up. It then stood on its tip and crashed to the ground. The cause of the accident was that the canopy came loose during takeoff, presumably as a result of damage to the rear canopy hinge.

As late as April 1945, ten operational Natters were lying in wait for an enemy bomber group near Kirchheim an der Teck. But they waited in vain, as the American bomber offensive was over. At least thirty-six 36 Ba 349 Natter devices were manufactured and twenty-two were tested, four of which were manned. At the end of the war, fourteen devices were still available. Ten were intentionally destroyed, the remaining four being captured by American troops in Austria, three of which were taken to the United States and the other to the Soviet Union.[18]

Before these events unfolded, Dr. Joseph Goebbels, the Minister for Public Enlightenment and Propaganda, advocated for a heroic project of self-sacrifice, intending to use it for propaganda purposes. On June 11, 1944, he expressed to his colleague von Oven that if he, Goebbels, was the head of the Luftwaffe, he would have issued an appeal to the young men of Germany, signed by distinguished individuals in the Luftwaffe, urging them to volunteer as suicide pilots.

Goebbels insisted on personally boosting the morale of the SO men of KG 200 in their endeavors, encouraging them with impassioned words. However, pressure from other sources was also at play.

On March 17, 1945, Karl Wahl, the Nazi regional leader of Swabia in Bavaria, sent Martin Bormann, head of the Nazi Party Chancellery, a personal, confidential letter to his Munich address, in which he demanded that Rhine bridges near Remagen, which had fallen into American hands, be attacked by one or two dozen airmen and destroyed in an act of self-sacrifice. He wasn't just interested in tactical success. Rather, he emphasized the propaganda effect of such heroic actions: "If the people's faith in victory is not to be shaken any further, then something special must gradually happen. The German people would breathe a sigh of relief if the radio reported that all the bridges near Remagen were destroyed by airmen who sacrificed themselves."[19]

The Japanese Ohka bomb is said to have had a certain relationship with the Natter. Also made of wood, series production of the Ohka glide bomb began towards the end of 1944—as did the Natter. The existence of the Ohka was initially kept top secret. Japanese naval aviator Captain Okamura quietly gathered pilots willing to make sacrifices around him. In just under six months, they prepared for the tactic of conscious self-sacrifice at Kohnoike airfield, northeast of Tokyo.[20] The attack group, which belonged to the 721st Air Squadron, was given the name *Kamikaze*, although this honorary title actually only belonged to the special operations corps under Admiral Ohnischi. Organized self-sacrifice by pilots of the Luftwaffe or the Waffen-SS did not take place, meaning the dubious glory of consciously sacrificing volunteer airmen for military purposes fell not to German but to Japanese commanders.[21]

A final effort was made to employ individuals willing to sacrifice themselves. According to Himmler's new ideas, these were to be selected from those who were weary of life, unwell, or deemed honorable criminals—a sort of lost group. The objective was to use them to demolish the Oder River bridges, hindering Russian soldiers from advancing further. However, this plan ultimately remained a mere intention. According to an entry from February 24, 1945, in the war diary of the Luftwaffe High Command, the training of volunteers in KG 200, apart from thirty-four whose training was well advanced, had to be stopped at this point due to a lack of aviation resources. It was suggested that airmen who became available should be transferred to the paratrooper units.[22]

On March 1, 1945, Baumbach, in his capacity as a lieutenant colonel and squadron commander, issued an order for the mobilization of forces from KG 200. This directive outlined the mission to target the railway bridges spanning the Vistula near Warsaw, Deblin, and Sandomierz. The second group of KG 200, led by First Lieutenant Pilz under the flying unit command, was assigned to this task. The group included a weather reconnaissance aircraft, nine target finders, six Mistel Is, eight Mistel IIIs, and three reserve aircraft—noticeably lacking, however, was any self-sacrificing man.

(Note: (1.) The Mistel I was a unique and unconventional composite aircraft used by the Luftwaffe. It consisted of a small, piloted aircraft mounted on top of a larger unmanned explosive-filled aircraft. The concept behind the Mistel (German for "mistletoe") was to use the larger aircraft as a flying bomb, guided by the pilot in the smaller aircraft. (2.) The Mistel III was a variant of the Mistel series. Similar to other Mistel configurations, the Mistel III comprised a smaller piloted aircraft mounted on top of a larger unmanned explosive-filled aircraft. In the case of the Mistel III, the upper component was typically a Focke-Wulf Fw 190 or a Junkers Ju 88, while the lower component was a modified Ju 88 filled with explosives. The Mistel III was developed with the goal of creating a powerful long-range bomber capable of carrying a heavy payload. The pilot in the upper aircraft would guide the combined unit to the target, detach from the larger aircraft, and then control the upper component back to safety. The larger lower component, acting as a flying bomb, would continue on its trajectory to the target.)

While the Mistel project, including Mistel III, was an interesting concept, practical challenges and the changing dynamics of the war limited its operational use. The Mistel III was not widely deployed in combat, and as the war progressed, the development and use of such composite aircraft became less significant. The command center of KG 200 was situated at Stendal air base, west of Berlin. Interestingly, this very base would soon become the covert location for Colonel Herrmann's Sonderkommando Elbe ramming unit. During this period, KG 200 remained highly resolute and committed to its objectives.

In a document titled "Bridge Fighting Project," dated March 5, 1945, the department identified Bridge Representative Baumbach under paragraph eleven: "Weapons and methods of combat in a sudden attack on the most important Oder River bridges in the initial days of an enemy offensive on the Berlin area." The operation was to involve the use of old models such as the Bf 109 and Fw 190. The specified explosives included a BM 1,000lb bomb and a hull-filling load of 10kg of phosphorus. In April 1945, an SO unit at the Jüterbog air base with around forty men was given the task of directing aircraft loaded with explosives or bombs directly against the Oder bridges. This was intended to stop the Russian advance. According to research by Zweites Deutsches Fernsehen (Second German Television) filmmaker Peter Hartl, between April 16 and 19, thirty-six death pilots flew missions and destroyed seventeen Oder crossings without even beginning to stop the Russian advance.

According to paragraph three of the same document, the self-sacrifice operation was expected to culminate in a large-scale SO mission, along with an increased "mistletoe" use and a large-scale bomb squad operation. In the event of failure in these ambitious bridge demolition projects, the plan was to promptly initiate preparations for a war of sabotage against subsequent enemy-held bridges. This implied an underground and guerilla-style resistance.

However, the Russian advance thwarted this plan. The operation against the Oder River bridges unfolded exclusively as a Mistel mission. When contrasting the sole visible self-sacrificing group of the Luftwaffe in Prenzlau and Friedenthal with the ramming command of German fighter pilots established in Stendal, it is not implausible to consider that some of those self-sacrificing individuals may have hesitated in executing their initial decisions, opting instead to join the ramming association at a later point. Pure glider pilots faced challenges in handling complex Bf 109 or Fw 190 fighter aircraft. Yet the Me 321 type (originally a large-capacity glider) had already prompted the question of who could best pilot this voluminous structure: a motorized pilot or a glider pilot? Following several attempts, assessments from notable glider pilots tipped the scales in their favor. Back when the idea was taking shape, Göring had expressly ordered General Korten to check those willing to sacrifice themselves in case this tactic was decided upon.

Nevertheless, it is impossible to overlook the distinct contrast between Colonel Herrmann's planned ramming operation, executed as a tactical military maneuver, and the underlying intention conveyed through the use of fighter aircraft weaponry. Regardless of whether or not Herrmann's actions were deliberate, and despite what a general staff officer might later record in the Supreme Command of the Luftwaffe's war diary, Herrmann—influenced by Hitler's ideology—believed that the deployed men had a chance of survival. However, the grim reality was that the pilots in KG 200, designated as true death flyers, self-sacrificers, and total-war combatants, were destined to give up their lives when deployed. There exists a profound alignment in both spirit and tactical concept, and even a striking similarity between the Ohka bomb and the V-4. The German self-sacrificing men and the Japanese *Kamikazes*, particularly those of the Jinrai Butai (Godly Thunder Corps) under Rear Admiral Ugaki, shared an extraordinary closeness, despite harboring no mutual aspirations. While Herrmann's subsequent ramming command cannot be linked to plans of self-sacrifice, another precursor did emerge in the form of a distinct aviation unit: the special combat force of the *Sturm* (Storm) fighters.

At about the same time that glider pilot First Lieutenant Heinrich Lange developed the idea of self-sacrifice in flying operations, one of the oldest German fighter pilots at the time, Major von Kornatzki—an officer on the staff of the II Fighting Corps—produced another idea that would apply the *Sturm* concept in air combat. *Sturm* attacks meant particularly difficult, dangerous operations that were usually only assigned to selected officers, non-commissioned officers, and men. Such elite units were characterized by extraordinary boldness in attack.

When the National Socialist idea became a movement, their leaders immediately tried to recall German military traditions with which to connect. They referred to paramilitary organizations, such as the Brown Shirts, as Sturm Detachments-S. A. In the military, individuals or units who had committed themselves particularly hard in battle were allowed to use the *Sturm* designation: for example, *Sturm* divisions of the infantry, *Sturm* gun divisions, and *Sturm* units of the navy, in particular the *Sturm*-Vikings who had a self-sacrificial character. A *Sturm* badge was established as a medal for the infantry, and at the end of the war there was the Volkssturm ("People's Storm"), the last contingents to be raised with defeat for the Nazis fast approaching.

The Luftaffe initially lacked the capability to execute genuine attacks employing storm tactics. It was only when American day bombers flew in significant numbers, and the hedgehog formations embraced the individual bomber tactic of all-around fire, that German fighter pilots began to question the approach. Suddenly, there was a call for shock tactics, attack points, and *Sturm* fighters to disrupt the armed bomber groups. Major von Kornatzki, the first to highlight this necessity and provide a solution, had served as an adjutant in 1934 under then-Major Ritter von Greim. The latter, who briefly held the position of the last field marshal and commander-in-chief of the Luftwaffe in April 1945, should be noted for his advancement. Adolf Galland, then a general of fighter pilots, agreed to the *Sturm* idea that was brought to him in the winter of 1943/1944.[23]

However, he softened the original idea: Kornatzki had first thought of radical ramming operations, as Colonel Herrmann was later to implement. According to Lange, Kornatzki's idea was to recruit self-sacrificing men for a ramming mission he was planning. However, this was impossible because former glider pilots did not have the necessary powered-flight training. Soon after Galland's approval, the first test squadron of the JG 1 fighter wing flew special aircraft *Sturm* operations in southern France, figuring out the best attack tactics. The pilots of this experimental unit were all old hands; they had been flight instructors and the intention was that they should now gain new courage and self-confidence before being transferred back to front-line units. But there were a few pilots who lacked the usual fighting spirit, and these had to prove that they met the requirements. Although the experimental operations failed to achieve spectacular success, Galland, to whom many pilots had written asking him to found special ramming squadrons, issued a general appeal to all fighter pilots to voluntarily join assault formations.[24]

In May 1944, Lieutenant General Schmid, then in command of the I Fighter Corps, transferred from Treuenbrietzen near Berlin to Salzwedel Hertiber, the current location of Group IV from Bär's JG 3 Udet. There, he enlisted men for a significant new unit. The first sixty-eight pilots then officially introduced a novel form of attack—the *Sturm* airborne assault. This marked the initial stride toward adopting battle group tactics. Formally the 4th Fighter Wing, JG 3 Udet transitioned into the 4th Sturm JG 3 Udet. In July of the same year, Galland instructed the 11th Group of JG 300 to become the second German *Sturm* group, now known as the 2nd Sturm JG 300.[25]

The third and final *Sturm* group took shape under the leadership of Major von Kornatzki, the originator of the *Sturm* concept, who was later promoted to lieutenant colonel. Arising from JG 4, it was designated 2nd JG 4 and, notably, was not integrated into Major Walther Dahl's special JG 300 wing, likely as a gesture of consideration for the courageous and deserving senior officer.

Leaders among the fighter pilots, deeply rooted in military tradition, deemed it fitting to adopt specific criteria from renowned assault formations in other branches of the armed forces. These principles included voluntariness, elitist attitudes, and solemn loyalty. Indeed, members of the Luftwaffe's *Sturm* groups were required to pledge "to engage the enemy at close range and, if the bomber cannot be downed by on-board weapons, to destroy the enemy through ramming."[26] However, it appears it was essential to temper the notion of voluntariness to some extent. As integral members of squadrons, groups, and units, fighter pilots were influenced by a compelling desire to safeguard themselves. Primarily, they aimed to maintain a level of comfort to avoid disapproval from comrades or superiors. Group motivation and loyalty contributed to both individual and collective achievements. The successes achieved through the inevitable fragmentation of fighter units in aerial combat also benefited the victorious group.

Those immersed in aviation culture avoided needlessly provoking disapproval from fellow group members. If the group volunteered, an individual was certainly not excluded. The same applied to granted withdrawal options. According to the document, anyone volunteering to become a member of a *Sturm* group had the freedom to request a transfer if the harsh realities became too daunting. This was intended sincerely, yet it contributed to fostering a proud, elite association of German pilots. *Sturm* fighters submitted written declarations of commitment. Their vow was sealed by a handshake with the general. Promotion and award structures adapted to the delicate task. Rapid advancement to higher ranks and medals were in prospect, but neither age nor rank was to play a role in the distribution of KG 200 veterans' association appointments.[27]

Galland underscored the necessity of establishing *Sturm* units around the turn of the year 1943/1944 when the elite fighter tactic gained prominence.[28] In reality, within the Luftwaffe, particularly at fighter schools and in supplementary groups, it was for a time regarded as prestigious to be transferred to and be part of a *Sturm* group. The emergence of the nickname "Ramm-Dahl" for Major Dahl, the commander of the *Sturm* fighters, occurred on September 13, 1944, after he intentionally rammed a four-engine day bomber while leading a *Sturm* wedge. This happened without any hidden motives, merely fully recognizing the daring nature of the act.[29]

However, an indeterminate minority held a low opinion or had little regard for this approach. Occupants of enemy bombers derogatorily referred to the *Sturm* fighters as *Totenkopf-Jäger* (death's-head fighters), perhaps drawing parallels to the SS, an organization that had employed the skull symbol from its inception and whose members gained renown for their combat bravery. It is plausible that bomber crews, upon inspecting German hunting aircraft tailplanes, occasionally discovered skulls indicating successful *Sturm* fighters. These fighters, having engaged in ramming maneuvers, would typically have the customary vertical white 15cm bar, denoting a kill, painted on them.

In the relatively cumbersome attack wedge, as impressive as it looked, *Sturm* fighters were exposed to the strongest defensive fire. The question that arose at the beginning was what means could best be used to protect pilots and aircraft from this hail of fire. The choice of assault aircraft remained the heavyweight Focke Wulf Fw 190, series A-8/R2 and R8. An armored oil cooler and windscreen made of bulletproof glass were already standard features of this well-established fighter aircraft, which was popular with the troops.

In addition, for *Sturm* purposes, armor plates 6mm thick were mounted on the firewall, which separated the cabin from the engine, and on both sides of the cabin. A 9mm bulletproof plate was placed behind the pilot's seat, complemented by 40mm bulletproof glass at the top. The triangular side windows were also the same thickness. The standard armament already consisted of two Type 151/20 2cm cannons and two 13mm Type 131 machine guns, all controlled by the air screw circuit shot. Two additional Type 151/20 cannons were installed to increase firepower, which were later replaced by even more powerful calibers, namely two Mk 108 3cm machine cannons. Projectiles from additional weapons remained outside the propeller circle. Experience has shown that fuel consumption doubles in air combat. Consequently, in order to ensure approximately three hours of flight and combat time, the amount of fuel carried was increased to 960 liters with the help of a 300-liter droppable tank under the fuselage and an additional container with a capacity of 110 liters behind the normal fuel tank in the hull.[30]

The standard Fw 190 A-8 weighed 4.5 metric tons, including ammunition and fuel. In contrast, the specialized aircraft of the *Sturm* groups ultimately reached a flying weight of 7 tons. To offset this substantial increase in weight, which was not particularly favorable for fighter aircraft, a robust 14-cylinder twin radial BMW 801 engine was newly designed and implemented. This engine boasted a maximum power of 2,400hp.

Galland wrote that he admired "the spirit of the German fighter pilots," who "with the consequence of self-sacrifice rammed attacking day bombers."[31] But by this he only means German assault fighters and not Herrmann's later ramming command, a fighter pilot group specially set up for this purpose.

The association made by Galland between the *Sturm* idea and the *Kamikaze* would likely be accurate if he had been aware, toward the end of 1943, that his Japanese allies would adopt such tactics a year later, in October 1944. This was when formations, later named *Kamikaze*, would come into play. As established, the first organized *Kamikaze* attack did not occur until October 25, 1944. However, Galland had already conceived the *Sturm* idea in autumn 1943, around the same time as those individuals committed to self-sacrifice. Intentional self-sacrifice was not thought of in the fighter camp. The undeniable, explicit ramming order for *Sturm* fighters was again somewhat weakened by Galland; he thought that the bombers would have fallen under fire anyway if the pilots had made a determined approach at short range. In fact, ramming remained the exception for *Sturm* fighters.

Similar to infantry close-quarters combat, assault fighter pilots were to aim to minimize the distance to the enemy. The guiding principle was to get close enough until the bomber was brought down. Equipped with powerful weaponry and bombs in close proximity, even less experienced, younger pilots would succeed in launching or colliding with bombs. The *Sturm* concept involved coordinated attacks in tightly formed battle formations. The entire group would unite to create a *Sturm* wedge, with the leader at the forefront, reminiscent of the great battles of the Germanic peoples of antiquity and the Dark Ages. Flying in an almost synchronized manner, the fighter unit approached the enemy bomber groups from slightly behind and above. Only in the final moments, when the more loosely organized bombers permitted, would the attacking wedge disperse into individual strikers, each pilot executing the concluding phase independently. During such an attack, *Sturm* fighters naturally had to reckon with a massive threat from American escort fighters. At the time of the *Sturm* attacks, the escort ratio was already one fighter covering every two bombers.

Despite their massive and formidable nature, the specially equipped Focke Wulfs faced slim odds in surviving engagements against enemy fighters, as subsequent events unfortunately demonstrated. Consequently, strict orders were given to avoid direct encounters with Allied escorts; the primary focus was on targeting bombers. Two substantial *Sturm* groups were accompanied by two lighter escort groups featuring conventional Bf 109 fighter aircraft. One of the light groups operated as an altitude group, flying at an elevated altitude behind the densely packed ramming formation to preempt potential attacks from the enemy. The other accompanying group divided its efforts to protect both flanks.

Roger E. Freeman dates the first mission using *Sturm* tactics to April 29, 1944. More than 700 four-engine daytime bombers of the U.S. Eighth Air Force transported 1,402 tons of bombs to Berlin on that day. Near Magdeburg, Freeman reports, around 300 German fighters, including the 4th *Sturm* Fighter Wing, JG 3 Udet, under the command of Captain Moritz, had lined up for battle.[32] On May 25, fighters from the same squadron intercepted eighteen aircraft from a bomber group en route to Berlin. According to Galland, the commander of the fighter pilots at the time, the *Sturm* fighters performed exceptionally well.[33] Encouraged by this success, he aimed to establish a *Sturm* group in each of the nine Reich Defense squadrons by September 1944. His strategic concept was known as the Großer Schlag ("Great Blow").[34]

On July 7, 1944, a diverse American bomber group, comprising 756 Flying Fortresses and 373 Liberators, conducted a mission to attack fuel plants in Böhlen, Merseburg, and Lützendorf, as well as aircraft factories in Leipzig, and headed towards Oschersleben, where an AGO Aircraft Works manufactured 22 percent of all Fw 190 aircraft.[35] This mission led to a significant aerial confrontation. A Wehrmacht report dated July 8 acknowledged the event and cited that *Sturm* fighters had successfully downed thirty bombers. According to American sources, twenty-three bombers—predominantly B-24 Liberators, notably a significant number from the 492nd Bomber Group—were lost in this engagement.

On July 19, 1944, a Wehrmacht report highlighted the *Sturm* groups again, recognizing them with a notably high commendation. In this instance, the specialized fighters successfully brought down forty-nine four-engine bombers, with no information available regarding ramming successes. Another noteworthy engagement occurred during a four-minute encounter on August 16, when twenty Fw 190s from the 4th *Sturm* fighter wing, JG 3 Udet, downed six Flying Fortresses of the 91st Bomber Group while they were bombing Halle an der Saale. However, six *Sturm* fighters were lost in the process.[36]

The German special unit suffered a severe setback in August 1944 when it was intercepted and attacked by P-51 Mustangs. In this encounter, fifteen *Sturm* fighters were brought down, having no chance to execute their ramming tactics.[37] Lieutenant Colonel von Kornatzki, the initiator of the *Sturm* fighters, fell at the forefront of his attack formation on September 11, 1944, only the second assault attack of his group. Unfortunately, his creation did not endure for long. Despite initial successes, where surprise certainly played a significant role, the *Sturm* groups were unable to achieve the decisive breakthrough they sought. The constant and escalating superiority of American air fleets extinguished any prospect of sustained, long-term success for them.

E. J. Hoffschmidt and W. H. Tantum IV offer a contrasting perspective. They perceive the formation of *Sturm* groups as an expression of desperation, indicting a leadership that lacked innovative strategies. The deliberate and organized avoidance of enemy fighters by those steadfastly pursuing them, with the sole objective of eliminating bombers at all costs, had a profoundly psychological impact on American fighter pilots. Their self-confidence soared, while German pilots increasingly grappled with a growing awareness of their inferiority and isolation.[38] On numerous occasions, American fighters trailed behind *Sturm* units, successfully shooting down one aircraft after another, all the while without the cumbersome Fw 190 or accompanying Bf 109 fighters engaging in dogfights or attempting to evade them.

Following the Bodenplatte Operation along the Western Front on January 1, 1945, the *Sturm* group of the JG 4 fighter wing was reduced to a remnant of nine aircraft. Adolf Galland recalled the results of the operation:

> The *Luftwaffe* received its death blow at the Ardennes offensive. In unfamiliar conditions and with insufficient training and combat experience, our numerical strength had no effect. It was decimated while in transfer, on the ground, in large air battles, especially during Christmas, and was finally destroyed. Operation Ground Slab [Bodenplatte] was the conclusion of this tragic chapter. `In the early morning of January 1, 1945, every aircraft took off. They went into a

large-scale well-prepared, low-level attack on Allied airfields in the north of France, Belgium and Holland. With this action, the enemy's air force was to be paralyzed in one stroke. In good weather this large-scale action should have been made correspondingly earlier. The briefing order demanded the very greatest effort from all units. According to records, about 400 Allied airplanes were destroyed, but the enemy was able to replace material losses quickly. In this forced action we sacrificed our last substance. Because of terrific defensive anti-aircraft fire from the attacked airfields, from flying through barrages intended for V1 bombs, and from enemy fighters, and because of fuel shortage, we had a total loss of nearly 300 fighter pilots, including 59 leaders. Only by radically dissolving some units was it possible to retain the remainder.[39]

The situation worsened the next day during a mission in the Kaiserslautern area, resulting in a catastrophe: only two aircraft returned from fifteen, and one of those was severely damaged, sustaining over forty hits. As the war neared its end, *Sturm* groups, like nearly all fighter units, found themselves engaged in desperate ground operations, representing the final buildup. A concise entry in the *Kriegstagebuch* (KTB, "Combat Log") on March 31, 1945, reported the release of the *Sturm* groups by the Luftwaffe High Command for Air Fleet 6 for aerial use, especially attacks on locomotives.

Only after the war was the effectiveness of the *Sturm* tactic appreciated. Relying on authentic American sources, Freeman suggests that the campaign of the U.S. Eighth Air Fleet could have taken a disastrous turn if *Sturm* fighters had appeared just a year earlier.[40] In February 1945, Colonel Herrmann reintroduced the *Sturm* concept; however, this time, he insisted on ramming. The specialized equipment that *Sturm* fighters were accustomed to was no longer required, nor was time-consuming preparations. Instead of employing attacking wedges, ramming swarms and formations of four took their place, and the commanders themselves ceased flying.

In the fall of 1944, as the first pilots of organized *Kamikaze* naval and army units deliberately plunged to their deaths on American warships, the Japanese pilots developed the skills to defend themselves against American B-29 bombers with an interesting ramming method. During the Pacific air war, spontaneous ramming attacks occurred, without any orders or organization. In the summer of 1944, for instance, Lieutenant Naoschi Kanno encountered a solitary B-24 Liberator while on a patrol flight. Upon attacking, and witnessing the bomber withstand multiple hits without crashing, the Japanese fighter pilot opted for a frontal ramming attack. It took three attempts before he successfully struck and destroyed the tail section, just above the hull of the Liberator. The bomber, without its rudder, then fell into the sea. Kanno, who briefly lost consciousness during the forceful impact, managed to regain control of his spiraling aircraft and return to base, albeit with significant damage.[41]

During the night of September 5/6, 1944, a Japanese J1N1 Gekko two-engine night fighter engaged a Liberator. When the onboard weapons proved ineffective, the two Japanese aviators—pilot deck officer Yoschimasa Nakagawa and upper deck officer Isamu Osumi—resorted to ramming to bring down the bomber. Nakagawa skillfully maneuvered his aircraft as close as possible to the Liberator, eventually lodging one of the Gekko's propellers into its fuselage. Despite being severely damaged, the American bomber managed to stay airborne for a while before crashing around 1 a. m. south of Samar and sinking into the Pacific. Nakagawa suffered injuries to his right eye from glass splinters due to a broken canopy. Nevertheless, he successfully landed his battered aircraft.[42]

In terms of organized and methodical ramming operations, the initiative came from pilots in the Japanese army. Similar to some German fighter pilots, they attacked frontally against fast B-29 bombers operating at altitudes of approximately 11,000 meters. The Japanese pilots positioned themselves immediately in front of the target, controlled their aircraft until the last moment, parachuted out after releasing the canopy, and let the stabilized fighter hurtle into the bombers.

Unlike *Kamikaze* pilots, who targeted ships with the intention of giving up their lives, German pilots initially attempted ramming attacks on incoming bombers without a firm commitment to sacrifice themselves, hoping to survive if possible. However, only a few managed to survive. Fortunate circumstances and an almost inhuman cold-bloodedness had to collaborate at high altitudes to provide any chance of survival for Japanese ramming pilots against attacking aircraft.

Japanese aircraft carriers acknowledged this harsh reality, leading to a significant shift in strategy. Consequently, they abandoned the idea of bailing out to save pilots for future flights and instead extended the principle of *Kamikaze* to American bombers. Methods of ramming against bombers, whether or not involving the sacrifice of the aircraft, were neither universally ordered nor recommended by the Japanese high command. The decision was entirely left to the discretion of the pilot. To Japanese leaders, it appeared more strategic to preserve valuable airplanes in anticipation of an American invasion of the Japanese homeland. A bomber, as large and modern as it may have been, seemed relatively less valuable compared to the prospect of expending the same effort to destroy a significant enemy warship, possibly an aircraft carrier.[43]

During that period, soldiers faced the fundamental question of death, a pressing concern for those whose lives were defined solely by warfare, bloodshed, and destruction. Despite apparent differences in East Asian and German terminology, a comparison of the mindset and motivation of Japanese and German pilots is evident. Aside from some profound reflections and premonitions in mysticism, there is little equivalent to Zen in the German intellectual and religious context. Parallels, however, may arise from the simultaneous glorification of steadfastness, fanatical fighting spirit, and masculinity.[44]

In World War II, German military leaders drew support from traditional symbols, particularly in terms of military prestige, which had been popular since the wars of German unification and carried considerable trust among the people. Uniforms played a crucial role in this context. The deep penetration of German sentiment and thinking into the populace, even against their will, is illustrated by the demonstrated commitment of soldiers. Despite their aversion to ambivalent worldviews, they forgot themselves and willingly sacrificed themselves when it came to defending their homeland.

Similar to all states prioritizing long-term survival, the National Socialists in Germany placed significant emphasis on shaping the youth. Nurturing a younger generation immersed in Nazi ideology appeared more promising for ensuring the continued existence of the movement and its leaders than a potentially challenging and uncertain upbringing. All educational institutions were dedicated to serving the regime, tasked with instilling a new, martial set of ideals. From an early age, young Germans were indoctrinated to perceive themselves as special, privileged, and belonging to a particular race. Only Aryan, meticulously chosen, predominantly German literature was permitted, but works from the classics, such as those of Homer that portrayed heroic times in Greece, also carried significant validity.

School education in the Third Reich aimed specifically at shaping young men to be robust, assertive, and resistant. From the outset, armed conflict with other ideologies was deemed inevitable. The youth were repeatedly taught that the will to defend equated to the will to live, considering the latter as the primary and most potent law of nature. The strength of defense, in turn, was believed to be nourished by the collective will to protect oneself. The spiritual foundation for military strength included the concept of community among the people, emphasizing that the power of the people would reach its pinnacle only when everyone united in a shared community spirit, directing their will toward common goals. This message was ingrained in the minds of the youth.

Most of the fighter pilots who willingly joined the inaugural German ramming unit at the outset of the final year of the war had been in the Hitler Youth. There appeared to be an inseparable connection between aviation and National Socialism. Privately, only a few could afford the expensive training required to become an aircraft operator. Starting at barely 10 years old, they began constructing their first model aircraft in school workshop classes. Model assembly groups in the *Jungvolk* ("Young People"—boys aged between 10 and 13) and *Pimpfen* ("Cubs," or "youngsters"—boys from the ages of 6 to 10) had captivated them at a formative time, casting a spell over them. The Flieger-HJ (the flying section within the Hitler Youth), one of the numerous specialized formations within the youth wing of the Nazi Party, offered cost-free, well-organized training, including glider pilot courses provided outside of vacation periods with the opportunity to obtain coveted glider licenses.[45]

6
Creation of Sonderkommando Elbe

Hans-Joachim Herrmann's original strategy involved deploying a massive force of a thousand fighters simultaneously, aiming to eliminate entire bomber formations from the skies over Germany with a single powerful strike. The young colonel essentially adopted Galland's plan for the "Great Blow" in a modified form, incorporating Komatzki's idea from 1943. Herrmann, drawing on his illustrious past as the former commander of the Wilde Sau, referred to it as the war of focus. During operational briefings, increasingly held in February 1945, he consistently recalled the experiences of those formidable airmen and emphasized his leadership experiences at that time. His objective was to implement both the principal idea and mobility in day-fighter missions using weapons. He placed considerable hope in the technical superiority of the new jet fighters, particularly highlighting their high flight speeds. This advancement allowed for the swift assembly of a substantial number of jet fighters from various places, even from distant locations, concentrating them at a single focal point to intercept daytime bombers. He stressed to the officers during briefings the importance of countering an attacking focal point with a defensive focal point, advocating for the concentration of robust forces followed by their united and rapid deployment.

As early as the spring of 1944, when the looming catastrophe of a German defeat became apparent, Göring had urged Galland's pilots to volunteer for the defense of the Reich. The planned "Great Blow" was set to involve eleven combat units, despite the acknowledged vulnerability of deploying large masses of fighters. Approximately a thousand aircraft were intended to participate in the operation. An estimated 500 of them would engage in combat operations, undergo refueling, and reload ammunition to be thrust into battle for a second time. By shooting down enemy bombers and blocking escape routes to Sweden or Switzerland, between eighty and 100 additional night fighters were anticipated to prevent any escaping aircraft. Here too, the ambitious goal was to destroy entire bomber groups.

Herrmann was given approval to create Sonderkommando Elbe and immediately began selecting pilots from units across Germany. He specifically chose those pilots who were experienced in close combat and were willing to undertake a suicide mission. These pilots were given extensive training in air-to-air combat and ramming tactics, with an emphasis on precision and timing. They were also instructed on the technical modifications made to their aircraft. The unit was expected to make a one-way trip, with the pilots bailing out just before impact if possible.

In addition to the selection and training of pilots, significant modifications to their aircraft were required in order to carry out their mission. The planes were stripped of their armaments and ammunition to reduce weight, and the fuel tanks were partially emptied to further lighten the aircraft. The front section of the plane was reinforced with steel plates to withstand the impact of a collision, and the canopy was modified to make it easier for the pilot to bail out at the last minute. The aircraft chosen for the mission was the Focke-Wulf Fw 190 fighter, which was highly maneuverable and had a top speed of over 400mph. However, the planes were also prone to engine failures, which could prove disastrous during the mission.

Preparation for Sonderkommando Elbe's mission faced numerous challenges, both technical and logistical. One major challenge was the shortage of pilots, as the Luftwaffe had suffered significant losses in the preceding years of the war. The selected pilots were often inexperienced or had not flown in combat for months, which posed a risk to the success of the mission. Another difficulty was the modification of the aircraft, as the changes made to them were experimental and had not been tested in combat. Additionally, the lack of resources and funding meant that the unit had to make do with whatever equipment and supplies were available, which often meant using outdated or damaged planes.

Despite these challenges, Sonderkommando Elbe was given the go-ahead to launch its mission in April 1945. The plan was for the unit to take off in small groups and intercept Allied bomber formations, using their modified planes to ram into the enemy aircraft. The mission was to be carried out in two waves, with the first wave consisting of 170 fighters and the second comprising 210 fighters. The mission was to take place in the skies over Berlin, where Allied bombers were expected to attack in large numbers.

The mission was a high-risk operation, with the pilots facing almost certain death. Despite this, the pilots were highly motivated and believed that their sacrifice would help turn the tide of the war in Germany's favor. The lack of experienced flyers also meant that the Sonderkommando Elbe pilots had to undergo intensive training in a short period of time to fly the planes they would use in the mission. They were trained to fly single-engine fighters, which were vastly different from the multi-engine bombers they had previously flown. The pilots were given only a few weeks to master the new planes, during which they had to become proficient enough to fly them in combat situations.

The training took place in several locations, including Jüterbog, Grossenhain, and Frankfurt an der Oder. It was conducted by experienced pilots who were pulled from active duty to serve as instructors. They trained the pilots in the techniques of dive-bombing and other tactics that would be used during the mission. In addition to the training of the pilots, the men also had to prepare the planes they would use in the mission. The planes were stripped of their armament and all non-essential equipment to make them lighter and more maneuverable. They were then fitted with additional fuel tanks to increase their range, allowing them to fly deeper into Allied-held territory, but these were emptied before attack runs to improve performance. The planes were also painted with a yellow and black striped pattern to differentiate them from other German aircraft and avoid friendly-fire incidents.

In addition to its audacious nature, the Sonderkommando Elbe mission involved meticulous planning and coordination to maximize its chances of success. Intricate preparation laid the groundwork for the execution of this high-stakes aerial mission. The need for surprise and evasion of Allied radar detection was recognized. To achieve this, the pilots were instructed to take off in small groups of three or four planes. This aimed to minimize the probability of detection by enemy radar, providing the element of surprise that was crucial for the success of the mission. Flying at a low altitude during the initial phase of the mission further contributed to the stealthy approach. Low-altitude flight reduced the visibility of the aircraft on enemy radar screens, allowing the German pilots to approach their targets undetected. The element of surprise was a paramount consideration, as the success of the mission hinged on catching the Allies off guard.

Once the initial approach was completed, the pilots would climb to a higher altitude. This maneuver served multiple purposes. Firstly, it allowed the German pilots to gain a strategic vantage point for identifying and engaging their targets effectively. Secondly, the ascent was part of the plan to form a single-file line, a formation chosen for its precision and streamlined approach to the attack. The single-file formation was a critical aspect of the mission's strategy. It enabled the German pilots to precisely coordinate their attacks, ensuring a concentrated assault on the Allied bombers. This formation also facilitated quick and agile maneuvers, crucial for evading defensive fire from the targeted Allied aircraft.

The final phase of the mission involved a daring dive on the selected targets. The pilots were given explicit instructions to aim for the engines and cockpit of the Allied planes. Targeting these vulnerable areas maximized the chances of inflicting critical damage and downing the bomber. The success of the mission relied on the precise execution of these attacks, requiring skilled and determined pilots willing to carry out these high-risk maneuvers.

Luftwaffe Pilot Training

Despite having a group of highly skilled and experienced pilots at the beginning of the war, Germany struggled with pilot training; this ultimately became the biggest failure of the Luftwaffe,[1] contends historian James S. Corum.

In comparison to other air forces—such as the USAF, RAF, and even the Soviet air force—the majority of Luftwaffe pilots were technically inferior, especially as the war progressed. The gap in training between the Allied and German schools grew larger over time; by 1944, replacement pilots in the Luftwaffe were so inadequately trained that they were easily taken down in large numbers by Allied bomber gun crews without the help of fighters, according to Corum. These inexperienced or poorly trained pilots struggled to handle challenges like engine failures, rough field takeoffs or landings, bad weather, or heavy cloud cover.

The issue with wartime pilot training in the Luftwaffe can be attributed to cultural and disciplinary problems. Two separate studies examine aspects of discipline in flight training and pilot culture within the Luftwaffe during this time. A paper by Roger Bohn, "Not Flying By The Book," looked at the adoption of better flying methods and procedures, such as checklists, during World War II and beyond, up to the midwar implementation of the standardized Luftwaffe flight procedure system.[2] The human factor in flying is a significant cause of accidents, and the Luftwaffe lost thousands of aircraft due to non-combat causes during the war. For instance, in February 1944 alone, over a thousand Luftwaffe aircraft were lost in accidents, with a good proportion being attributed to inadequate training, as noted in David Isby's book *The Decisive Duel*.[3]

During World War II, as aircraft became more complex and the need increased for training large numbers of new pilots, some air forces recognized the necessity of developing standardized procedures and checklists to maintain and enhance military effectiveness. However, very few air forces implemented such practices. The Luftwaffe did not adopt this approach; indeed, its organizational culture would not have permitted it. For Luftwaffe pilots, accidents and surviving them were almost a point of pride. This attitude had little to do with the intensity of the air war. As early as 1935, Werner Mölders, the leading German fighter ace in the Spanish Civil War, noted in his diary that many accidents were due to a lack of discipline. Furthermore, biographers of Adolf Galland observed that accidents among the macho German fighter pilots were a daily occurrence in 1938.[4]

Prior to World War II, the Luftwaffe was mainly composed of individualistic fighter pilots, who prized their independence and did not adhere to strict discipline. Experienced pilots had developed their own methods and decision-making skills, but new pilots did not have this luxury. Accidents were a common occurrence due to the absence of standardized procedures, checklists, and written documentation. Gunther Rall, who was converting to the Messerschmitt Bf 109—at the time one of the best fighter planes in the world—had almost 200 hours of flight experience, but he operated without any checklist, not even a basic memorized one like that used by the RAF. The Bf 109 was a difficult machine to fly because of its narrow undercarriage and required a lot of attention from the pilot to perform correctly. Take-off accidents were frequent, and once in the air, the pilot had to carry out several actions, such as retracting the undercarriage, adjusting the engine and propeller, cranking up the flaps, and trimming the aircraft for level flight.

If the pilot forgot or mixed up any of these actions, it could lead to a crash. Even after landing, the Bf 109 had a few more tricks up its sleeve, as any slight mistake by the pilot could result in a somersault or crash.

It is noteworthy that the high number of accidents in the Luftwaffe during World War II was mainly due to factors other than combat. According to Ernst Stilla's study, General Milch complained about the lack of aviation discipline in 1943 and cited the high loss rates during transfer flights, which were around 20 percent between May and September 1942. In contrast, the Americans had only six aircraft losses out of 1,200 during transport flights across the Atlantic in September 1944. In retrospect, standardized procedures and checklists could have helped mitigate these losses, but Luftwaffe commanders saw no value in these developments. This neglect was surprising given that aviation checklists were already in use by the United States at the time, with *Life* magazine even publishing an article on the B-17 checklist in 1942. The Luftwaffe's failure to adopt such procedures turned out to be a crucial oversight in managing technological change in aviation.[5]

The Luftwaffe failed to adopt best practices in instrument training, which was a critical area. The Luftwaffe mainly operated in good weather conditions in 1940 and continued to do so throughout the war. The only way the Luftwaffe was able to use fighter aircraft to intercept bombers in bad weather was by putting bomber pilots trained on instruments into fighters from spring 1943. The day-fighter arm of the Luftwaffe had trouble with bad weather throughout the war. Perhaps one of Adolf Galland's biggest mistakes as *General der Jagdflieger* was his failure to realize the importance of instrument training for single-engine day-fighter pilots until it was too late. This attitude was typical of prewar fighter pilots who did not believe in fighting over the Reich against planes that flew in clouds. This lack of instrument training put Luftwaffe pilots at a severe disadvantage as the air war intensified. Fighting often took place over long distances above cloud cover, and disoriented fighters had to go below the cloud and land wherever they could. This led to many additional losses and a wide scattering of aircraft due to insufficient navigational aids.

The aircraft of the latter part of World War II had an incredible variety of weapons, including machine guns, cannons, and rockets. Knowing how to fire these weapons accurately was essential to success in aerial combat. If an enemy airplane was flying straight and level directly in front of him, traveling in the same or the opposite direction, a pilot had only to wait until the airplane was in his gunsight before firing his weapons. However, most of the time, a pilot approached and attacked the enemy at an angle, and deflection shooting was the only way he could hit the target. Deflection shooting called for the pursuing pilot to shoot at a point in space just ahead of the flight path of the enemy plane. This was known as "leading." With the right amount of deflection, the bullets would reach that point at the same time as the enemy plane. Deflection shooting was difficult, especially for the jet- and rocket-powered Luftwaffe aircraft, as at speeds of over 500mph, it was hard to judge distances and there was little time to aim and fire. The low muzzle velocity of their cannons and rockets also hindered pilots' ability to score hits with deflection shooting.

In the latter part of 1943, the Luftwaffe had suffered a significant loss of pilots, with 1,100 fighter pilots already having been lost in the first six months of the year, equating to about 60 percent of the original number. This figure rose, with another 15 percent lost in both July and August. Out of the more than 100 Luftwaffe pilots who were credited with over 100 victories during the war, only eight started flying after 1942. The loss of pilots had two major consequences: new pilots, even if well-trained, were inexperienced, and they were more likely to suffer accidents and casualties.[6]

The Luftwaffe's leadership had stripped away many experienced instructors, and pilot training programs were heavily curtailed. By early 1944, the average Luftwaffe fighter pilot's training was shortened to 160 flight hours, and then further shortened to only 112 hours. By spring of that year, *B-Schule* advanced combat training was disbanded, and pilots were sent directly into first-line service after *A-Schule* primary flight training. In contrast, the average USAAF or RAF fighter pilot's training consisted of 225 flight hours. This lack of training had a severe impact on German survival rates. During the first five months of 1944, Luftwaffe fighter units experienced a complete turnover of pilots, rendering the German aircraft production achievements in 1944 meaningless.[7]

Sonderkommando Elbe Pilot Training

The pilots were tasked with a daunting and dangerous mission, and their training was essential to their success. The selection process for the pilots was rigorous, as the pilots would be sacrificing their lives for the mission. "Hajo" Herrmann, the leader of Sonderkommando Elbe, was responsible for selecting the pilots. He chose experienced pilots who had proven themselves in combat, as well as those who were willing to give their lives for the mission.[8] The selection process involved several criteria. Firstly, the pilots had to be highly skilled and experienced, with a minimum of 500 hours of flight time.[9] They also had to have experience in aerial dogfights, as this was essential for the success of the mission. Furthermore, the pilots had to be in good physical and mental health, as they would be under intense pressure during the mission. Finally, the pilots had to be highly motivated and committed to the mission, as they would likely be sacrificing their lives.

Herrmann personally interviewed all of the pilots who were selected for the mission.[10] He wanted to make sure that they understood the risks involved and were fully committed to the task in hand. Herrmann also made sure that the pilots were aware of the fact that they would not be returning from the mission. The selection process was highly secretive, and the pilots were not told about the details of the mission until they had been selected. This was to prevent leaks and ensure that the mission remained a secret. The pilots were given strict orders not to discuss the mission with anyone, not even their families.

Once the pilots had been selected, they underwent rigorous training to prepare them for the mission. They were trained in the tactics that they would use, including the ramming technique. They were also trained to fly the planes that they would be using during the mission. The training was intense and lasted for several weeks.[11] The selection process for the pilots was not without controversy. Some pilots felt that they had been unfairly passed over for acceptance. There were also concerns that the selection process was biased towards certain pilots who had personal connections to Herrmann. However, it is generally agreed that Herrmann did his best to select the most experienced and committed pilots.

Overall, the selection process for the pilots was rigorous and highly secretive. Those who were selected had to meet strict criteria, including being highly skilled and experienced, in good physical and mental health, and highly motivated and committed to the mission. The training that the pilots underwent was intense and designed to prepare them for the challenges that they would face.

Colonel Herrmann's special command conducted clandestine operations in a secluded section of Stendal air base, guarded by a manned barrier. Nestled in a distant corner of the base, these hidden activities unfolded between March and April of 1945. Some 300 volunteer pilots experienced an extraordinary and almost fairy-tale-like existence amid Luftwaffe stone structures and barracks. This unique and idyllic life stood in stark contrast to the surrounding conditions. The airplanes remained just as they had arrived, adorned with old, predominantly foreign signs or devoid of any signage.[12]

The ancient symbolism of their Japanese allies, embodied by fighter flying, was often much richer and more profound than the case in Germany. During the ceremonial induction of new *Kamikaze* pilots, Japanese marines were adorned with white robes featuring embroidered pink cherry blossoms on the back, while army aviators donned black attire adorned with embroidered gold and green dragons. All *Kamikazes* wore a reproduction of cherry blossom as a symbol of purity, considering it the foremost among flowers, much like the warrior was regarded as the best of men. In a symbolic gesture representing their spiritual resolve, the Japanese named their massive *Kamikaze* attacks off Okinawa *Kikusui*, meaning "floating chrysanthemum." The term evoked the imperial chrysanthemum crest and served as an allegory for self-sacrifice.[13]

During the tumultuous final months of the war in Germany, a multitude of rumors and slogans circulated regarding miracle weapons and specialized armaments. Amidst this chaos, the transfer of a few hundred fighter pilots to Stendal went largely unnoticed. The true nature of the purported Elbe training course remained shrouded in secrecy until the day of the event. Unfortunately, numerous Allied intelligence services discovered the reality of the situation well in advance, significantly undermining the intended psychological impact on American bomber crews. All individuals, either directly or indirectly engaged in the organization and administration of this special unit, maintained strict confidentiality. Anything that might have been disclosed publicly appeared to be absorbed, perhaps not regarded seriously. There were only a handful of points of interaction with the outside world, such as the kitchen and the guards, making it relatively easy to control access. However, the primary reason the secret of the new unit and its objectives remained completely unknown was likely attributed to the strict discipline observed by members of the Sonderkommando command itself.[14]

The overall situation serves as evidence of the impeccable level of secrecy. The regular unit fighter pilots were taken aback upon learning about the objectives of these unfamiliar individuals who had been present in the area for several days, only finding out on the day of the operation.

Contrary to the customary wartime breakfast featuring diluted substitute coffee, damp and hard-to-digest commissary bread, margarine that was stretched thin, and spread, the pilots' table was suddenly adorned with delicacies: freshly aromatic white bread, genuine butter, sausage, cheese, eggs, and even coffee beans—all in abundance, leaving no one overlooked. These delights continued at lunch and dinner. Everyone helped themselves to whatever they wanted—a world of abundance had opened up. Supplies rolled in from apparently inexhaustible sources. The transformation of the overall mood was inevitable, with well-fed stomachs. The remarkable food conditions undoubtedly elevated the status of the young unit, and it was clear that they enjoyed special privileges. Personal pride swelled, and from the outset, the usual distinctions between enlisted personnel and officers seemed to blur; at least the officers were part of the same lineup. Membership of the new unit held more significance than rank itself.[15]

At Stendal, Colonel Herrmann observed a distinct deficiency, particularly in his perspective. To his disappointment, there were insufficient individuals among the volunteers who could be considered representatives of success. The shortage lay in leaders with front-line experience and with significant medals. Consequently, there was a lack of luster, charisma, and magnetic appeal. However, experience had demonstrated that there were still influences of almost undiminished fascination, especially among younger crews.

Herrmann efficiently addressed the issue by issuing orders within his own sphere of influence. Thus, during the night from March 25 to 26, a few classified directives were transmitted through Luftwaffe teleprinters. Acting on behalf of the commander of the 9th Aviation Division (J [for *Jagd*]), Major I. G. Wetterer instructed commanders and squadron captains under his command to oversee and execute a special mission, the successful completion of which carried high expectations. The directive specified individuals with front-line experience and accolades, explicitly stating at least the German Cross in gold. The exact nature of this special operation was not disclosed. The marching orders were issued the following day, designating Stendal as the destination. The officers summoned were instructed to report to Major Köhnke at the Sonderkommando Elbe training course for an introduction to the task, with the expected command duration ranging from ten to fourteen days.

The Prussian military roster did not exist in the Elbe training course. In its place, only a calendar of events was published, which drew attention to lectures or films. Nobody was forced to take part. But the fascination of the company was so strong that everyone seemed to be taking part in events. The lecture halls were always full. Despite the intended camouflage of the Elbe training course, events with a distinct educational purpose transpired. Some of the presentations provided had an evident bias, including anti-Semitic remarks made by the then-prominent workers' professor, Wilhelm Heinrich Börger, a Nazi Party functionary and *SS-Brigadeführer* (general major). Some of the films on offer had the same intentions: *Jud Stifl*, *The Eternal Jew*, *The Rothschilds*—films that were shown in all cinemas anyway and that everyone knew.[16]

A distinguished radio commentator, Professor Hans Härtel from the Ministry for Popular Enlightenment and Propaganda, examined the circumstances within the opposing camp in his lecture. He highlighted significant tensions among the so-called Allies and expressed optimistic expectations about this. An intriguing perspective surfaced concerning the upcoming ramming operation. Härtel expressed hope that a successful Sonderkommando Elbe operation by the individuals at Stendal might not merely be seen as a victory, but that the American bomber fleets might suddenly vanish from the sky. The professor did not entertain the idea of Germany achieving final victory. What appeared crucial to him was creating space for negotiation, obtaining time, and garnering prestige through the most remarkable military success, regardless of the means. According to Härtel, actions such as the upcoming ramming operations would undeniably compel the Western powers to engage in negotiations. Himmler, he added, having already extended his resources, could thus significantly contribute to Germany's cause with the military advantages at his disposal. The planned ramming operation was deemed a substantial trump card.[17]

Several films consistently depicted Germans with a resilient character, showcasing scenes of heroic resistance by noble minorities against brutal enemy forces. Patriotic films such as *Bismarck* and *The Great King* were crafted to appeal to the German spirit. The pilots were given an understanding of the challenging nature of the impending mission through the official suggestion that they should make arrangements for their affairs. This led to the formulation of wills, which were then notarized, and farewell letters were written on paper that had been provided. Some even participated in long-distance weddings. Certain individuals mentioned that they had joined the NSV winter relief organization and redirected their military pay. The NSV (Nationalsozialistische Volkswohlfahrt) was a social welfare organization in Nazi Germany. The term "winter relief" referred to the organization's efforts to provide assistance and support, particularly during the winter months when needs were often heightened. Members of the NSV were involved in various charitable activities, including helping those in need, supporting families, and contributing to the wellbeing of the community. In the given context, individuals mentioned transferring their military pay to support the NSV's winter relief efforts, indicating a commitment to contributing to social welfare initiatives during challenging times.[18]

The activities undertaken by the men were far from conventional, carrying a somber and gloomy tone. Nonetheless, a positive atmosphere persisted. Coarse jokes, particularly directed at the officials' unimpressive meticulousness, served to conceal inner emotions. Nobody wanted to die. In the extensive discussions about the most secure and effective attacking and ramming techniques, a gradual convergence began to take place. Newcomers, including pilots with limited front-line experience or those recently graduated from school, joined the ranks and mingled with the more seasoned veterans. However, the latter were not significantly older themselves, also trying to discern how to perform ramming missions. With the passage of time, tactical details began to surface.[19]

An operational altitude of 11,000 meters was deemed suitable for leading the ramming formations. This could be ensured from considerable distances by the single informed and prepared ground location in Treuenbrietzen. The on-board radios utilized operated exclusively in the ultra-shortwave range, meaning their range aligned with optical visibility. The higher the altitude, the greater the distance over which ultra-short waves could be received; approximately 200km at a medium altitude. It was known that Allied jamming aircraft flew in large bomber formations in order to zero in on German radio communications. Lively German communications thus offered Allied specialists the opportunity to assess the strength of a fighter operation and take appropriate defensive measures.

As the ramming pilots grew more accustomed to their mission, the course management lessened. The seeming superficiality, even nonchalance, might have reflected the perspective of those dealing with this intense matter. Certainly, individuals with the same outlook were involved—some of them combat-experienced, brave, and resolute pilots. These pilots, ready for unconventional combat tactics like ramming a formidable adversary, were no longer willing to relinquish the freedom of decision-making and the mobility they had acquired. This autonomy was a distinct allure of the special operation.

Within the *Schwarm* (swarm), consisting of two squads with four pilots operating four ramming aircraft, a collective and binding course of action had to be agreed upon. The *Schwarm* autonomously selected their leaders, with every member having an equal and valid vote, irrespective of rank. In cases of disagreement, the voice of the *Schwarm* leader took precedence, and any uncertainties were resolved by the command leadership. The composition of the *Schwarm* was beyond external influence; individual pilots had the freedom to decide with whom they wanted to form groups, making their personal choices for the challenging journey into the unknown. Thus, within the diverse assortment of groups of four, a formation method without any complications emerged. Despite its unconventional and non-Prussian nature, the process proceeded smoothly.

Colonel Herrmann, who had a demanding role as the commander of the 9th Aviation Division (J), maintained a reserved yet observed and respected presence at the center. His authority remained unquestioned. Abruptly, he could appear, engage in a few words, provide encouragement, offer advice, issue orders, and then vanish again. He tirelessly commuted between Stendal and Neubiberg, the headquarters of the 9th Aviation Division (J).[20]

Even during that time, the training of aircraft pilots placed a significant burden on German taxpayers and the populations of occupied countries. Conversely, the war presented young men with the opportunity to undergo aviation training without having to concern themselves too much with expenses. It appeared that there was ample funding available. The expectation of the Sonderkommando Elbe pilots was that their fighter aircraft would be successfully launched, ascend to the designated altitude, maintain controlled altitude flight, operate all equipment accurately, respond to the flight leader's signal, stay within the *Schwarm*, and identify the enemy promptly to execute the required actions. They were expected to fly the attack in such a way that penetration and destruction were achieved. Such a special mission without landing required neither exceptional talent nor excellent training. The men had to act like normal pilots and be courageous. If someone had greater skills or more experience, all the better.

The radical ramming technique, despite its imperfections and crudeness, proved more suitable for a situation where one aimed to continue fighting while still in the air, compared to the more refined conventional tactics. It is acknowledged that the Japanese invested considerably less time and resources in training compared to their German allies.

Amidst the haste of preparations, there was scarce opportunity to delve into the effects of the impact of ramming materials on the human body, let alone satisfactorily address and resolve these complex issues. Moreover, there was considerable doubt about the wisdom of bluntly exposing the ram pilots to harsh physical consequences. People were also certain that the psychological strain on pilots, regardless of their apparent resilience, was evident. The quicker the deployment and recruitment, the more favorable it seemed.

Certainly, the likelihood of pilots successfully escaping with their lives hinged significantly on selecting the appropriate aircraft. The unique objective of the forthcoming mission was to inflict severe damage on the enemy by employing fighter planes as ramming devices, with the pilots seated inside. There was no consideration given to the idea of the distorted machines making a return.

Over the years, a misguided aircraft policy simplified the Luftwaffe leadership's selection process. While German engineers generated a plethora of intriguing designs in test facilities and factories, the pilots, with only a few exceptions, continued to operate the traditional Bf 109 and Fw 190 models. Journeying to Leipzig, specifically to the Erla and A. T. G. (Allgemeine Transportgesellschaft) plants, where a substantial portion of Bf 109 components originated, or to Focke Wulf in Berlin-Johannisthal or Bremen, where the leaders of the ramming command could have feasibly visited, were potential destinations for information excursions. Meaningful discussions on the ramming capabilities of the heavy fighter engines might have also taken place, given the proximity of BMW production facilities in Basdorf, north of Berlin, and in Spandau, as well as Daimler-Benz's locations in Marienfelde near Berlin and in Genshagen, south of Berlin, producing aircraft engines for fighter planes on their assembly lines.[21]

Sturm fighters, precursors to the ramming command, were equipped for special operations, with Fw 190s modified for ramming purposes. In the limited instances of ramming engagements, the broad and powerful engine did not pose a disadvantage; indeed, the substantial disk of the 14-cylinder double stem provided a more effective impact on the target, minimizing the risk of penetration into the pilot's compartment. The Focke Wulf's heavy, air-cooled and therefore bulletproof radial engine also offered natural protection when approaching a target. Only put into service with the Luftwaffe in 1941, the Fw 190 had more modern technical attributes than the Messerschmitt Bf 109. At ground level it was clearly superior, around a ton heavier than its competitor.

However, all the benefits that the Fw 190 had over the Bf 109 were nullified by a significant drawback: its performance sharply declined at altitudes exceeding 7,000 meters. Beyond this threshold, the Fw 190 became more vulnerable to enemy aircraft, making it easier prey for adversaries. Given that the intended ramming operation was planned at an altitude of 11,000 meters, the deployment of Fw 190s had to be reconsidered due to this critical issue, highlighting the lack of thought regarding suitable aircraft types. During the final air battle of World War II in Europe on April 7, 1945, the sudden appearance of Fw 190 fighters as ramming machines can likely be attributed to the prevailing urgency and haste under which the ramming command operated. It became impractical to provide instructions to all Fw 190 pilots to adopt the Bf 109 type. Consequently, some pilots continued to fly their standard Focke Wulf models. Additionally, amidst the chaotic nature of the battle, pilots from other fighter units spontaneously decided to emulate their counterparts and engage in ramming as well.

Colonel Herrmann was familiar with both standard aircraft types, as well as with Ar 234 and Me 262 jets. The situation with so-called "long noses" was completely different than with normal Fw 190s. Rather than utilizing the low-altitude BMW radial engine found in the standard fighter planes, Focke Wulf-Werke introduced an advancement of the A series known as the Fw 190 D-9. This variant incorporated the highly potent, water-cooled, in-line engine 12-cylinder Jumo 213 A-1, designed for higher altitudes. To accommodate the elongated nose, the fuselage was extended. The introduction of the long noses into fighter groups had taken place in September 1944. The III Group of JG 54 Grünherz flew its first missions with this improved aircraft type. During the spring of 1945, JG 2 Richthofen was equipped with Fw 190 D-9s, earning widespread acclaim.[23] However, for the specific purpose of ramming operations, long noses were selected because the relatively rare D-9 model was not sufficiently available near the ramming command. Given the crucial role of a potent and destructive propeller in ramming, the use of wooden propellers on the D-9/13 types posed a significant disadvantage.[24]

One of the key challenges for the training of the pilots was the limited time available to prepare them. They had to be trained in just a few weeks to carry out a mission that was extremely dangerous and required a high level of skill. The pilots had to be in excellent physical shape to withstand the physical demands of the mission, and also mentally prepared for the dangers they would face.

The second stage of training focused on mastering the specific techniques that would be required for the mission. The pilots were trained in a range of skills, including low-level flying, attacking ground targets, and evading enemy fire. Low-level flying was particularly important, as the pilots would need to fly close to the ground to avoid radar detection and surprise the enemy. The pilots were trained to fly at extremely low altitudes, often just a few meters above the ground. This required a high level of skill and concentration, as any mistake could result in a crash and probable death.

Attacking ground targets was another key skill that the Elbe pilots had to master. They were also, of course, trained to use ramming to attack enemy bombers. This involved flying directly at an enemy plane and then veering away at the last moment, causing the two aircraft to collide. Ramming was an extremely dangerous tactic, putting the pilot at risk of being killed or seriously injured. However, it was seen as a necessary tactic for the mission, the only way to ensure that the enemy planes were destroyed.

The third stage of training focused on teamwork and coordination. According to Herrmann, the pilots were trained to work together in small groups, with each having a specific role to play in the operation. The pilots had to be able to communicate effectively with each other and to follow orders quickly and efficiently. The success of the mission depended on the ability of the pilots to work together as a team.

One of the key challenges in training the pilots was the shortage of planes. German industry was struggling to keep up with the demands of the war, and the Luftwaffe was severely short of aircraft. This meant that the pilots had to train using whatever planes were available, even if they were not the same type they would be using on the mission. The pilots were trained on a range of planes, including the Messerschmitt Bf 109, Focke-Wulf Fw 190, and Messerschmitt Me 262. This meant that the pilots had to be adaptable and able to fly a range of planes with different capabilities.[24]

As we have seen, another challenge in training the pilots was the shortage of experienced flyers. Many of the Luftwaffe's most experienced pilots had been killed in combat or were already assigned to other units. This meant that Sonderkommando Elbe had to rely on less experienced pilots who had fewer flight hours and less combat experience. To compensate for this, the leadership implemented a rigorous training program that focused on advanced aerial combat techniques, such as deflection shooting and dive-bombing. Pilots were also trained in flying the Fw 190 and Me 109 at high speeds and low altitudes, which were essential for the success of the operation.

The training program was led by experienced pilots such as Herrmann and included intensive physical training to prepare the pilots for the demands of flying at high speeds and making high-G maneuvers. The pilots were also trained in the use of a new weapon, the Hs 293, a radio-controlled glide bomb that was designed to be dropped from the Fw 190 at high speed. Despite the rigorous training program, the pilots were still at a disadvantage due to their lack of experience. This was especially true for the less experienced pilots who had never before flown the Fw 190 or Me 109. Many of these pilots had only a few weeks of training before they were sent on the mission, which was not enough time to become fully proficient in these aircraft.

Furthermore, the pilots were not trained in how to bail out of their planes in case of emergency. Instead, they were simply instructed to crash their planes into the enemy aircraft, which further increased the risk of injury or death. They knew that the odds were against them, but were willing to make the ultimate sacrifice in the name of the Fatherland.

The training and instruction of the pilots was a challenging process due to a shortage of experienced flyers, limited resources, and time constraints. Nevertheless, the pilots received intensive training in advanced aerial combat techniques and the use of new weapons, which were essential for the success of their mission.

The aircraft were usually modified Messerschmitt Bf 109s, which had their armament removed and additional armor plating added to protect the pilot. However, due to the shortage of planes in the Luftwaffe, the unit also used a variety of other aircraft for training, including Fw 190 A-8s and Ju 87 Stukas.

The planes were also fitted with a wooden or metal nosecone, which was filled with explosives to increase their destructive power upon impact. Preparing a Sonderkommando Elbe aircraft was a complex process that involved several steps. First, the aircraft had to be modified to remove its armament and add additional armor plating. This was typically done by ground crews, who would work to make the aircraft as sturdy and durable as possible. Next, the nosecone of the aircraft was modified to accommodate explosives. This involved carefully measuring the amount of explosives needed to ensure that the aircraft would be as destructive as possible upon impact. Once the nosecone was filled with explosives, it was sealed to prevent any leaks.[25]

The planes were stripped of their armor and non-essential equipment such as radios in order to make them lighter and faster, increasing their maneuverability. The guns were removed to further reduce weight. Some planes were fitted with an additional fuel tank to increase their range, but this made them even more vulnerable to enemy fire. The planes were also fitted with an explosive charge, which the pilots could use to destroy their own aircraft if they were unable to hit a target. This was seen as preferable to bailing out, as the pilots risked being shot by Allied fighters or captured by ground forces.

In addition to their modified planes, the pilots were issued with special protective gear, including thick leather jackets and helmets, to protect them from the high-speed impact of the mission.

As soon as pilots arrived at the Stendal air base, they were involved in their secret mission training. Payrolls went into the drawers of the office. No contact was allowed with people outside the fence. The camp was shielded from the outside world, but from the beginning psychological barriers were more effective than a more symbolic fence. The excitement of anticipation accompanied the pilots. Occasionally, they ventured outside the enclosed zone for brief hikes in laid-back gatherings, dressed in attire of their choice. They encountered only a handful of civilians, exchanging greetings as they passed by. Within the camp, there was the typical coming and going of individuals who had recently crossed paths. People sought to establish connections, primarily aiming to gather information. Navigating this small world was easily accomplished due to the familiar surroundings.

Soon, newcomers found their way to the canteen, to the barber, to the photographer who took passport photos for front-line flight IDs, to the toilets and all those facilities without which even this most unusual collection of personnel could not get along. A homogenous group gradually formed from individuals.

Luftwaffe fighter wings not only had numerical designations but were also bestowed with distinctive names. For instance, JG 3 identified itself as Fighter Wing Udet in honor of the renowned fighter and aerobatic pilot Ernst Udet, who later achieved prominence as a general aviation expert.[26] JG 26 adopted the name Schlageter, paying homage to the National Socialist hero of the German Revolution, Albert Leo Schlageter. As for JG 54, it ultimately carried the title of the Grünherz (Green Heart), created by Luftwaffe pilot Hannes Trautloft from Thuringia, symbolizing Thuringia as the green heart of Germany. Such naming practices played a crucial role in establishing and preserving traditions. Each fighter wing aspired to achieve the distinction of the highest mission numbers, and wing leaders competed for top positions in both the takeoff and combat performance rankings. The names assigned to fighter wings were often reflective of their emblems or wing badges, which adorned nearly every squadron aircraft. These badges were accompanied by special paintings and unique lettering on various aircraft, although this became less common towards the end of the war when the significance diminished. The more successful a fighter pilot proved to be, the more lenient their superiors were, with airmen identifying themselves as aces through distinctive markings painted on their aircraft. More solemn in nature were the regimental flags awarded to each squadron.

(Note: Each *Geschwader* (or "wing") was made up three or four *Gruppen* ("groups") and typically comprised between 108 and 120 aircraft. A *Staffel* ("squadron") consisted of twelve to fifteen planes. I. Gruppe consisted of Staffel

1, 2, and 3, II. Gruppe of Staffel 4, 5, and 6, III. Gruppe of Staffel 7, 8, and 9, and so on.)

Diverging from the established customs of traditional German squadrons and in stark contrast to the Japanese approach, the pilots of Sonderkommando Elbe consciously abstained from adopting such symbolism. The hurried construction, relatively underdeveloped group cohesion, efforts to maintain secrecy, and external challenges all contributed to the fact that none of the pilots who embarked on their challenging flight on April 7, 1945, operated under a distinctive symbol, apart from the Swastika, perhaps.

7
Use of Pervitin by Sonderkommando Elbe Pilots

The use of drugs to enhance pilot performance was common during World War II. One such drug was Pervitin, a form of methamphetamine that was used by both Allied and Axis pilots to stay alert and focused during long flights. The use of Pervitin by Luftwaffe pilots has been the subject of much speculation and debate.

Pervitin, also known as methamphetamine hydrochloride, was first synthesized in Japan in 1919, being introduced to Germany in the early 1930s.[1] It was marketed as a treatment for depression and fatigue, but its potent stimulant effects soon made it popular as a recreational drug. During World War II, Pervitin was widely used by soldiers and pilots on both sides of the conflict to stay alert and focused during long periods of intense activity.

The use of Pervitin by Sonderkommando Elbe pilots was documented in several sources, including the memoirs of Hans-Joachim Herrmann and other members of the unit. According to Herrmann, the pilots were given Pervitin in order to enhance their performance and keep them focused during the mission. Its use was voluntary. Herrmann wrote: "The morning of the attack, the pilots were given a pill to keep them awake and alert. We knew that it was a form of methamphetamine, but we didn't care. We were willing to do whatever it took to complete the mission."[2] Other members of the unit confirmed the use of Pervitin, with one pilot stating that he was given two pills to keep him going.

The effects of Pervitin on the pilots are difficult to assess, as there is limited information available on their physical and mental states during the mission. However, we can draw on the experiences of other pilots and soldiers who used the drug during the war to gain some insight into its effects. Pervitin is a potent stimulant that increases alertness, reduces fatigue, and can produce feelings of euphoria and wellbeing. However, it also has a number of negative side effects, including increased heart rate and blood pressure, loss of appetite, anxiety, and insomnia.[3] In high doses, it can cause paranoia, hallucinations, and delusions.

The use of Pervitin by German pilots during the war has been linked to a number of crashes and accidents. In one well-known incident, a pilot who was under the influence of Pervitin crashed his plane into a mountainside, killing himself and his crew.⁴ Other pilots reported experiencing severe mood swings and hallucinations after using the drug. Despite these risks, Pervitin continued to be widely used by German soldiers and pilots throughout the war. According to one estimate, over 35 million tablets of Pervitin were distributed to German soldiers during the war.⁵ The drug was seen as a way to enhance performance and boost morale, and its use was encouraged by military authorities. The use of Pervitin was at the discretion of the JG commanders, and most did not require it.

During World War II, German society and the Nazi military became intertwined with the use of Pervitin. This methamphetamine-based substance played a significant role in both civilian and military contexts, offering temporary benefits of increased alertness and combat-readiness. However, its rampant use also brought about severe consequences, highlighting the darker side of its widespread availability.

In the late 1920s, the pharmaceutical company Temmler introduced Pervitin to the German market as a prescription medication. It was initially marketed as a treatment for various conditions, including depression, fatigue, and asthma. The drug's stimulant properties gained popularity, leading to its widespread availability and usage in German society. Recognizing the potential benefits of Pervitin, the Nazi military incorporated it into their operations. German soldiers were issued Pervitin tablets, particularly pilots and tank crews, to combat exhaustion and enhance combat performance. The drug helped overcome the physical and mental strains of warfare, allowing soldiers to remain awake for extended periods, march long distances, and fight without rest, contributing to the success of the Blitzkrieg strategy during the invasion of Poland in 1939.

Pervitin was not limited to military use; it permeated civilian life. It became readily available over the counter, and individuals from various professions—including factory workers and medical personnel—relied on the drug to combat tiredness and increase productivity. Pervitin became known as a miracle drug, enabling individuals to work longer hours and meet the demands of wartime production. While Pervitin offered short-term benefits, it came with severe side effects and addictive properties. Users experienced increased energy, reduced fatigue, and heightened alertness, but prolonged use led to detrimental consequences: insomnia, hallucinations, paranoia, aggressive behavior, and physical and mental deterioration plagued those who became dependent on the drug.

The widespread availability and use of Pervitin in German society had far-reaching consequences. It revealed the ethically questionable practices of the Nazi regime, exploiting a drug to push soldiers and civilians beyond their limits. Moreover, the normalization of drug use for productivity and combat effectiveness created a culture of dependence, blurring the boundaries between medical treatment and abuse. As the war progressed, Pervitin's availability decreased due to supply shortages and increased regulations. The military began recognizing the negative consequences of drug use, leading to stricter control measures. Soldiers faced the risk of addiction, with withdrawal symptoms further compromising their combat effectiveness. Additionally, the long-term health impact on both soldiers and civilians began to emerge, shedding light on the dangers of drug abuse.

In the case of the Sonderkommando Elbe pilots, the use of Pervitin was likely seen as a necessary risk. The mission was a desperate and dangerous one, and the pilots knew that they would be facing overwhelming odds. Taking Pervitin may have been seen as a way to give them a physical and mental edge during the mission, but it also had its downsides. Side effects such as paranoia, aggression, and hallucinations could have increased the danger. Additionally, the long-term effects of Pervitin on the pilots' health and mental state are not fully known.

Despite these potential risks, it is clear that the pilots were willing to take them in order to carry out their mission. In the end, the operation was not successful in terms of achieving its stated goals of destroying a significant number of Allied planes. However, it demonstrated the willingness of the Luftwaffe and its pilots to resort to desperate measures in the face of overwhelming odds in a bid to turn the tide of war. The use of Pervitin by Sonderkommando Elbe pilots was a reflection of the dire circumstances facing the Luftwaffe in the waning days of World War II, with a crippling shortage of experienced pilots, planes, and fuel.

Long-term use may have contributed to postwar health challenges for those who relied on Pervitin. Prolonged use of stimulants can result in psychological dependence. Pilots may have experienced difficulties readjusting to normal life after the war, the absence of Pervitin-induced performance enhancement possibly leading to feelings of inadequacy or lethargy. Adapting to civilian life and dealing with potential physical and mental health issues could have been significant long-term challenges. The use of stimulants like Pervitin by Luftwaffe pilots contributes to the historical understanding of the conditions and challenges faced during World War II. It sheds light on the complex relationship between the military, medical science, and ethical considerations surrounding the use of performance-enhancing substances.

While Pervitin may have provided short-term benefits in terms of performance during wartime, the long-term consequences were detrimental to the health and wellbeing of those who used it. The physical and psychological toll on individuals could extend well beyond the wartime period, impacting their post-war lives and contributing to broader discussions about the ethical use of drugs in military contexts.

8

Eighth Air Force Target List for April 7, 1945

Despite having a substantial and expanding synthetic fuels production capacity at the onset of World War II to supplement its limited domestic crude oil resources, German industry faced challenges in meeting the military's fuel requirements throughout the conflict. The scarcity of fuel became apparent when Germany implemented fuel rationing from late 1940 to the spring of 1941, aiming to accumulate reserves for Operation Barbarossa. Recognizing the critical nature of the fuel shortage, General Walter Warlimont, the head of the German military's operations staff, expressed concerns in June 1941 in his paper "War Potential 1942." In this document, he highlighted that the supply of oil would be one of the weakest points of the German economy potentially affecting the operational capabilities of the armed forces, armaments industry, and deliveries to allies.[1] British and American leaders recognized Germany's supply challenges, understanding that a reduction in the enemy's fuel levels would hamper the operational effectiveness of German mechanized forces, whether on land, at sea, or in the air.

In the autumn of 1944, equipped with huge numbers of heavy bombers and long-range fighters, the United States Army Air Forces was in a position to deliver a decisive blow to the enemy's vital transportation and oil sectors. Formations consisting of over 1,000 heavy bombers conducted attacks with impunity, completely annihilating oil refineries, synthetic oil plants, bridges, and railroad marshaling yards throughout Germany. By early 1945, following months of relentless assaults, the strategic bombing campaign had wreaked havoc on Germany's transportation system and severely curtailed its oil production. This extensive destruction left the Wehrmacht significantly weakened due to shortages of supplies and fuel. With its air force vanquished and its infrastructure utterly devastated, Nazi Germany ultimately succumbed to Allied ground advances from both the east and the west in May 1945.

Oil storage facilities presented a prime target for the U.S. Air Force during the war. The disruption of Germany's capacity to manufacture and distribute fuel was a crucial objective for the Allies. Severing the fuel supply chain had a domino effect, hampering the mobility and effectiveness of Nazi military operations. Targeting such vital infrastructure aimed to weaken the German war machine and undermine its ability to sustain prolonged conflict.

Mission 931 on April 7, 1945 included 1,315 USAAF bombers and 898 fighters that were dispatched to hit airfields, oil and munitions depots, and explosive plants in central and northern Germany. All primary targets were bombed visually. The Eighth Air Force target list for the day included a number of industrial and transportation targets in Germany.[2] The 3rd Air Division Intelligence Annex to its field order was used to justify targets for bombing:

Intelligence Report CQ-2038 (Büchen)
Despite 2nd Air Division's attack of March 25th, the majority of storage tanks remain intact. Photographic coverage shows two of the nine tanks in the central section severely damaged, and another probably damaged. The southern and central tank areas have not yet been covered over with a protective cover of earth and concrete as has the northern tank area. This accounts for the MPIs (Mean Point of Impact) being placed upon the two most vulnerable tank areas. [In fact, the raid of March 25 mentioned had been something of a disaster, bad weather causing the 1st and 3rd Air Divisions to be recalled, leaving the 2nd Air Division alone to attack the oil facilities at Ehmen, Hitzacker, and Büchen. Only fifty-seven bombers had actually attacked Büchen.][3]

Intelligence Report GN-3773 (Güstrow)
This ordnance depot has shown marked activity on recent (photographic) cover and is the most important depot of its kind in this portion of Germany. It is sufficiently close to the Eastern front for the Russians to be well aware of its importance. A successful attack will not only be a tactical aid to the ground troops but will also strengthen the diplomatic ties between the Allies.[4]

Intelligence Report GU-3910 (Parchim)
This is an operational field for both jet aircraft and conventional single-engine fighters. Recent cover has shown between 75 and 100 aircraft on this field, including both Me 262s and Ar 234s. About two weeks ago P-51s were able to confirm the operational use of GU-3910 by jet aircraft when they trailed three Me 262s, which had been attacking 8th Air Force bombers in the Hamburg area, back to this field and destroyed them as they were landing. [This seems to refer to March 25 when P-47s of the 63rd Fighter Squadron, 56th Fighter Group, chased six or seven Me 262s which had attacked a 2nd Air Division formation. The victims on this occasion were Me 262A-1s belonging to the 7th Fighter Wing. One of the successful American pilots was Captain George E. Bostwick, who would also be actively involved in the mission of April 7.][5]

Intelligence Report GU-4277 (Kaltenkirchen)
This Me 262 operational base was being used by a Group of Fighter Wing 7 at last report. Recent cover has shown both Me 262s and a moderate number of other types of aircraft on this field.[6]

Intelligence Report GH-5556 (Neumünster)
This marshaling yard has been assigned as the secondary priority target for all of the 2nd Air Division's 32 squadrons as well as 6 Groups of this Division. Operations Officers should brief Lead crews concerned of this fact. [While every effort was being made to destroy the factories, industrial plants, and workshops, the bombers still had to ensure that any material produced by surviving facilities could not be moved by rail.][7]

Enemy Air Opposition
All forces will be crossing the area where approximately 200 tactical fighters are located. These are not expected to react but are capable of opposing the bombers anywhere east of eight degrees. There are approximately 250 fighters located in the area south of Bremen. Most of these aircraft are thought to be non-operational. Forces on GU-3910 and GN-3773 (Parchim and Güstrow) are reminded that 2nd Air Division was attacked by 30–35 Me 262s in target area on 4th April. Also near target area are six operational jet fields, each of which has ten or less Me 262s. Weather is against take-off and assembly of large numbers of enemy aircraft.[8]

B-17 bombers were sent to hit the following:

Büchen Oil Storage Depot (Primary Target) (36 B-17s)
Büchen, situated in the scenic Neckar-Odenwald district of Baden-Württemberg, carries a rich historical significance. Nestled within the captivating Odenwald region, the town is strategically positioned about 80km southeast of Frankfurt and 60km northeast of Heidelberg. Amid its picturesque landscapes, Büchen played a notable role during World War II due to its oil storage tanks, which held immense importance.

The oil storage tanks of Büchen presented a prime target for the Eighth Air Force during the war. Disruption of Germany's fuel manufacture and distribution system was one of the Allies' main aims, as breaking the fuel supply chain could cripple the mobility and effectiveness of German formations. Bombing this vital infrastructure seriously weakened the ability of the Nazi war machine to keep functioning.

The strategic positioning of Büchen relative to major urban centers and industrial hubs made it a logical target for the intensive bombing campaigns carried out by the Allies. The town's role as a transportation and logistics hub heightened its importance in the eyes of the strategists.[9]

Güstrow Ordnance Depot (Primary Target) (104 B-17s)

The Güstrow Ordnance Depot emerged as a high-priority target for the Eighth Air Force during the climactic days of World War II. Situated in the northeastern reaches of Germany, in close proximity to the town of Gustrow, this depot held a critical role in the German war effort. Housing a substantial cache of munitions and military supplies, the facility was a linchpin in the logistical backbone of the Nazi war machine.

In a determined bid to disrupt the enemy's capabilities, the Eighth Air Force orchestrated a formidable aerial assault on the target on April 7, 1945. This audacious mission involved a formidable force of approximately 600 bombers and fighters, an awe-inspiring manifestation of Allied air power. The squadron of bombers, laden with a staggering 1,300 tons of bombs, roared across the skies toward the Gustrow Ordnance Depot.

The thunderous bombardment unleashed upon the depot and its surroundings left an indelible mark. The sheer force of the assault shattered the facility's infrastructure, reducing storage facilities and supply lines to smoldering ruins. The devastation was a testament to the unwavering determination of the Allies to dismantle the logistical backbone of the Nazi war machine. The strategic significance of Gustrow as a distribution center for military resources rendered its obliteration an imperative step in crippling Germany's ability to keep on fighting.[10]

Kaltenkirchen Airfield (Primary Target) (143 B-17s)

Kaltenkirchen Airfield, a pivotal asset for the Luftwaffe situated in the northern expanse of Germany, etched its name into the annals of World War II history. Positioned just 15 miles north of the bustling city of Hamburg, this airfield held strategic importance as a hub for Luftwaffe operations. The mission was clear: to unleash an unrelenting barrage of destruction upon Kaltenkirchen Airfield. In an awe-inspiring display of aerial power, the bombers bore down upon their target, carrying a payload exceeding 2,000 tons of bombs.

The symphony of destruction that ensued left an indelible mark on the airfield and its surroundings. As the bombs rained down, the area was devastated, reducing aircraft, buildings, and other crucial facilities to rubble. The once-bustling hub of Luftwaffe activity was left desolated, its functionality brought to a grinding halt.[11]

Neumünster Marshaling Yard (Secondary Target) (37 B-17s)

Neumünster Marshaling Yard, nestled in the heart of northern Germany near the town of Neumünster, was a linchpin of wartime logistics. A critical cog in the vast machinery of the Wehrmacht, this marshaling yard played a pivotal role in coordinating the movement of troops, supplies, and equipment. The bombers descended upon their target, unleashing a storm of destruction.

The impact on the marshaling yard was catastrophic. Tracks were twisted and shattered, buildings reduced to rubble, and the very foundations of the logistical lifeline undermined. The devastation served as a testament to the Allied air forces' relentless pursuit of disrupting the German military's ability to function effectively. The destruction of transportation hubs like that at Neumünster struck at the heart of the Nazi regime's ability to sustain and reinforce its front lines.[12]

Parchim Airfield (Primary Target) (134 B-17s)
Parchim Airfield, in the northern expanse of Germany near the town of Parchim, held strategic significance as a pivotal stronghold for the Luftwaffe. Amidst the orchestration of the Allied forces' grand finale, Parchim emerged as a target of paramount importance, drawing the gaze of the Eighth Air Force on the fateful day of April 7, 1945.

The B-17s heading for Parchim were carrying over 1,200 tons of bombs, primed to shatter the airfield's strategic potency. The airfield's runways, buildings, and infrastructure were left in smoking ruin.

The attack on Parchim was part of the Allied forces' relentless campaign which aimed to erode the very bedrock of Germany's military might. Parchim's key role as a bastion of the Luftwaffe made it an obvious target, and its airfield was left showing the terrible scars of battle.[13]

Salzwedel Airfield (Target of Opportunity) (1 B-17)
Salzwedel Airfield, in the northeastern German state of Saxony-Anhalt near the tranquil town of Salzwedel, bore witness to the ebb and flow of conflict during World War II. The strategically located airfield enabled the Luftwaffe to target the Allied forces advancing through the region.

On April 7, 1945, the U.S. Eighth Air Force orchestrated a symphony of destruction against Salzwedel Airfield involving masses of B-17 and B-24 bombers. Fighter escorts flew in harmony with the bombers, ensuring their protection from Luftwaffe fighter planes throughout the perilous journey. A relentless torrent of destruction rained down upon the airfield's facilities and aircraft, dealing a further crippling blow to the German war machine.

The effects of the mission reverberated far beyond the airfield. By dismantling the infrastructure and weakening the defenses at Salzwedel, the Eighth Air Force laid a crucial foundation for the relentless advance of Allied ground forces.[14]

Schwerin Marshaling Yard (Secondary Target) (48 B-17s)
The marshaling yard in Schwerin was an important transportation hub for the Wehrmacht, coordinating the movement of troops, equipment, and supplies. The bombing raid was part of a larger Allied effort to disrupt German transportation and supply lines in the final stages of the war. Despite heavy anti-aircraft fire from German defenses, the Eighth Air Force destroyed much of the marshaling

yard, fatally disrupting German operations in the area. Overall, the raid on the Schwerin Marshaling Yard was considered a great success.[15]

(Note: Of the 503 bombers on the mission, fourteen B-17s were lost and 117 damaged. One airman was killed, five were wounded and 117 were listed as missing in action. The formation was escorted by 317 P-51 fighters, two of which were lost with their pilots listed as missing in action. One Mustang was damaged beyond repair. The P-51s claimed to have shot down thirty-one German aircraft.[16])

B-24 bombers were sent to hit the following:

Düneburg Explosive Works (Primary Target) (168 B-24s)
Düneburg Explosive Works was a target of the Eighth Air Force on April 7, 1945. The explosive works were located near the town of Düneburg in northern Germany, a significant facility for the production and storage of explosives and munitions. Over 900 tons of bombs were dropped on the facility, causing significant damage to its infrastructure and setting off numerous explosions. The destruction of facilities like Düneburg hindered the German military's ability to produce and store explosives and munitions, thereby reducing units' effectiveness in battle.[17]

Krummel Explosive Works (Primary Target) (128 B-24s)
Krummel Explosive Works was a target of the Eighth Air Force on April 7, 1945. The explosive works were in northern Germany, near the town of Krummendorf, another important facility for the manufacture and storage of explosives and other munitions. The bombers dropped a total of over 1,400 tons of bombs on the works, which caused severe damage to the facility.[18]

Neumunster Marshaling Yard (Primary Target) (26 B-24s)
Neumunster Marshaling Yard, located in northern Germany near the town of Neumunster, was a critical Wehrmacht transportation hub. Over 1,300 tons of bombs were dropped on the yard, causing significant damage to its tracks, buildings, and other facilities. The destruction of transportation hubs such as that at Neumunster hampered Germany's ability to move troops, supplies, and equipment to the front lines.[19]

(Note: Of the 322 bombers on the mission, fourteen B-17s and three B-24s were lost, with forty-four damaged and one damaged beyond repair. Six airmen were killed, seven wounded, and twenty-five missing in action. Escorting the formation were 252 P-47s and P-51s. Two P-51 Mustangs were lost, their pilots listed as missing in action. One P-51 was damaged beyond repair. The fighters claimed the shooting down of thirty German aircraft.)

Eighth Air Force Target List for April 7, 1945

Four hundred and forty-two B-17s were sent to hit the following:

Fassberg Airfield (Target of Opportunity) (twelve B-17s)
Fassberg Airfield in northern Germany, a target of the Eighth Air Force on April 7, 1945, was an important base for the Luftwaffe during World War II. The bombers dropped a total of over 1,000 tons of bombs on the airfield, causing significant damage and destroying many aircraft on the ground. By attacking airfields like Fassberg, the Allies aimed to limit the Luftwaffe's ability to carry on air operations and provide support for ground troops.[20]

Hitzacker Oil Depot (Primary Target) (115 B-17s)
Located in the town of Hitzacker in northern Germany, this was one of the major storage facilities for fuel and oil used by the German military during the war. The depot was an important target for the Allied forces because it supplied fuel for German tanks, planes, and other military vehicles. The bombers encountered heavy anti-aircraft fire, but still managed to drop their bombs on the target. The attack caused significant damage to the depot and disrupted the flow of fuel to the Wehrmacht. However, the Eighth Air Force suffered losses as well, with several aircraft shot down or damaged by the German defenses. Nevertheless, the attack on the Hitzacker oil depot played a role in the eventual defeat of Germany.[21]

Kohlenbissen Airfield (Primary Target) (93 B-17s)
Kohlenbissen was a military airfield used by the Luftwaffe during World War II. Located near the town of Holzminden in Lower Saxony, it was primarily used for training purposes, although it was also a base for fighter and bomber squadrons. It was equipped with concrete runways and various support facilities, including hangars, maintenance buildings, and barracks for personnel. It was reported that all bombs hit their target.[22]

Lüneburg Airfield (Secondary Target) (92 B-17s)
Lüneburg Airfield in Lower Saxony was primarily used by the Luftwaffe for training and as a base for fighter and bomber squadrons. The airfield was targeted by Allied bombing raids on several occasions during the war, including attacks by the RAF and USSAF. The raids caused significant damage to the airfield's facilities and aircraft, although it was not completely destroyed.[23]

Uelzen Marshaling Yard (13 B-17s)
The marshaling yard was an important transportation hub located in the town of Uelzen, Lower Saxony. The mission was part of the ongoing effort to disrupt German military operations and infrastructure. The Eighth Air Force carried out a bombing raid on the marshaling yard, using B-17s. The mission was supported by fighter escorts to protect the bombers from German fighters. The attack was

successful, with many of the rail tracks and other facilities destroyed, which helped to disrupt German transportation and logistics.[24]

Wesendorf Airfield (107 B-17s)
Located near the town of Wesendorf in Lower Saxony, the airfield was used by the Luftwaffe to launch attacks against Allied forces advancing through northern Germany. The mission on April 7th, 1945, involved B-17 bombers supported by fighter escorts. The attack was deemed a success, with much of the airfield's facilities and many aircraft destroyed.[25]

(Note: Of the 432 bombers on the mission, twenty-seven B-17s were damaged. One airman was killed and three were wounded. Meanwhile, 209 P-51 Mustangss escorted the formation without loss. In addition to the bombing missions, four B-17s flew scouting missions, and twenty-three P-51s escorted twelve F-5 aircraft on photo-reconnaissance missions. The F-5 Photo Lightnings were based on the P-38G aircraft.)

9
The Attack on April 7, 1945

From March 2, 1945, onwards, conventional German fighter planes had not significantly confronted the heavy bombers of the Eighth Air Force. The Allies possessed limited knowledge about the actual condition of the Luftwaffe. There were reports of entire flying units disbanding, and accounts from returning bomber and fighter crews depicted the severe and practically fatal setbacks the Luftwaffe continually suffered. Photographs brought back by Allied reconnaissance aircraft revealed abandoned air bases. This, along with the overall confidence in victory, served to bolster the conviction of American airmen that the Luftwaffe had already been obliterated.

As had happened on numerous occasions before, on April 3, 1945, not a single German fighter intercepted the bombers of the 3rd Air Division, let alone hindered their bombing mission over the northern German city of Kiel.[1] Despite the likelihood of this occurrence being considered unlikely, it prompted the headquarters of the Eighth Air Force to issue Field Order Number 1887A on the same evening, urgently cautioning all units against any understandable relaxation of vigilance. The silence was disconcerting, especially considering the favorable weather predicted by meteorologists.

The potential for cloud cover, particularly medium stratification, could facilitate jet fighter attacks from above and below, as past experience had shown. Purely on paper, the Germans could also deploy strong units of single-engine fighters from the Berlin and Leipzig area. However, the current condition of these formations and recent experiences with conventional German fighters made it appear highly doubtful in the opinion of the Allied staff officers whether the heavy bombers had to reckon with major enemy forces. On April 4, during renewed bombing missions targeting Kiel and Eggebeck, the Eighth Air Force encountered only limited opposition near Hamburg. A handful of Me 262 jet fighters and a few Fw 190s attempted to engage, but aside from an unfortunate collision between two B-17 bombers, the Eighth had no casualties to lament on that day.

The German operations command issued a relocation order to the Stendal pilots in the middle of the night on April 5. The organization still worked excellently.

In the subdued confusion of the transfer, the pilots hurried to the waiting trucks. Engines started, doors slammed, and shouts were suppressed. The men stared into the darkness. The procession departed the small oasis of prosperity with a low, resonant noise. The air was chilly, and the rigid seats offered little comfort. Amidst the haze of cigarette smoke, thoughts surged forward. A sense of unease cast a large shadow.

During that evening, robust military trucks transported ramming pilots from Stendal to specific operational sites in the Altmark area. Meanwhile, the thirty pilots slated for take off from Stendal remained stationed there. Additional planned locations in the state included Sachau, the base of Group 3 of Fighter Wing 301, as well as Gardelegen, utilized by Group 4 of Fighter Wing 301 and Group 2 of Fighter Wing 54. Solpke and Salzwedel were also designated, serving as bases for the remaining units of Fighter Wing 301. Others were the Delitzsch airfield near Bitterfeld and Mortiz near Eilenburg, northeast of Leipzig.

With the departure of the individual units from the special command, the ramming operation had progressed to its subsequent phase. Along the periphery of the runways at the berths of the host fighter groups, a consistent scene unfolded: remarkably, numerous undamaged standard Bf 109 and Fw 190 aircraft, along with a few Me 262s, were scattered about, undergoing various movements—being rolled, pushed, and braked. Mechanics diligently worked on the engines, conducting checks and preparing the aircraft for active duty. Tanker trucks traversed from one machine to another, supplying the scarce fuel. The atmosphere was bustling with activity. The deteriorating situation on the Eastern Front necessitated an escalated deployment of fighter groups to safeguard the ground forces.

Despite the vastness of the flight fields, there was, as always, a heavy smell of gasoline and fuel hanging over the hustle and bustle. Calls from waiting staff, guards, and other personnel mingled in the lines of aircraft taking off and landing, with echoes of music blowing from loudspeakers set up all around. Engines roared; dust swirled into a cloudless, cold blue-gray sky. Owing to exceedingly significant losses in recent weeks and months, the personnel of conventional fighter squadrons found themselves acclimatizing to the continuous turnover of aircraft pilots. Some newcomers were duly observed. Consequently, on the night of April 4 to 5, the pilots of Sonderkommando Elbe could inconspicuously blend in across all designated operational zones. Strict directives were issued for the thirty-man groups to remain discreetly restrained.

Scattered clusters of three or four individuals engaging in casual conversations were scarcely noticed, offering glimpses into the daily routine of those fully committed to the mission. Individuals strolled amid rare jet fighters, around lounges and barracks, surveying the aircraft prepared for ramming and anticipating the as yet uncertain day of the operation. A few superficial jokes about the regular fighter groups were unavoidable. Fellow pilots who knew each other from other associations or from flight schools, suddenly found themselves facing each other. But the great secret was kept.

The issue of fuel took on a new significance. There was only enough for a one-way flight. With no possibility of a return journey, the entire fuel supply was allocated for the outbound flight, encompassing waiting time and the impending attack. Due to the strategic timing, the ramming units' deployment was intended to commence as soon as the certainty of enemy incursions arose. This adaptable combat strategy aimed to position the core force of the impending German attack—namely, the ramming fighters—into the most advantageous starting positions possible. The plan outlined that the ramming formations would ascend to designated holding areas above the Elbe region, awaiting the final operational order at an altitude of approximately 11,000 meters. The river whose name the unit bore was destined to play a significant role in the fate of many young pilots.

On the morning of the Friday after Easter 1945, April 6, while the ramming pilots were having breakfast, they were electrified by a rumor of an imminent mission. In contrast to the consensus of the Luftwaffe command staff, Colonel Herrmann independently designated Saturday, April 7, as the day for the ramming unit to become operational. However, the entry in the Situation Book of the Wehrmacht command staff dated April 4, 1945, reveals that the high command had already earmarked a squadron of 150 aircraft in the Stendal area for a two-part operation.

With the deployment date seemingly confirmed for April 7, there was a noticeable shift in the mood and demeanor of the pilots. Many of them moved about with somber expressions, preoccupied with thoughts of impending events. Some engaged in idle activities, their appetites waning in anticipation of what lay ahead. The night of April 6 to 7 was spent sleeplessly by some; the awkwardness of their situation just wouldn't go away.

The Eighth Air Force's strategic attack against targets in Germany on April 7 was the one of its last missions in the strategic air war in Europe.[3] The American command planned operations by large formations against five jet fighter bases in northern and central Germany. Reinsehlen, Kohlenbissen (a field airfield east of Munster and north of Faßberg), Wesendorf, Kaltenkirchen, but especially Parchim—which was repeatedly targeted by bombs—were considered objects of the highest order of urgency. Kaltenkirchen hosted the 1st Group of Fighter Wing 7, while the 3rd Group of Fighter Squadron 7 with the integrated 4th Group of Fighter Wing 54 was located in Parchim. Both jet fighter groups were later to intervene in the air battle.

American mission planners believed that, besides encountering jet fighters, they would also come across another mysterious aerial unit based in Parchim, which could thwart their participation in a crucial night mission against Russian crossing points on the Vistula. However, this intelligence turned out to be inaccurate. In reality, a target group from Kampfgruppe Helbig, comprising eight Mistel Ju 88/Fw 190 teams, was awaiting orders to take off from Parchim. These aircraft, affiliated with the KG Fighter Wing 30, were part of the major operation named Iron Hammer, involving other Mistel units in Oranienburg, Rechlin-Lärz, and Peenemünde, which was initially never intended to take place, but the units were kept in readiness. Further primary targets for the Allied bombers were two large ammunition factories near Hamburg on the Elbe, Düneburg and Krümmel, as well as two underground fuel depots near Btichen and Hitzacker, and an important Wehrmacht equipment depot in Güstrow.

The initial intention was to include Rechlin in the series of attacks. But this important Luftwaffe research facility was now east of the bombardment line agreed with the Russians and was thus taboo. There was no time left to let the issue be settled by the United States Military Commission in Moscow. As a result, the operational staff acted immediately, in accordance with the Plan of Attack on German Communications. They designated the east–west railway connections of the Reichsbahn to the Ruhr area as priority targets. In addition, they selected traffic facilities in the area known as Zone 1 as secondary objectives. These targets included the towns of Neumtinster, Schwerin, Ltineburg and Uelzen, as well as Salzwedel airfield—coincidentally, one of the launch sites used by the ramming command.

At the commencement of the final air battle of World War II in Europe, two special Flying Fortresses conducted weather reconnaissance over the sea northwest of Land's End in western Cornwall, from where Atlantic weather fronts moved east, impacting operations targeting Germany. Simultaneously, two other Fortresses followed a standard route for the same purpose, and five de Havilland DH98 Mosquitos reported weather conditions over England, Holland, Denmark, and Berlin. As the bomber fleets embarked on their mission, twenty-nine Mustangs and three Flying Fortresses served as designated weather scouts. At 5 a.m., three out of the original four special Liberators modified for weather reconnaissance or electronic warfare took off.

The Allied 2nd Air Division, with some units still equipped with B-24 Liberator bombers, received the mission to destroy targets in Düneburg and Krümmel. Ten heavy bomber groups were organized into four combat wings, protected by a combination of fifty-eight P-47 Thunderbolts and 229 P-51 Mustang fighters, totaling seven fighter groups. Meanwhile, the main portion of the force, comprising thirteen heavy bomber groups, was allocated to target Güstrow, Parchim, Kaltenkirchen, and Büchen. These bomber groups belonged to the 3rd Air Division, organized into four combat wings, all utilizing B-17 Flying Fortresses. Their escort included six fighter groups with a total of 358 Mustangs. Considering the heavy losses suffered by the bomber groups in particular of the 3rd Air Division, individual radio call signs appear like bad omens: "Fireball" (13th Combat Bombardment Wing), "Vampire" (45th Combat Bombardment Wing), and "Hotshot" (4th Combat Bombardment Wing). The third and final large bomber formation of the day was to be twelve heavy bomber groups from the 1st Air Division. Starting exactly at noon in four combat wings, they launched a raid against targets near Reinsehlen, Hitzacker, Kohlenbissen and Wesendorf.[4] These bombers were protected by two P-51 Mustang groups.

The Attack on April 7, 1945

Due to favorable weather conditions over Germany on April 7, well-coordinated and intense attacks were launched against the bombers by at least fifty Luftwaffe jet fighters east of Bremen. Based on available information, the leading bomber formations were deemed particularly vulnerable. Consequently, it was mandated that all U.S. fighter groups adopt a defensive formation and stay close to the bombers. Deep attacks, which had become popular among fighter pilots due to the perceived helplessness of the German defenses against American aerial forces, were strictly prohibited on April 7.[5]

On that sunny spring Saturday, Colonel Herrmann awaited the initial reports from listening services at his command post in Treuenbrietzen. Anticipating a significant American attack due to the clear weather, he promptly ordered high operational readiness for the entire special unit. Across various deployment sites, situation briefings were conducted.

Preceding the massive assembly of the U.S. bomber force, which emitted a constant drone as it advanced toward its designated targets, the primary American fighter escorts detected enemy aircraft. The B-24 Liberators belonging to the 2nd Air Division were accompanied by the 56th Fighter Group, piloting P-47 Thunderbolts. In the vicinity of Celle in Lower Saxony, north-central Germany, situated at the southern boundary of the 2nd Air Division's flight path, the lead P-47 aircraft intersected the trajectory of two Bf 109s that were heading towards the bomber formation at an altitude of approximately 30,000 feet.

Meanwhile, approximately forty planes had been gathered on the square in Prague-Klecan. According to fighter pilot Walter Otto's recollection, there were an equal number in Gabel, all consisting of brand-new machines without paint and weapons. Fellow pilot Kurt Ahrens recalled his aborted takeoff in Klecan:

> Transportation from the accommodation to the air base by bus. There are about 50 Me 109 G-14 planes ready to take off. We go to the machines scattered about, with around 27 in front of me. All engines are started. Everyone in front of me taxis towards the takeoff in quick succession, without any issues. The senior officer signals for me to turn off the engine. No one behind me is called to take off. I exit and return to the accommodation. The Elbe mission was over for me.[5]

The same experience befell Obergefreiter Hans-Dieter Eitle, who waited in vain for the command to start his engine. Lieutenant Emst-Hermann Rtibsam, the leader of the second-to-last group, faced misfortune as well. During takeoff, his right landing gear leg collapsed, causing the wingtip to touch the ground and tear off. Among those who initiated takeoff was Herfried Breinl. After approximately thirty minutes of flight, the order to abort was issued. Breinl and his comrades returned without encountering the enemy. Bf 109 pilot Werner Zell recounted:

> Following a restless night for most of us, marked by little sleep and anxious anticipation of the events to unfold the next day, the moment finally arrived.

Following the customary wake-up call, signaling the commencement of the daily routine of washing and shaving, everyone convened in the breakfast room to partake in the final pre-flight meal together and receive the situational briefing. Another unexpected development awaited us there. The tables were arranged in a horseshoe shape and seated in the center were several highly decorated officers in full dress uniform, adorned with the Knight's Cross around their necks.[6]

The "highly decorated officers" were expected to set a positive example, but Zell did not witness any of them ascending into a cockpit and joining them. They briefed the pilots on the situation, indicating that German intelligence services had identified the anticipated arrival of a substantial bomber group along with heavy fighter protection. The flight was likely to target northern Germany. Consequently, Magdeburg was designated as the rendezvous point for the Rammjager groups, from where the flight to the attack target would commence. The critical factor emphasized was the unwavering adherence to the close-approach formation under all circumstances. The following debriefing information was based on Lieutenant Hans Bott's notes:

At the commencement, there is a waiting area for the first three *Schwarm* leaders, with a provision for the aircraft to stop and move to the reserve aircraft behind the takeoff in the event of a failure. During takeoff, keep the stick on the stomach (due to additional treatment) and avoid taking off too early. Trim at 0, with flaps at 15 degrees. If the engine fails to start, there is no maintenance, and all ammunition remains. Methanol is not effective beyond 8,000 (three times 10 minutes). Codename for identification: Werewolves. Wait in the waiting room but be prepared to attack immediately if the crowds are already present. A call from the waiting room will signal the attack with the keyword: "To the Werewolves, line up for the attack," providing information about the location of the bombers. If a cloud layer obscures the waiting room, search for an alternative location through the cloud hole. Don't forget the additional [fuel] container. During ascent, not all maneuvers involve loops, but there are many straight stretches to ensure the *Schwarm* flyers do not have to face the sun. Maintain a speed above 250km/h during ascent. Upon spotting an enemy formation, the *Schwarm* flyer should move forward and wobble, ensuring that enemy sightings involve wing movements. If visibility is compromised, return to the waiting room and cross the bomber stream. During an attack, avoid exceeding 450km/h. Do not jettison the cabin prematurely. When launching, open the lever first, then pull the emergency button while bending forward. Upon exit, decelerate to 250km/h, then sharply push the stick forward. Record the precise time of the attack. Note that enemy fighters do not target the bombers. If the speed is excessive, veer to the side. In the event of a spin, deploy the landing gear.[7]

Due to poor visibility in England, the start time actually had to be postponed twice. Originally, the heavy bombers and their escorts were supposed to set off on their dangerous journey from 7.30 a.m. It was thought that the bombing would then take place at approximately 11 a.m. The final start time was 10.30 a. m. Just like in Horsham Saint Faith, a village in Norfolk where the 458th Bomber Group had prepared for the mission with fifty-two Liberators, anywhere on the English airfields it was possible to take off in any number of directions depending on the wind conditions. In Horsham, for example, there were three tracks available.

As flares cleared the aircraft for take-off, Flying Fortresses, Liberators, Mustangs, and Thunderbolts roared above eastern England, gathered over prescribed radio beacons, and formed huge streams of fighting machines heading towards Germany. The take-off, assembly, and planned formation of 1,315 heavy bombers and 898 fighters did not go as scheduled. The 388th Bomber Group had gotten away from the field well and was now gathering at the intended height. When forming up, however, because it had arrived a minute too early, it unintentionally pushed aside the 452nd Bomber Group, which consequently did not follow the wing leader. All bombers in the lead 45th Combat Wing climbed together to an operational altitude of 5,500 meters. In the 13th Combat Wing, there were problems for a while with the classification of the 95th and 390th bomber groups.[8]

Even though the 4th Combat Wing was supposed to be the final group in the formation during the flight, it reached the designated assembly point approximately one minute ahead of schedule. On the other hand, the 93rd Combat Wing, which was slated to take the third position in the column, experienced a delay of around a minute and a half. To address these discrepancies, a somewhat confused S-curve maneuver was initiated. Despite this, the 93rd Combat Wing had to veer away to allow the last group to properly position itself. Consequently, once the turn was executed, the individual bomber groups found themselves quite widely spaced apart. Navigators encountered challenges with orientation, with one group deviating approximately 3km off course. By the time the 93rd flew over the coast of the continent, there was already a time gap of seventeen minutes between the first and last bomber groups.[9]

According to the operational plan, the initial intention was for the first two large bomber fleets to depart from the English coast almost simultaneously. However, the entire 2nd Air Division deviated from this plan by initially following a northward course at a 90° angle after passing Cromer. At that point, no one could have predicted that this deviation would spare the division from experiencing the challenging circumstances faced by the 3rd Air Division, which now occupied its original position. Unexpected easterly winds set back the 2nd Air Division by an additional two to eight minutes before it even reached the Dutch island of Texel. The gap eventually expanded to between fifteen and twenty minutes by the time they reached their respective destinations over Düneburg and Krümmel. In contrast, the first branch of the 3rd Air Division flew exactly according to schedule. At an altitude of 2,500 meters, there were forecast northeasterly winds with a speed of 20 knots. North of Amsterdam, the coast was reached a few minutes earlier than planned. So it happened that not the 2nd Air Division, but the correctly and cleanly flown 3rd Air Division received a warm reception over the lake of Steinhuder Meer, 30km northwest of Hanover.

If a fleet of 700 aircraft typically extended for approximately 100km,[10] the bombers heading towards their targets on April 7 were expected to be distributed over twice that length, as later observations confirmed. Under decentralized leadership, IA officers guided groups and squadrons from squadron command posts as they approached enemy units, using radio communications. On April 7, Luftwaffe fighter control officers of the 1st Fighter Division in Döberitz, with the codename Koralle, assumed command over deployed personnel from German fighter groups in collaboration with 9th Air Corps. Command responsibilities naturally changed as soon as formations entered neighboring airspace areas. Fighter divisions and their control centers had formed the foundation of the Reich air defense since the fall of 1942.

The communication known as the Y-guide, involving VHF radio communication between ground-based radio stations and those on board fighter planes, was facilitated through on-board radios of the FUG 16 ZY type, utilizing the *Reichsjägerwelle* (fighter communications radio) in the frequency range of 38.5 to 42.3MHz. This control system incorporated synchronous grid square designations. The flight cards on board featured double letters that corresponded to analogous designations on large glass panels. These panels were situated in the central area of spacious, bomb-proof concrete bunkers, serving as fighter control centers, also known as the *Kampfoper* (battle opera). *Reichsjägerwelle* translates from German to "imperial hunting wave" in English. The term is historical and refers to a radio broadcast initiative during the Nazi era in Germany. It aimed to promote and glorify hunting activities, aligning with the regime's emphasis on traditional and outdoor pursuits. The broadcasts typically featured hunting-related content, including discussions, stories, and advice, and were part of the broader propaganda efforts to shape cultural and recreational activities in line with Nazi ideology.

In this location, primarily situated deep underground, hundreds of men and women tirelessly worked in continuous day and night shifts, serving as day or night reporters. These individuals operated devices that received signals from radio measuring instruments (radar) directed towards distant enemy positions along the coast or borders. The intercepted movements of enemy formations were disseminated across an extensive network and displayed on aircraft monitoring devices in the fighter control centers. Rows of air intelligence assistants, known as *Blitzmädchen* ("Lightning girls"), were seated one behind the other, and their information was promptly projected onto oversized glass maps using light spitters. Simultaneously, bearings were determined through radio measurement methods to ascertain the respective distances to on-board transmitters. This information helped establish the current location, flight altitude, and flight direction of the German fighter groups.

As the morning of April 7 dawned in Germany, it presented a stark contrast to the weather conditions in southeast England, being remarkably beautiful with clear skies, no wind, and cool temperatures. The pilots in Germany partook of their pre-flight meals with a mix of emotions. In the combat barracks, members of ramming squadrons and fighter pilots from host units met for the first time. Then, finally, the veil was lifted from the mystery that had surrounded this strange group of pilots during the last few days. Only then did regular fighter pilots learn what that day was about. The announcement was a bombshell. After the general excitement had subsided, they received final instructions. There was only one channel to tune in to—*Reichsjägerwelle*, 40.9 MHz. Call signs were "Vulture" and "Falcon." This was followed by millibar values for the altimeter setting. An extensive high-pressure area meant temperatures of minus 40 degrees could be expected at altitudes of around 11,000 meters, or rather lower. Following a general overview of the prevailing weather situation and guidance on high-altitude behavior, concise reports were provided on the weather conditions across Germany, southeast England—the launch area of the Eighth Air Force—and the Sonderkommando Elbe launch area. Additionally, there were predictions regarding expected weather developments. The meteorologist's announcement indicated that the upcoming coordinated major strike would benefit from ideal weather conditions.

Assumptions about the possible behavior of the enemy were made, listed, and discussed. If there was to be a start at all in England because of the bad weather there, it would probably not be until midday. The possible flight areas would probably be at heights of around 8,000 meters or less. This was followed by information about the type and sequence of start of the *Schwarms*, the assembly point, and once again an insistent emphasis on formation. The breaking up of the ramming formation was the worst thing that could happen. Aircraft commanders and their replacement pilots were assigned. Then they started preparing the maps for the expected operational area. After completing the flight preparations, the ramming pilots went to the berths. There, a lengthy wait began. The alarm group waited outside the takeoff area, where the pilots were observed in anticipation within their aircraft. Due to the morning pause, the canopies were open, and time seemed to stretch endlessly. All of a sudden, in the middle of the nervous fiddling, the division order for the ramming *Schwarm* burst out: thirty-minute standby! Aircraft attendants approached the planes and stood ready. Reports of the enemy situation and changes in the weather came from the Stako facility; positions, courses, distances, probable operational areas. The duration of an approach to the enemy and the expected fuel consumption were then determined and noted.

Somewhere, an engine was ignited, producing a rattling sound as it ran, briefly howling before falling silent again. Shortly thereafter, at approximately 11:10 a.m., the command to take a seat was issued. Two attendants then quickly boarded each ramming machine, ready to crank the momentum starter upon receiving the signal. They willingly and kindly assisted the pilots in maneuvering into the tight seats, providing reclining straps that individuals used to secure themselves even more cautiously than usual. In the seated position, all the instruments—oil pressure, fuel gauge, temperature, clock, altimeter, parachute seat, oxygen supply, quality of the FM reception—had to be checked and calibrated correctly. Ring circuit devices were delivered to the leaders' planes, and the ring line was now activated for reporting. Suddenly, the order to commence starting the engines was given.

The commander's voice came through the headphones: "Birds of prey and falcons are gathering over Friedrich Caesar ... heading 190° to combat altitude 10,000, general direction Heinrich Dora [that was Magdeburg] ... Good luck!"[11] Without delay, the canopies swiftly shut. Various sounds ensued, distant calls, humming, clicking, and a rising howl from the momentum starter that drowned out all other noise. The cabins were filled with the smell of glycol, gasoline, and oil. A strong pull on the starter handle—powerful engines brought 1,600hp to life, the pistons began to work, heaving heavy three-blade propellers around the long axles with a loud noise. A little later, the motors were checked; then throttle back, the braking process ended. After releasing the spur locks, a short, grateful nod was given to the waiters. People waved. The planes of the ramming *Schwarms* now lumbered clumsily to the take-off. Finally, the start waver raised the flag: free to take off.[12]

Getting more and more up to speed, the fighter planes rolled in, accelerated, raced across the grass runways without regard to the wind direction, became faster and faster, hopped, then flew. With a single press of a button, the landing gear retracted into the wings on both the left and right sides. Inside, red indicator lights illuminated on the four-lamp device. The ascent was now underway at 2,600 revolutions per minute. The flaps were raised, and fellow pilots from the ramming formations gradually maneuvered their machines closer together, creating a crowded scene of aircraft. With a successful start, the ramming operation on April 7 had finally begun. In Stendal and Gardelegen, the ramming hunters roared past standard bearers. The imperial war flag flew violently in propeller gusts. The operations managers are said to have stood by, raising their right hands in a German salute.

After a long collection flight, the planes of the ramming *Schwarms* closed up. They set off towards Magdeburg. As is typical in military formations, many individuals experienced a powerful and comforting sense of camaraderie. Having comrades beside them felt reassuring. On this particular day, formations remained more tightly knit than usual, with a distance of approximately 20 or 30 meters between each airplane. The pilots wondered if the limited fuel supply would even allow them to get close to the bombers.

Upon reaching altitudes of approximately 4,000 meters, the German pilots took meticulous precautions by equipping themselves with breathing masks to protect their noses and mouths. They were concerned about altitude sickness,

Damage to B-17 No. 43-38514. (*American Air Museum in Britain*)

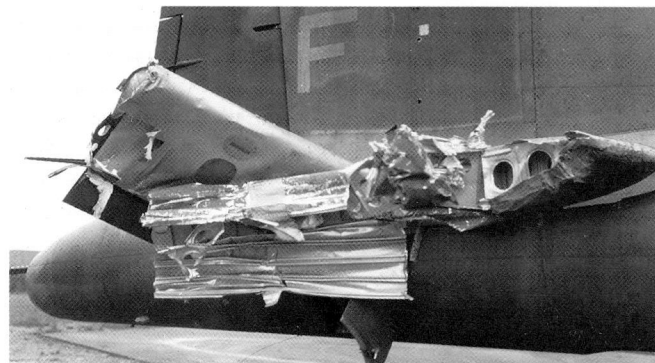

Boeing B-17 *Gold Brick*, damaged by flak on April 7, 1945. (*Eighth Air Force Archives*)

B-17 41-24406 *All American*, rammed by an Fw 190 on January 2, 1943. (*Dave Osborne, B-17 Fortress Master Log*)

A Luftwaffe officer inspects a crashed B-17. (*Maxwell Air Force Base*)

Luftwaffe ground crew positioning a Messerschmitt Bf 109G-6. (*Maxwell Air Force Base*)

Ground crew fitting a P-51 with fuel tanks. (*Maxwell Air Force Base*)

B-17 ground crew loading bombs. (*Eighth Air Force Archives*)

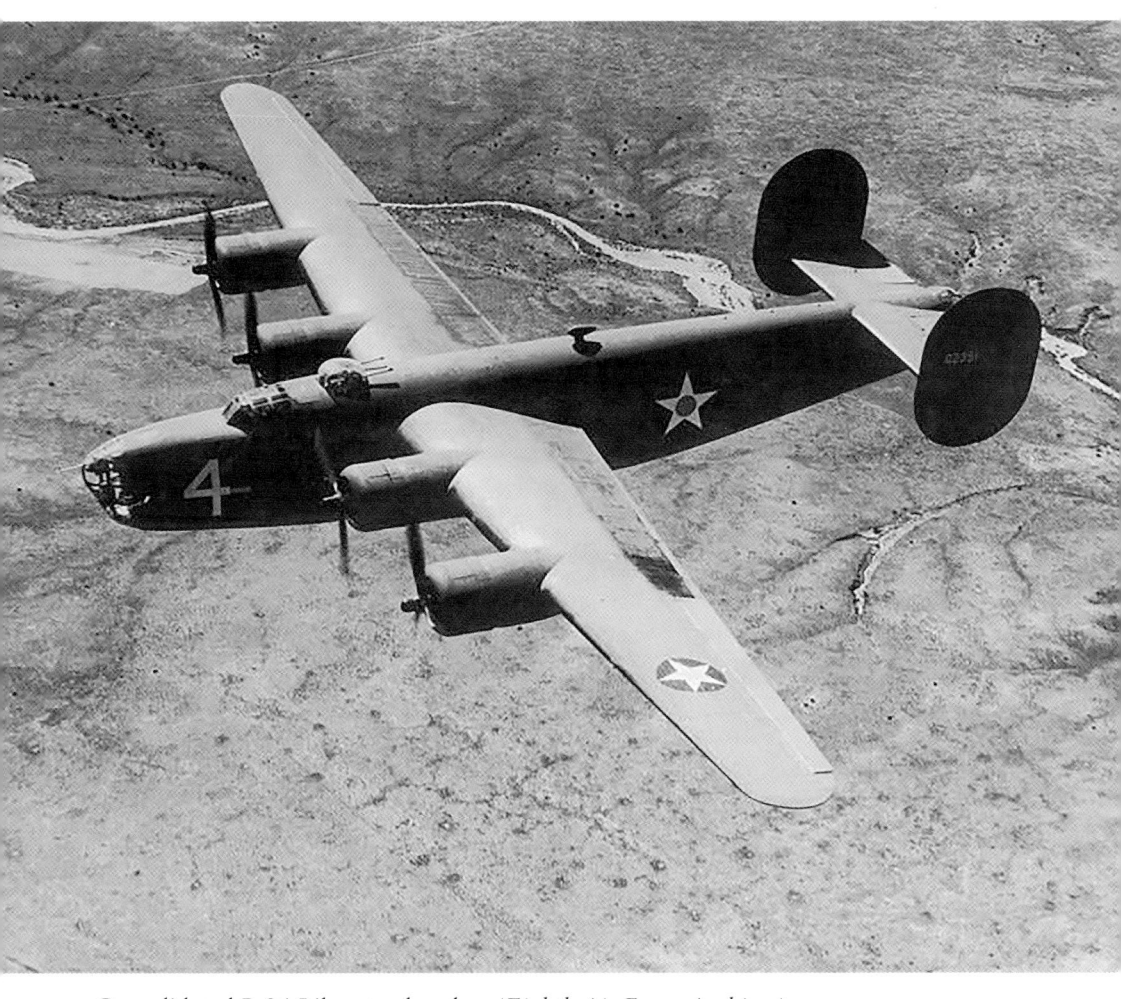

Consolidated B-24 Liberator bomber. (*Eighth Air Force Archives*)

B-17s releasing their bomb loads. (*Eighth Air Force Archives*)

Me 262 jet fighter. (*Luftwaffe Archives*)

Messerschmitt Bf 109G. (*Luftwaffe Archives*)

Focke-Wulf Fw 190A. (*Luftwaffe Archives*)

Bomber crew mission briefing. (*Eighth Air Force Archives*)

North American P-51D Mustang. (*U.S. Air Force Archive*)

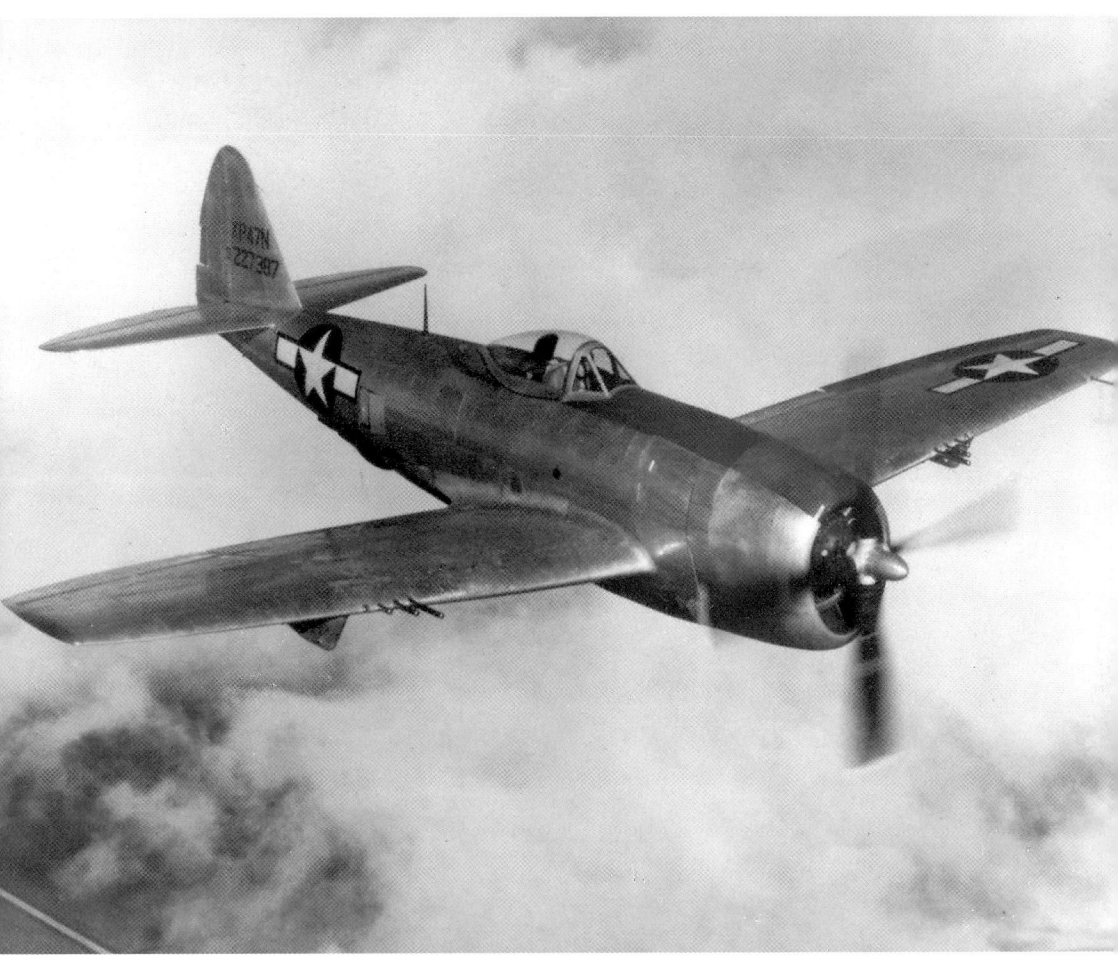

Republic P-47N Thunderbolt. (*U.S. Air Force Archive*)

Luftwaffe Bachem Natter. (*General Arnold's Report of German Weapons, 11/8/1945*)

Adolf Galland. (*Courtesy of Colin Heaton*)

Hans-Joachim "Hajo" Herrmann. (*Courtesy of Colin Heaton*)

Walther Dahl. (*Courtesy of Colin Heaton*)

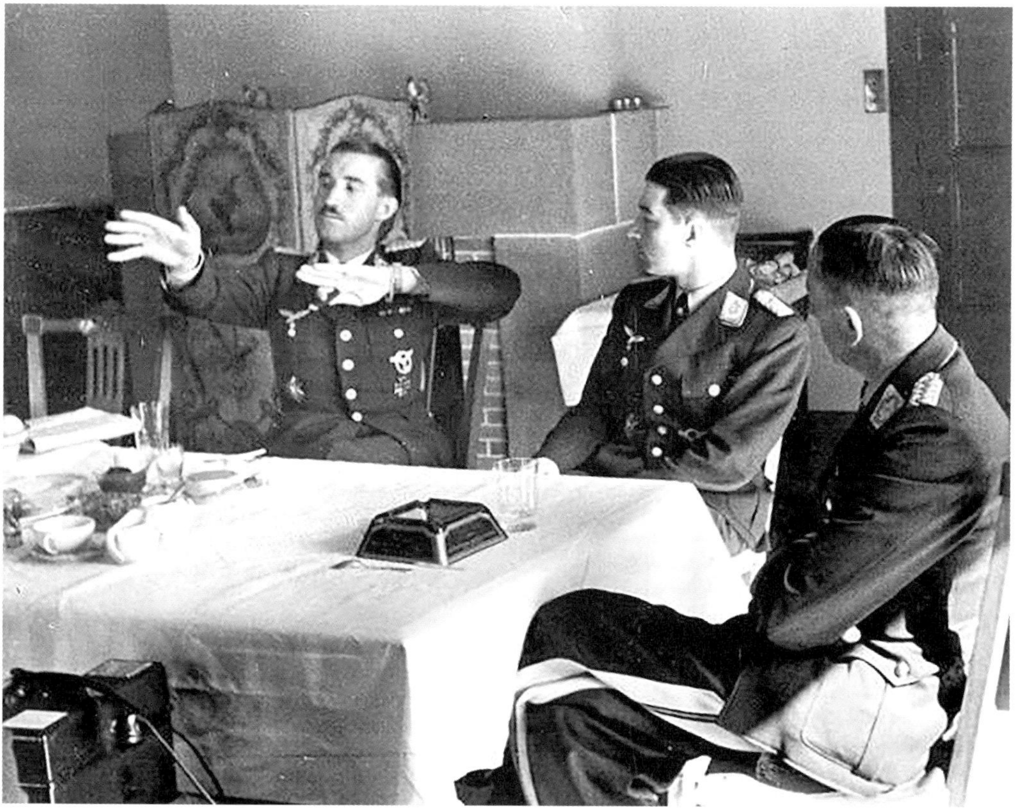

Galland describing fighter tactics. (*Courtesy of Colin Heaton*)

Galland receiving the Diamonds award to his Knight's Cross from Hitler. (*Courtesy of Colin Heaton*)

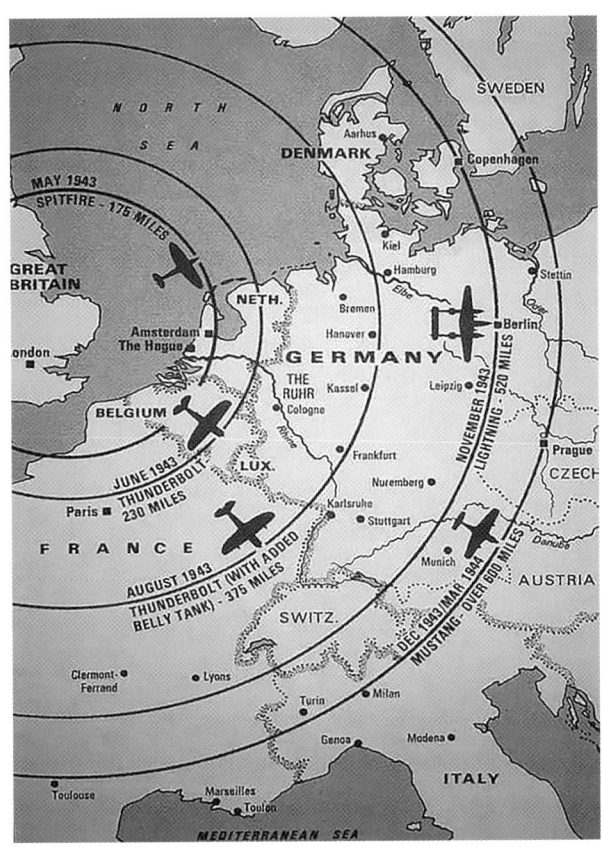

Allied fighter escort chart.
(*Eighth Air Force Archives*)

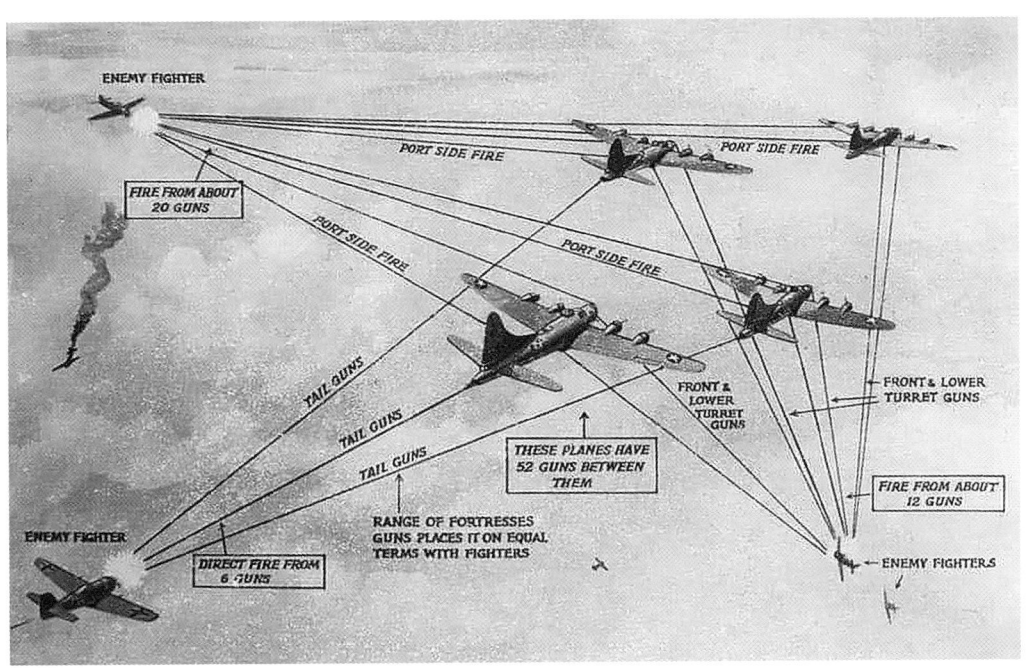

B-17 gun coverage chart. (*Eighth Air Force Archives*)

Martin B-26 Marauder. (*U.S. Air Force Archive*)

BV 40 glider fighter. (*Messerschmitt-Bölkow-Blohm Image*)

Pilot Klaus Hahn. (*War Hero Biographies, German Military Archives, Freiburg*)

Flight Captain Hanna Reitsch. (*Reitsch Collection*)

Bf 109 pilot Werner Zell. (*War Hero Biographies, German Military Archives, Freiburg*)

Wing Commander Wolfgang Falck. (*Courtesy of Colin Heaton*)

Werner Mölders and his Bf 109 D-1 during the times of the Condor Legion. (*Luftwaffe Archives*)

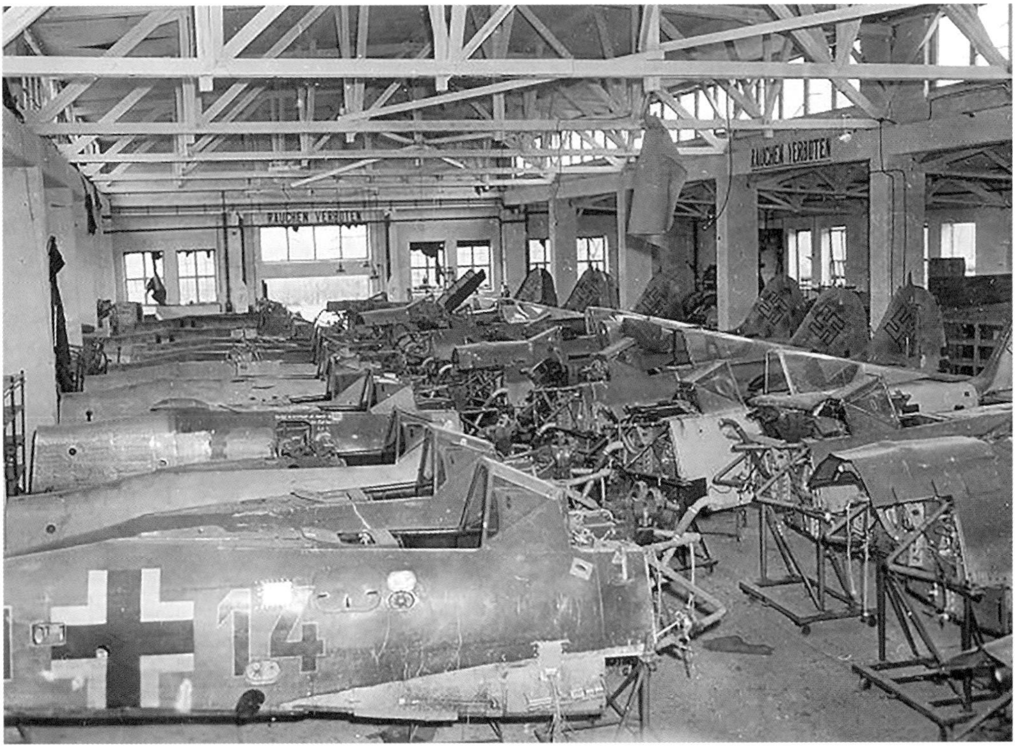

Focke-Wulf Fw 190 fuselage assemblies at Kolleda, Germany, in 1945. (*Luftwaffe Archives*)

Messerschmitt Bf 109 assembly line in Augsburg, Germany. (*Messerschmitt-Bölkow-Blohm Image*)

Sonderkommando Elbe pilots receiving ramming instructions. (*Luftwaffe Archives*)

A B-17 rammed by an Me 109G on January 2, 1943. (*American Air Museum in Britain*)

a condition caused by oxygen deprivation. Even slight increases in atmospheric air at altitudes exceeding 4,000 meters could trigger this ailment. Consequently, aviators diligently ensured the proper functionality of their breathing apparatus and performed regular checks to mitigate the risk of altitude sickness.

The urban area of Magdeburg served as a gathering place for the fighters of Sonderkommando Elbe, with the city center designated as the endpoint. Advancing from Sachau, Stendal, Gardelegen, Salzgitter, and Solpke, the formations of ramming fighters were somewhat dispersed. Favorable visibility conditions facilitated early detection, and a direct line of sight was swiftly established among most of the groups. Upon reaching the designated meeting point, a ground command was issued to commence in four minutes with a heading of 270 degrees. The ramming fighters curved towards the departure point and flew off at a fairly precise time. Everyone made sure to adhere to the ordered course and specified speed as precisely as possible in order not to endanger the intended spatial and temporal concentration, which was repeatedly presented as crucial.

The jet fighters employed integrated fighter course controls, ensuring accurate navigation. The ramming units were explicitly instructed to steer clear of engagements with enemy fighter groups and instead to approach large wings of U.S. bombers. However, German fighter units operated under different guidelines, with leaders having the ultimate decision-making authority. Typically, the order to attack was issued promptly upon being detected by the enemy. However, on this particular day, when the primary objective was to integrate the German attack formation of ramming machines closely into the enemy bomber stream, certain German jet fighters chose to initially steer clear of confrontations with enemy escort fighters, despite their superior capabilities. The emphasis was on strategically building up the impact of the mission.

Based on the location and trajectory updates, it seemed that the enemy air forces were converging directly toward each other. All senses heightened in anticipation. According to the intelligence, potential targets for the bomber fleets included Kassel, Braunschweig, and possibly Hanover. The tension now reached its peak. Suddenly, a passionate female voice came through the headphones of the German ramming pilots, addressing them with "Comrades!" The voice continued, urging the pilots to think of their wives, mothers, and children in the bombed cities. The emotional appeal resonated deeply, causing some hands to grip the control stick even tighter. The bombers soon became visible. Shiny metal hulls glinted in the sunlight. The airwaves were now filled with concise and periodic reports from German pilots indicating the sighting of enemy bomber groups approximately 10km away, flying on a course of 40 degrees.

The communication "March church tower" (indicating the current altitude of 9,000 meters) and the instruction to "Stay on the balcony!" (advising pilots to maintain the current approach altitude) were exchanged among the other fighters, but these radio messages were concealed from the ramming pilots. They exclusively received the *Reichsjägerwelle* frequency and were only exposed to combat slogans. The constant presence of the female voice, intense and almost unbearable, persisted. At this moment, the leader of the conventional fighter group signaled the message "Enemy sighted!" The ramming formations drew even closer together, following the given order. Brief, intense glances were exchanged among neighboring aircraft. Then, the eagerly anticipated, wished-for, feared, and cursed signal resounded: "To all vultures and hawks—attack freely—victory is assured."[13]

Simultaneously, all fighters launched their attacks, with over 200 planes descending upon the bombers. The jet fighters now had approximately forty minutes to engage in combat and then return. Operating at attack speeds of 800km/h, a distance of around 150 meters was maintained within the *Schwarms*. To the surprise of American interception fighters, alongside brief and encrypted German combat communications, they suddenly encountered marching music in their headsets. The "Horst Wessel Song" played, and phrases such as "Germany over everything" resonated. Interwoven with patriotic tunes on the German fighter radio frequency were unprecedented, stirring cheers from a woman's voice. This voice poignantly evoked the images of women and children amidst the rubble of bombed German cities, passionately urging the fighters to "fight to the last for Germany" and pleading for them to "save the fatherland."[14] The Americans lacked a direct explanation for this radio traffic. Apparently they were at a loss and did not know what to make of it. In any case, no warning was given to the bomber fleets.

The ramming fighters, originating from Gardelegen and Stendal, headed north by northwest, ascending towards the assembly point above Dömitz, east of Ltineburg. The Elbe River stood out distinctly in the sparkling sunlight. Unlike the units from the Leipzig region, which were initially supposed to converge via Magdeburg, the flight duration was relatively brief. The initial aircraft reached the vicinity of the northern bomber stream, including the Liberators from the 2nd Air Division, around noon. The aircraft flew scattered, either in flocks or groups, attempting to maintain visual contact since, unfortunately, the pilots did not communicate with each other; more importantly, they could not communicate. The attacking fighters typically searched for their targets within the now clearly visible large stream of bombers, either in groups or individually, which made the task of the American escort fighters easier.[15]

Just before noon, the initial ramming fighters struck the southern section of the 2nd Air Division's bomber stream. The protecting P-47 Thunderbolt aircraft were from the 56th Fighter Group based at Boxted Airfield, north of Colchester in Essex. North of Celle, pilots from the 63rd Fighter Squadron spotted a pair of Bf 109 aircraft. In the course of 2nd Lieutenant Charles T. McBath's attack on the two ramming fighters, one aircraft successfully escaped into the sunlight, but the other was shot down. Witnessing impacts in the right wing, the unidentified German pilot attempted to evade the projectiles from the P-47. However, it was too late, hits to the cockpit and fuselage sealing the fate of the Bf 109. The aircraft plummeted vertically with a long trail of smoke, eventually exploding as it hit the ground. McBath could not confirm the deployment of a parachute. Approximately fifteen minutes later, northeast of Düneburg, Lieutenant James W. Ayers from the 334th Fighter Squadron, 4th Fighter Group, engaged a lone Bf 109 with his P-51 Mustang. Following concentrated fire on the cockpit, fragments flew from the body of the German aircraft and the canopy, the Bf 109 descending rapidly. The unidentified pilot ejected but fell to the ground without his parachute opening.[16]

Meanwhile, the main contingent of the ramming command, which had gathered in the Magdeburg area, was also nearing the bomber stream in the Steinhuder Meer region. Radio transmissions from the Americans were filled with warnings about enemy fighters being spotted all around. Around 12.15 p.m., Captain Charles McGraw of the 351st Fighter Squadron, 353rd Fighter Group, and his formation approached the Luftwaffe fighters attacking the bomber stream east of Steinhuder Meer. When a Bf 109 descended directly above McGraw towards the bombers, he pursued it. As the unidentified ramming fighter realized the threat behind him, he abandoned the attack on the bomber formation to seek refuge in a cloud bank. However, McGraw caught up, firing at the aircraft's fuselage and tail section. Other P-51s also closed in, targeting the Bf 109, whose tail assembly was severed. The plane descended, engulfed in flames, with no parachute observed by the Americans. Once again in proximity to the 2nd Air Division's bombers, McGraw found himself some 80km northeast of Steinhuder Meer, roughly over the Südheide Nature Park, with another Bf 109 tailing him as it attacked the bombers. Under fire from the Mustang, the Bf 109 caught fire, lost part of the fuselage, and crashed. The unknown pilot climbed out and parachuted to safety.[17]

In the interim, Me 262s from JG 7 and possibly KG (J) 54 had joined the fray in the Bremen/Lüneburg area. At 12.34 p.m., a first B-24 crashed near Schollen near Bremen, having been targeted by an Me 262. In the Nienburg region, pilots from the 63rd Fighter Squadron, 56th Fighter Group—known as "Zemke's Wolfpack"—flying P-47 Thunderbolts, identified a lone Me 262 attacking the rear formation of the 2nd Air Division. Captain George E. Bostwig later reported pursuing the Me 262 and scoring a hit in the cockpit area, though without any apparent effect. Within minutes, two contrails were reported near the bombers. Captain Bostwig approached one of the aircraft, initially mistaking it for an old Bf 109 E with a non-retractable tail. He opened fire on the enemy, registering hits on both wings and the fuselage. The Bf 109 descended with a coolant stream. First Lieutenant Eugene W. Andermatt observed the pilot dropping the canopy and climbing out, but the parachute failed to deploy. This was possibly the Bf 109 K-4 flown by Sergeant Gerhard Böhnke, which went down near Neddenaverbergen. While tracking the second contrail, it was revealed to be a lone P-51, which Bostwig pursued and thereafter encountered a formation of five Bf 109s.

As a Bf 109 rapidly approached Captain Bostwig, initiating a dive, he pursued it towards the ground. Just before it crashed at high speed into a pond, the American pilot saw the pilot leaping from his doomed fighter. Bostwig skillfully maneuvered his P-47 to avoid a collision and then used the onboard camera to capture photographs of an oil slick on the pond, providing evidence of his "kill." In all probability this aerial victory for Bostwig was at the expense of Warrant Officer Werner Lindner's Bf 109. Lindner had managed to parachute out of his aircraft as it crashed but was found dead days later in the large ponds near MeiBendorf in Winsen/Aller.[18]

At 12.20 p.m., U.S. radio transmissions began reporting the appearance of Me 262s from JG 7, and a Mustang was downed by the jets over Nienburg. The bomber formation, the 29th Combat Bomb Wing consisting of the 93rd, 446th, and 448th bomb groups, was positioned somewhere south of Bremen across the Weser River at this time. The bombers were under the escort of P-51s from the 479th Fighter Group, with the 434th, 435th, and 497th fighter squadrons, led by Major Robin Olds, who was now directing his 434th Fighter Squadron towards the Me 262s. According to Olds, these jets were in perfect formation, diving towards the bombers. However, the twelve Me 262s once again refrained from engaging in combat, instead employing tactics to lure the American fighters away from the bomber formation. The downing of an Me 262 was later claimed by 2nd Lieutenant Melton O. Thomson of the 434th FS, 479th Fighter Group. He claimed to have seen his gunfire striking the cockpit, with parts detaching and the aircraft descending steeply. Captain Verne E. Hooker of the 435th FS, 479th FG, was also credited with shooting down one of the attacking Me 262s in the area southwest of Bremen.[19]

Bf 109s and other aircraft arriving at the combat area had reached the 2nd Air Division bomber stream consisting of B-24 Liberators in the greater Lüneburg, Soltau, and Verden area and pounced on the four-engine bombers from their advantageous position. The U.S. central command later admitted that the actions of the German pilots had been considered for some time, though it had never before manifested in such a striking manner. They concluded that the pilots appeared to have been coerced into engaging in suicidal assaults.

It was 12.18 p.m. when numerous contrails from fast aircraft were noticed over Hanover, heading northwest. Immediately the airwaves buzzed with warnings to bomber and fighter crews of the Eighth Air Force. It was assumed that four large German fighter formations were on a course of 320°. Messages warning the aircrews to beware of intense antiaircraft fire in the Dümmer area increased the general excitement of the Americans. The radio traffic increased to the point of confusion; people often forgot to switch from transmission to reception, which caused considerable frequency interference. In the middle of the conversation burst an ominous warning about unmarked P-51 Mustang fighters that were allegedly shooting at their own bombers.[20]

To the west of Hanover, near the former traditional interception point for German fighter forces in the zone over Dümmer and Steinhuder Meer, a large number of German fighters once again descended upon the leading bomber groups of combat wings 45, 13, and 93 from the 3rd Air Division.

The Attack on April 7, 1945

Colonel Batson, the commander of the 452nd Bomber Group, which was the highest group in the 45th Combat Wing and bore the brunt of the initial attack, identified the first enemy contact at coordinates 52.30 north and 09.00 east, slightly west of Stolzenau over marshy terrain between the Weser River and one of its minor tributaries. This location was approximately above what is now Federal Highway 441. For the first time in the history of German fighter aviation, mixed combinations of standard Bf 109 and Fw 190 fighters and Me 262 jet fighters attacked together.[21]

Without hesitation, four sizable formations aggressively approached the bombers from altitudes ranging between 5,500 and 9,000 meters, originating from the southern direction. Initial reports from American eyewitnesses provide varying details regarding the strength and composition of the German fighter squadrons, citing estimates ranging from seventy to eighty Bf 109s and Fw 190s to just a handful of Me 262s.[22] According to American sources, the initial assault by the German units involved at least one Arado Ar 234, identified as a jet reconnaissance aircraft and light high-speed bomber, along with another rare aircraft type.[23]

There were a total of 184 ramming fighters, predominantly Bf 109s, and fifty-one Me 262 jet fighters. A highly effective collaboration among various units laid the groundwork for the successful execution of the planned major assault against American bomber formations. The strategy of engaging enemy bombers head-on originated from the tactics employed by JG 2 Richthofen. This unconventional form of attack had been refined to the point of maturity, prompting others, particularly esteemed and successful fighter pilots, to adopt and prefer its use. Launching a rapid frontal assault demanded strong nerves and advanced flying skills, as unanticipated reactions from targeted enemies could lead to disastrous collisions. Fighters employing this tactic typically initiated gunfire from a distance of approximately 200 meters. Facing them were formidable twin machine guns mounted in rotating chin turrets on Flying Fortresses or in nose cockpits on Liberators. The accelerated approach speeds significantly compressed the actual combat time to just under a few seconds.

Despite wearing antiaircraft-fire jackets in the style of chain mail, along with protection from steel helmets and solid shell seats made of durable metal, crew members in the bomber cockpits had little chance of surviving direct fire from German fighters.[24] Understandable fear gripped them as soon as they realized that German fighters were forming up for a frontal attack. The crews found themselves questioning whether they would once again have to endure frontal assaults from enemy fighters. Unbeknownst to them, the Luftwaffe pilots soaring high above them took on a more audacious approach that day. The conventional attack method employed by standard German fighters involved daring maneuvers, approaching from behind a targeted four-engine bomber in formation at approximately 350km/h. The tactic involved maintaining weapon engagement until the bomber succumbed or ammunition was depleted, while keeping a vigilant eye on the rear gunner. To avoid such U.S. machine-gun fire, initiating the final phase of an attack from behind and shooting from a low angle was deemed most effective. Due to the relatively minor speed difference between bombers and standard German fighters, a pursuit attack from behind lasted two to four minutes, contingent on the speed of the attacker.

Upon receiving alerts, certain bomber pilots endeavored to enhance the defensive capabilities of their rear gunners by executing abrupt and erratic maneuvers. The restless, weaving motion of heavy bombers made them elusive targets. The attacking fighter had to get close enough to be successful. In order to shorten the period of time during which they were exposed to the enemy's massed defensive fire, German fighters attacked from above whenever possible. In doing so, they achieved a considerable increase in speed, which carried them through the barrage relatively quickly.

At approximately ten minutes after noon, some escort fighters affiliated with the 359th Squadron, a component of the 67th Fighter Wing responsible for patrolling and guarding to the east of the bomber formations, encountered a grouping of Me 262 jet fighters flying at relatively widely spaced intervals. Subsequently, they initiated engagement. A skirmish unfolded over Nienburg at altitudes ranging from 6,000 to 4,000 meters, resulting in the downing of a Mustang. While the pilot successfully climbed from his aircraft in time, his comrades were dismayed to witness the parachute malfunction, despite its initial deployment. The Americans were unable to impede the swift westward progress of the jet fighter squadron from JG 7. The 339th Fighter Group had extended its coverage towards the east in response to escalating reports of approaching Luftwaffe fighters. Unfortunately, it failed to attain a sufficient altitude, causing it to miss encountering the sizable German fighter group. In the meantime, chaos unfolded behind them. Later on, Colonel Burham L. Batson, the commander of the heavily damaged 452nd Bomber Group, voiced dissatisfaction with what he called "the completely insufficient fighter escort."[25]

The initial U.S. surprise upon hearing a German female voice in the radio communications swiftly turned to unease, and eventually terror, as the pilots from bomber groups 452 and 388 observed the concentrated presence of German fighter units. It became evident that the descending German fighters were aiming in their direction, heightening the sense of anxiety among the bomber crews.

Lieutenant William Richardson's B-17 Flying Fortress with the identification number 43-38868, from the 452nd Bomber Group, sustained serious damage and lagged behind the rest of the formation. Shortly thereafter, a Bf 109 struck the left side of the bomber, hitting between the side stand and the tail unit, resulting in the separation of the tail section from the fuselage. The B-17 fell approximately a thousand meters before exploding. The only survivors were the turret gunner and radio operator, who had been temporarily assigned to the crew from the 730th Squadron for this particular mission.[26]

Above the northern shore of Steinhuder Meer, approximately 6km west of Neustadt am Rübenberge, the Flying Fortress number 42-31366, piloted by Lieutenant Dave Owens, found itself directly in the path of the oncoming ramming fighters. A Bf 109, while executing a sharp turn with its engine roaring, crashed directly into the pilot's cockpit from behind and above. Striking at an exceptionally high speed, it demolished everything in its path, including the cockpit, before plummeting earthward. The bomber immediately entered a steep dive, with three of the crew members falling out of the wreckage in flames. Up to five parachutes were observed.

Chaos ensued, marked by cannon fire, the rapid fire of machine guns, screams, engines pushed to their limits, exploding shells, blasts occurring within both friendly and enemy ranks, and, most prominently, the thunderous roar of powerful bomber engines. Alarmed Mustang pilots raced back and forth, and everywhere one could see planes falling to earth. To the east of the Dümmer, a Bf 109 made an impact. The commander of the 78th Fighter Group reported witnessing between five and seven B-17s falling, with approximately fifteen parachutes descending simultaneously.[27] There was also mention of an Me 210 being engaged in the conflict.[28] Pilots from the 339th Fighter Group observed four incapacitated B-17s along the route between Celle and Uelzen. They also witnessed a Bf 109 colliding with a bomber near Uelzen, causing it to split in two. Despite the Bf 109 attempting evasive maneuvers, it succumbed to machine-gun fire from a P-51 belonging to the 78th Fighter Group. Impact fires were now visible throughout the area, with clouds of black smoke rising into the sky, marking a trail of devastation.

Lieutenant William Gill successfully maintained control of his Flying Fortress number 44-8531 until reaching the northern outskirts of Hamburg, despite significant damage inflicted during the initial German mass attack. However, when two engines eventually caught fire, Gill was forced to abandon the aircraft. According to other crews, the exit hatches on the two side compartments and the rear compartment were thrown off, and the aircraft entered a slow tailspin. Only two parachutes were visible, and it was noted that one crew member's parachute had become entangled with the tail wheel.

On the German frequency, there were now communications such as, "I'm illuminated, I'm illuminated; leaving the operational area, taking evasive action" (indicating being hit) or, "I darn!" (indicating weapon malfunction).[29] According to reports from aviators in the 55th Fighter Group of the Eighth Air Force, the Luftwaffe engaged in a game of hide and seek with the heavy bombers after the confrontation began over Steinhuder Meer towards Salzwedel. Employing evasive movements and swaying maneuvers, the bombers aimed to complicate targeting for the German fighters. Hundreds of Browning machine guns unleashed fire in response to the chaotic descent of the pursuing enemy aircraft. A Flying Fortress with black identification stripes and a large white "H," from the 388th Bomber Group, which had taken off from USAAF Station Number 136 in Knettishall,

Suffolk, that morning, now had to be abandoned after a Focke Wulf Fw 190 fighter drilled its way into it.[29]

In the highest formation of the squadron, Fortress 43-38869, nicknamed "Paula Sue," under the command of Lieutenant Robert Bare and manned by nine other crew members, flew alongside the formation of the 388th Bomber Group to the right of the lead aircraft. Unexpectedly, a Bf 109 collided directly with the left side of the B-17 and exploded upon impact. Similar to Lieutenant Richardson's aircraft from the 452nd Bomber Group, the bomber promptly disintegrated in the middle. The front section descended to the ground in a spiraling motion, while the tail section slowly slid downward. As the German fighter pilot refrained from firing any shots during the attack, he was presumed dead at this point, and the collision was officially categorized as a significant accident.[30] In actuality, the pilot was one of those who deliberately chose not to use weapons in favor of maintaining speed. The wreckage of the B-17 hit approximately where parts of Lieutenant Owen's plane were already lying, on the northern edge of Steinhuder Meer.

One of the Elbe men rammed and hit his head hard in the collision. With a shattered skull, he managed to get out of the plane before it plunged earthwards, and he was even able to deploy his parachute. But he was dead before he reached the ground. Civilians recovered his body. Out of the nine-man crew aboard Flying Fortress number 42-97105, piloted by Lew Hickman Jr., positioned as the second aircraft in the flight below the command staff of the 388th Bomber Group, five survived the crash of their bomber. A Bf 109 ramming machine had severed the right elevator and vertical tail of the bomber, causing it to exit the formation. Observers noted that the pilot managed to maintain control of the heavy aircraft for some five minutes, executing a full circle turn. However, this eventually evolved into a tailspin, prompting the surviving crew to bail out.[31]

As the leading formations of the 2nd Air Division progressed slightly north of the heavily targeted 3rd Air Division's path and later entered the combat zone, they maintained impeccable defensive alignment, guided by radio alerts. This strategic positioning facilitated the escort fighters from the 65th Fighter Wing in delivering optimal protection, as Major Frederick W. Glover from the 4th Fighter Group later acknowledged. On the flip side, the substantial concentration of U.S. fighters presented challenges, as the high-speed aircraft struggled to navigate without causing significant interference in the confined space.

Southeast of Bremen, isolated formations comprising three large Bf 109s, Fw 190s, and a few jet fighters unexpectedly encountered bomber formations from the 2nd Air Division. The American perception was that these were fragmented units from the initial concentrated encounter with the 3rd Air Division, which was flying slightly further south in a broad formation. Subsequent analyses also mentioned "surviving attackers from the first encounter along with the addition of some stragglers."[32] Meanwhile, JG 7 was fully engaged, and the onslaught of ramming fighters had not diminished in intensity. Major Robin Olds successfully targeted a Bf 109 after it had recently taken down a Liberator. Olds also damaged an Me 262 and claimed it as damaged. Captain Tronicke of I. KG 54 (a jet bomber unit) was mortally wounded and crash-landed his jet, White 8. Olds was never credited for the victory.

Approximately 24km northwest of Faßberg, a Bf 109 fighter set a Liberator ablaze, and promptly did so to another one, which then spiraled down to the ground. Eight American crew members managed to parachute to safety. Neither bomber had yet released their bomb load. Accompanying fighters from the 479th Fighter Group had to stand by and watch as a Flying Fortress, whose right horizontal stabilizer had been torn off, fell to earth 8km north of Hineburg from a height of 6,000 meters. One of the crew, whose parachute had caught on the bow, fell to his death. First Lieutenant Donald E. Kunkel survived the disaster that befell his bomber. His Liberator was crewed by thirteen individuals, including two additional H2X navigators.[33] (H2X, officially known as the AN/APS-15, was an American ground-scanning radar system used for blind bombing.)

The German ramming aircraft approached directly from behind and above, thundered closely over the formation, then immediately executed a high turn to crash into the leading aircraft. One ripped off the nose cockpit of Colonel John B. Herboth Jr., commander of the 389th Bomb Group's lead aircraft, B-24 number 44-49524, flinging it to the side before colliding with the second leading aircraft, where the turret gunner's position was situated just behind the pilot's cockpit. The flying turret tore through the fuselage, the propeller of engine number one detached, and engine number four caught fire, as did the radio cabin. The controls became unresponsive and the aircraft flipped over, slowly rolling onto its back. Lieutenant Kunkel later described how he tried everything possible to get it back under his control. Finally, he gave the order to get out. He shouted at the men to jump off, but they were no longer able to fight the powerful centrifugal forces. As the four-engine bomber rolled over onto its back, it shook violently and began to dismantle.

The flight engineer, who had not yet donned his chest parachute, was hurled against the instrument panel and lost consciousness. Another crew member prematurely deployed his parachute inside the aircraft and caught fire. Subsequently, the aircraft disintegrated, and Kunkel suddenly found himself outside. Kunkel could only observe a single other parachute descending amid the wreckage of his aircraft. Fortunate circumstances enabled Sergeant Heinrich Rosner, whose ramming tactics led to the crash of the two lead aircraft, to bail out and survive. This dramatic encounter marked his initial experience in live combat at the front. In recognition of his double success, the modest individual from the Fichtelgebirge was awarded the Iron Cross II and I Class, in addition to the German Cross in Gold, alongside non-commissioned officer distinctions. The 389th Bomb Group suffered 153 total losses, and they had lost their commander in action.[34] Colonel Claiborne H. Kinnard Jr. of the 355th Fighter Group reported that two Liberators fell victim to German fighters shortly before reaching their target. First Lieutenant Bruce O. Kilborn, the pilot of Liberator number 42-94870, lost his life along with five other members of his ten-man crew when fire from an Me 262 ignited the bomb bay at approximately 12.30 p.m. The resulting explosion ejected six individuals, among whom only Sergeant George E. Schmidt, a radio countermeasures specialist, survived. Two seriously injured individuals were promptly taken to hospital. Czech forced laborers witnessed one parachute descending and hoped to see another, but it had drifted too far away to be visible.[36]

Thirteen Me 262 jet fighters attacked aircraft of the 2nd Air Division until 12:45 p.m. in the area south by southeast of Bremen, Nienburg, and Hamburg. They fought in relaxed small units. A closed battle group of jet fighters was about 3km to the west at the same time. Unlike other Me 262 squadrons, which reluctantly engaged in combat with enemy fighters and eagerly sought to reach bombers quickly, these units actively pursued dogfights with the American escorts, aiming to compel them to release their extra fuel tanks. The Mustangs accepted the challenge, sparking a chaotic pursuit where the German fighters continually scattered, only to regroup and launch sudden attacks from various angles. They avoided close-quarter engagements due to their high speeds, which ultimately worked to their advantage.[37]

Shortly after, two entire escort groups had to depart from the bomber formation prematurely due to fuel shortages. In response, the American command promptly deployed another fighter squadron, previously operating freely in the Steinhuder Meer area as Force IV. Eight other jet fighters persistently engaged in attacks along the Nienburg to Hamburg route, resulting in reports of four being downed and four sustaining damage. A confrontation ensued close to Lüneburg involving a different German fighter squadron comprising fifteen Bf 109s and four Fw 190s. Twenty Bf 109s engaged in combat south of Bremen, while an additional ten confronted the Americans west of Faßberg. Another ten fighters emerged in the vicinity of Uelzen and Salzwedel.

First Lieutenant Bob C. Dallas, piloting a Liberator, had just managed to alert his crew about an approaching enemy fighter and provide targeting instructions. Meanwhile, Sergeant Kratoska, positioned at the left-hand firing station, observed a German fighter circling around the third aircraft in the formation. Without hesitation, the enemy fighter aggressively approached his bomber. Shortly thereafter, the fighter collided with the firewall of the left outer engine, smashing into the side of the cockpit and causing instant death to the pilot and navigator.[38]

The general excitement among the American aviators increased further when warnings about Mustang fighters that were said to have fired on their own bombers started floating through the airwaves. Major Glover from the 4th Fighter Group was astonished as he witnessed multiple P-51 Mustangs launching assaults on the Flying Fortresses of the 2nd Air Division. Around Soltau at 12.45 p.m., several American fighter planes, later described by Glover as probably being flown by Germans, circled the bomber formations, displaying unmistakably hostile intentions. Flying at different altitudes, five or six pairs of silver P-51s, operating without additional tanks, also engaged in attacks against their fellow fighters.[39]

Lieutenant Gilbert F. Talbot communicated via radio that his Mustang had been hit. A few minutes later, he could no longer control his aircraft and ejected in the vicinity of Dümmer. Initial distress calls referred to unmarked Mustang attackers, but the 355th Fighter Group subsequently reported, with utmost seriousness, sightings of Mustangs displaying German national insignia. Colonel Kinnard echoed this information and pinpointed the unusual occurrences in the airspace east of Bremen.[40] Interestingly, pilots from the same 355th Fighter Group had previously reported an unusual Supermarine Spitfire during the outbound journey, causing disruption to the bomber formation from the 2nd Air Division deep into Germany. Major Leonard Carson from the 467th Fighter Group also relayed an incident involving a Mustang with a distinctive white nose and a yellow or orange tail being downed by another Mustang around 1.00 p.m. Another Mustang was reported to be carrying out attacks on bombers north of Braunschweig. It was brought down by defensive fire at 1.20 p.m., the pilot successfully ejecting.[41]

Throughout the war, there is no confirmed evidence of the use of captured aircraft in combat. Errors may have occurred, as exemplified by Lieutenant Harry Gohsler. In a subsequent report justifying his actions during the operation of April 7, 1945, he explained:

> While operating, a formation from the 359th Fighter Squadron, 356th Fighter Group assigned to the 2nd Air Division, encountered twenty Me 109s surrounding a group of yellow-tailed B-17 bombers. As a flight leader, I engaged an Me 109. The pilot from their squadron, executing a shallow attack from the 6 o'clock direction, shot down a B-17, then turned around with the presumed wingman moving out from underneath. Both appeared to have been hit by the onboard fire from the Flying Fortresses. I flew through the fire, shot down a Me 109, and turned another ten degrees to address the presumed wingman. Only when raising the wings to disengage did I realize that the apparent enemy wing aircraft was a Mustang. I immediately ceased my attack.[42]

There was a tragic mix-up for Lieutenant David A. Mackenzie of the 339th Fighter Group. While maneuvering to position himself behind bombers with his flight, Lieutenant Kunz, a rear gunner, mistakenly opened fire on him from a distance of approximately 500 meters. The gunfire hit the underside of the fuselage and the engine of the fighter, causing immediate smoke and engine trouble.[43] In a separate incident, a Mustang sustained significant damage when B-17 gunners scored a total of fifteen hits on it. Captain Jenkins led the attack as Air Leader of the 13th Combat Wing, in Flying Fortress number 44-8548 of the 95th Bomber Group.

A lone jet fighter descended into the formation, defying combat instructions as if he only had relatively harmless British bombers in front of him. Approximately five minutes before reaching the turning point toward the target, another Me 262 appeared, traversing the formation from the 7 o'clock direction and promptly downing the fourth aircraft of the lead squadron's high flight. Amid intense gunfire, the yellow-striped Flying Fortress with the red nose band disintegrated like a fragile glass balloon[44]. Despite its name "Hard to Get," bestowed by the men of Fortress number 44-8225, a single Me 262, armed with four 3cm Mk 108 cannons, proved otherwise. Instantly, both the right wing and the fourth engine erupted in flames, compelling pilot Lieutenant William Kotta to activate the alarm bell. Subsequently, eight crew members promptly bailed out, and Kotta exited the plane a little later. The bomber crashed near the infamous Bergen-Belsen concentration camp, 2km east of Bergen along the single-track railway line.[45]

The 13th Combat Wing also found itself vulnerable to fighter attacks as it approached the turning points for the targets Btichen, Kaltenkirchen, and Neumünster. Major Gibbons led the 100th Bomb Group, which faced an assault of fanatical intensity from fifteen Bf 109s and one Fw 190 between 12:50 p.m. and 1:26 p.m. The German fighters approached from various directions, predominantly from the 9 o'clock position above, traversed the bomber formations, executed turns, and launched attacks in succession. A Bf 109 engaged in a ramming maneuver lost a wing upon colliding with the tail of B-17 aircraft number 44-38514, causing it to crash. Despite sustaining significant damage, the bomber managed to limp along, albeit with a third of the fin and the left elevator torn off to a stump. Deep dents were visible in the bomber's tail section from the impact of the fighter's propeller.[46]

The pilots of Sonderkommando Elbe had repeatedly reminded themselves of the three survival rules once they had survived a ramming:

Survival Rule Number 1
This emphasized the necessity of releasing the canopy, an action that had to be executed under all circumstances before a collision occurred. Consequently, the pilots involved in the ramming had to do so without the protection of the top and side coverings. The only frontal safeguard was the 6cm-thick armored window securely fixed within its metal frame. After surviving the initial impact of ramming into an enemy bomber, the pilot had to immediately adhere to the next survival rule.

Survival Rule Number 2
This rule was crucial—swift evacuation from the disabled aircraft. Driven by the instinct to survive, those who remembered the protocol were to promptly detach the breaker plugs from the communications cable, which were still attached to them through the hood. They were then to open the push button on the throat

microphone and, if they maintained composure, take a deep breath of oxygen. Subsequently, they were to tear off the breathing mask and unfasten the seat belts by pulling the zippers. However, significantly more effort was required to hoist themselves out of the seat, overcoming the resistance of swirling air and the weight of the seat parachute, which had to be lifted simultaneously with their body from the seat pan. Upon ejection, when a pilot found himself suspended at approximately chest height outside their aircraft, the force of suction took hold of the body. It was as if a colossal grip propelled the individual and the plane forward with tremendous momentum, reaching speeds of around 700km/h. In theory, this action involved a forceful push against the control stick, aiming to enable lateral movement and a descent past the hazardous tail section. Successfully clearing the tail section, the pilots were now faced with the imperative of the final survival rule.

Survival Rule Number 3
Amid a chaotic whirlwind, enduring sore limbs and almost suffocating conditions, they were not to lose consciousness. The standard bailout altitudes for German fighter pilots were typically around 7,000 or 7,500 meters. Parachutists required approximately fifty seconds to descend to the normal atmosphere at 4,000 meters without deploying the parachute. However, if they pulled their ripcords hastily or without control, driven by fear the moment they left their aircraft, they would descend toward the ground at a lethally slow pace, sealing their fate. Their chances of survival would be lost. Falling at a speed of 10 meters per second, it took five minutes to reach the rescue altitude of 4,000 meters. Five minutes without an oxygen supply would undoubtedly lead to death. Moreover, a deadly cold would set in, causing life-threatening frostbite, eventually leading to death by hypothermia. Frostbite coupled with a lack of oxygen meant a swift and painless demise. To escape this grim destiny, those who could manage it allowed themselves to free-fall for several thousand meters through the air. It was only at that point, when altitudes of approximately 4,000 meters appeared to be attained, that the pilots were to pull the square handle situated on the front left side of the wide belt. This action released the clasps and, subsequently, set the silk parachute free.

Unfazed by the German fighter planes, the massive American formation of 1,300 heavy bombers, escorted by Mustangs from the 479th Fighter Group, pressed onward towards its northern targets. Near Uelzen, they encountered ten conventional German fighters still equipped with additional tanks, indicating that they had taken off relatively recently. This sparked a fierce aerial conflict that unfolded from an altitude of 10,000 meters all the way to the ground. Another Bf 109 had attacked B-17 number 42-97071, named "Andy's Dandy," from the formation of the 100th Bomber Group from behind and above. Shortly before the fighter reached the Fortress, the bomber's left wing, which still contained half-full fuel tanks, broke off under fire. The Bf 109 could not avoid it, colliding with the wing and exploding. Seven parachutes were seen opening, although it was not clear whether all of them belonged to this one bomber.

Another Fortress was struck 10km northwest of Winsen/Aller and exploded. B-17 number 44-8334, piloted by Lieutenant William Howard and part of the 100th Bomber Group, also met its demise in the same vicinity. Engine number three ignited after being attacked by a Bf 109, causing the propeller to break off. Upon leaving the formation, the engine fire extinguished, but now one of the wheels was ablaze. In response, the pilot ordered an emergency jettison. After releasing the bombs, Howard executed a 180° turn and descended into the sparse clouds, seeking refuge from approximately fifty enemy fighters still present in the area, as reported by witnesses. Nothing was subsequently seen or heard of the aircraft.[47]

On April 7, 1945, the 100th Bomb Group, already branded as unlucky within the Eighth Air Force and having suffered 229 total losses, incurred another devastating blow. German jet fighters were responsible for bringing down the 230th Flying Fortress with a black rudder and a prominent white "D" on this fateful day of operations. Approximately 11km north of Gifhorn, the rear gunner of Flying Fortress number 44-8744, Sergeant Charles Stewart, witnessed with horror an oncoming ramming fighter at the same altitude. It seemed to have already sustained damage, but before Stewart could react, the enemy fighter had collided with the left wing, resulting in violent explosions. Evidently, both wings of the German aircraft exploded. Immediately, the left side of the bomber's fuselage caught fire from leaking fuel. Before disappearing into the clouds, five parachutes were counted; there were ten men on board.[48] The 385th Bomber Group, known as "Van's Valiants," had previously been commended twice for missions against Regensburg and Zwickau. When a ram fighter collided with a B-17 adorned with large red diamonds on the vertical stabilizer and red stripes on the wings and horizontal stabilizer, the group's total losses rose to 169 aircraft. North of Hanover, the 385th found itself under attack by Bf 109s employing their customary aggressive tactics. At 1:10 p.m., five Bf 109s descended upon them from behind, flying in formation, exploiting the advantage of the sun, but they only closed in to approximately 200 meters. Then at 1:25 p.m., a lone Bf 109 suddenly cut through the high squadron of the 385th Bomber Group, taking a hit and promptly colliding with a B-17 from the lower squadron. Both aircraft plummeted to the ground, engulfed in flames, and erupted in explosions.[49]

A young Sonderkommando Elbe pilot bravely launched an attack after releasing the canopy but miscalculated, causing him to miss the intended bomber. Unexpectedly, he then found himself amidst another group of enemy planes, and by sheer accident he collided with and passed through the fuselage of a B-17 bomber at high speed. Remarkably, the German pilot emerged unharmed, promptly deploying his parachute. As two Bf 109s approached the formation, one of them collided with a red-striped bomber number 2, which belonged to the leader of the high squadron. This aircraft sustained significant damage and was compelled to depart from the formation. However, it managed to make a safe landing on an emergency airfield in northern France. Meanwhile, another B-17 had to maneuver to evade the fighter attack, its engine aflame.[50]

Lady Helene, a B-17 with the serial number 43-38082, piloted by First Lieutenant Richard Druhot and part of the 490th Bomber Group, manned by a crew of nine, sustained significant damage during the initial attack by a Bf 109. The impact severely damaged the rudder, striking the aircraft's substantial frame just above the head of the tail gunner, Sergeant James Kyser. Additionally, the left wing was hit, resulting in engine number two catching fire, followed by the ignition of the right inner engine, number three. Despite attempts to extinguish the flames using the fire extinguisher initially appearing to be successful, they reignited even more vigorously. Kyser was the first to bail out, preceding Lieutenant Druhot, who was piloting the aircraft marked as number 4 in the leader squadron. Gradually, the entire crew exited the plane approximately 5km away from Sulingen on a heading of 326°, over the small town of Schollen. Nearly twenty-five minutes earlier, a B-24 from the 2nd Air Division had exploded in the same vicinity. The lower squadron also lost a B-17 due to a ramming attack from a Bf 109; their rubble fell to the ground north of Hanover. The German attack on this bomber formation lasted ten minutes.[51]

A P-51 Mustang from the 353rd Fighter Group sustained considerable damage from falling debris. Bringing up the rear in the 3rd Air Division column was the 4th Combat Wing. Despite the Americans noting a reduction in the German attack's materiel strength, the 486th Bomber Group lost a Fortress in the high group's position. Simultaneously, another B-17 from the 487th Bomber Group in the lead formation managed to escape destruction. In this instance, a Bf 109 pilot attempted a ramming maneuver against the tail section of the bomber but failed to bring it down. Subsequently, the wing of the German fighter was severed, causing it to explode.

Shortly after 1 p.m., the German jet fighters were instructed to disengage from the battle and return to their bases. However, the pilots observed American bombers with their escorts across their flight routes. The Me 262s of Fighter Wing 7 had to be redirected to alternative positions because it became evident that certain bomber groups were heading directly toward Parchim and Kaltenkirchen. In less than half an hour, almost 150 B-17s roared over the airfield of Fighter Wing 7. They arrived in two separate formations, carrying over 400 tons of explosive and incendiary bombs, causing extensive devastation. The runways were literally obliterated, meaning that not a single German aircraft could take to the air.

The air battle of April 7 was not yet over. Twenty-four kilometers east of Hamburg, a Mustang with a blue tail chased a German plane directly into a B-24, whose wing caught fire in the collision. Fighters from the 357th Fighter Group, tasked with safeguarding the 3rd Air Division, came across a Liberator from the 467th Bomber Group, located quite a distance west of Magdeburg. This aircraft, identifiable by its red and white diagonally striped rudder, had suffered combat damage, losing its right elevator and vertical tail. The German pilot executing the ramming maneuver believed he had successfully downed the bomber. Despite having its tail severed, the heavily damaged bomber managed to reach friendly territory. However, it had to be abandoned after the entire crew had safely disembarked.[52] This incident marked the forty-eighth total loss for Colonel Albert J. Shower's "The Rackheath Aggies," a bomber group renowned for their precision and accuracy within the Eighth Air Force.

At 2:15 p.m., the ground control of the 65th Fighter Group received a communication on Channel 8 reporting that a B-17 was coming back with three engines but was missing a meter-sized section in the left wing, taken away during a combat encounter with an Fw 190. At this point, there were scarcely any German fighters of the standard Bf 109 and Fw 190 visible. Some were seen heading east, and a few remaining escort fighters with sufficient fuel pursued them. Major Leonard K. Carson spotted two Bf 109s flying at high altitude during their sortie, spaced far apart. One was shot down at an altitude of around 11,000 meters near Salzwedel, and the other met a similar fate at approximately the same altitude further to the south, northwest of Magdeburg, in close proximity to the ramming fighters launch sites in Sachau and Solpke. About fifty minutes after the intense aerial battle, Lieutenant Warren Whitson Jr., whose Flying Fortress number 43-39070 had sustained damage, ditched his aircraft on the single-track Schwerin to Parchim railway line, 17km east of Schwerin. With the flaps deployed, the aircraft, part of the 493rd Bomber Group, veered left to slip under the low-level squadron. It managed to release its bombs approximately in the target area before the crew bailed out. Nine parachutes were spotted by other crews, but Whitson remained missing.[53]

In general, the heavy bombers of the Eighth Air Force managed to maintain a solid group formation despite the unexpected assaults from ramming fighters and jet fighters. This ability, combined with effective support and protection from accompanying fighters, ultimately subdued the intensity of the frenzied German attacks.

By late afternoon, the sky had finally reverted to its tranquil state. Only the unsightly marks of numerous smoke columns hinted at the recent battle. The landscape, however, bore witness to the grim aftermath of the preceding hours. Stretching across a wide expanse of terrain were the remnants of fighters and bombers, now reduced to worthless wreckage. In these clusters of twisted metal, the lives of young pilots and crew members had come to an end. In other locations, the melancholy sight of a dead or dying airman lay close to his parachute. For those fortunate enough to survive with non-fatal injuries, the days and weeks ahead promised a slow and often agonizing recovery. Young Luftwaffe pilots faced the prospect of many months in captivity at the hands of their adversaries. Both sides discovered that they had lost not only comrades but also friends.

Luftwaffe records claim that at least twenty-two to twenty-four American bombers were victims of Sonderkommando Elbe. Estimates of Elbe aircraft shot down that day by escorting American fighters varied between forty-seven and fifty-three, with the death of some thirty to forty Elbe pilots. Sixty of the 180 Bf 109s launched that day returned with mechanical problems. The rammings were played down by American authorities and had little effect on the bombing campaign.[54]

10
Sonderkommando Pilots

There is no complete roster of all the pilots who participated in the Sonderkommando Elbe mission, as records were not kept or have been lost over time. However, the following pages include some of the known pilots who participated in the mission, where biographies could be located.

Hans-Joachim Herrmann

Hans-Joachim "Hajo" Herrmann was a bomber pilot in the Spanish Civil War and a fighter pilot in 1943 when he created the Jagdgeschwader JG 300. He was born on August 6, 1913, in Königsee, near Erfurt, in the German state of Thuringia. He began his military career as an infantryman in the Wehrmacht but transferred to the Luftwaffe in 1936. Herrmann started out in the He 51, then flew the He 11 and Ju 88, and later the Me 262. Hajo had nine kills as a Wilde Sau pilot, but his medals were awarded for sinking over 70,000 tons of shipping as a bomber pilot. Herrmann was known for his aggressive flying style and willingness to take risks in combat. He was awarded the Knight's Cross of the Iron Cross with Oak Leaves and Swords, one of the highest honors in the German military, for his service and bravery in combat.

In March 1945, Herrmann was appointed to lead a new unit known as Sonderkommando Elbe. The unit was created in a desperate attempt by the Nazi regime to slow down the Allied advance in the final days of the war. The concept behind the unit was inspired by the Japanese *Kamikaze* pilots who had been causing havoc in the Pacific theater. The idea was for German pilots to fly their own planes directly into enemy aircraft in midair, effectively using their own planes as weapons. Herrmann was handpicked by the Luftwaffe high command to lead Sonderkommando Elbe because of his exceptional flying skills and leadership abilities. He was given the task of selecting the pilots for the unit and training them in the art of ramming enemy planes.

Herrmann was initially skeptical about the effectiveness of Sonderkommando Elbe and the idea of using suicide attacks as a military tactic. He believed that it was a waste of valuable pilots and aircraft that could be better used in conventional combat missions. However, he ultimately agreed to lead the unit because of his sense of duty to his country and his belief in the importance of defending Germany against the Allies. Under Herrmann's leadership, Sonderkommando Elbe underwent intense training in ramming techniques and combat tactics. The pilots were trained to fly a variety of planes, including fighters and bombers, and were given special training in ramming enemy planes. The unit was also equipped with special planes that had reinforced cockpits and were designed to withstand the impact of a collision.

Hans-Joachim Herrmann played a crucial role in the creation and leadership of the special unit. As a highly experienced and decorated fighter pilot, he was handpicked by the Luftwaffe high command to lead the unit and was responsible for selecting and training the pilots. Despite the failure of the mission, Herrmann remained committed to Sonderkommando Elbe until the end of the war. Hajo flew to Hungary in May 1945 to negotiate the release of some of his men. The Soviets captured him, and he was held captive in gulags until December 1955. Later, he became one of Germany's most successful attorneys.[1]

Karl-Heinz Anton

Anton's life journey unfolds as a remarkable testament to the tumultuous era of World War II and its aftermath. He was born on August 1, 1926, in the historic city of Nuremberg. In 1944, he embarked on a path that led him to the ranks of the Luftwaffe.

The crucible of war and his relentless determination saw Anton hone his skills as a fighter pilot, mastering the art of aviation amidst the turbulence of operations. His mettle was tested in battles in the skies over the Western Front. He etched his name in the annals of history in 1945. Selected to join Sonderkommando Elbe, he found himself confronting a perilous mission that demanded unparalleled bravery. April 7, 1945, would forever be etched in his memory, as he embarked on his maiden and sole mission with Sonderkommando Elbe.

In a daring act of self-sacrifice, Anton executed his mission with resolute determination, ramming his Bf 109G into an American bomber. Fate favored him that day: as his aircraft collided with the enemy aircraft, his instinct for survival enabled him to bail out and escape death. Captured by the Allies, Anton's destiny took a different turn. He found himself a prisoner of war, a chapter in his life marked by uncertainty and resilience as the war's conclusion beckoned the dawn of a new era.

With the war's end, Anton's journey continued on a different trajectory. Returning to his homeland, he ventured into the realm of business, channeling his indomitable spirit into endeavors beyond the battlefields.

He passed away on October 2, 2006, marking the end of a life that spanned eight remarkable decades. His legacy, a story woven with threads of courage, sacrifice, and resilience, stands as a testament to the indelible impact of individuals amid the turbulent currents of history.[2]

Joachim-Wolfgang Böhm

Böhm exemplifies the valor and sacrifice that defined the tumultuous era of World War II. Born on August 24, 1924, in the idyllic German town of Gießen, his early years unfolded against the backdrop of a Germany in turmoil. In 1942, while still in his teens, Böhm embarked on a path that would lead him to the Luftwaffe. Guided by unwavering determination, Böhm honed his skills as a fighter pilot on the Eastern Front, where he confronted the harsh realities of aerial warfare.

In 1945, Böhm joined the ranks of Sonderkommando Elbe. Tasked with disrupting Allied bomber formations through midair collisions, Böhm embraced a mission that demanded unparalleled bravery. On April 7, the stage was set for his moment of reckoning, as he embarked on his first and final mission with Sonderkommando Elbe. He carried out his mission with precision, ramming his Bf 109G into an American bomber. Following the midair collision, Böhm plummeted to the earth in his badly damaged fighter, wounded and battered.

On the ground, people rallied to his aid, working tirelessly for three hours to extricate him from the tangled metal, but he subsequently died from his injuries. Posthumously bestowed with the Knight's Cross of the Iron Cross, he was honored for his unwavering courage and service.[3]

Gerhard Böhnke

Gerhard Böhnke was born in Berlin on January 10, 1926. He joined the Luftwaffe in 1944, becoming a fighter pilot, a profession that demanded skill, courage, and unwavering determination.

He served on the Eastern Front, where his mettle was tested and his commitment solidified, surviving the challenges of aerial combat on many occasions. He was handpicked to join the ranks of Sonderkommando Elbe in 1945 and took part in the events of April 7.

He took off on that day in his Bf 109G, becoming involved in a perilous dogfight encounter with a P-47 piloted by Captain George Bostwick of the 63rd Fighter Squadron, 56th Fighter Group. Although Böhnke was able to bail out from his stricken aircraft, fate dealt him a cruel blow. Striking the tailfin of his fighter, he was rendered unconscious and his parachute failed to deploy. His body was later discovered southeast of Verdun. Gerhard Böhnke is believed to have been the first member of Sonderkommando Elbe to fall in action that day.[4]

Hans Bott

Born on 29 October, 1925, in the Bavarian town of Dillingen an der Donau, Hans Bott joined the Luftwaffe in 1943, serving amid the crucible of the Eastern Front. Handpicked to join the ranks of Sonderkommando Elbe in 1945, Bott was trained for the unit's daring mission to engage in mid-air collisions with Allied bomber formations.

On April 7, Bott took off in his Messerschmitt Bf 109G to attack a stream of American bombers. He executed his mission skillfully, successfully ramming his aircraft into an enemy bomber. However, he was killed as his own aircraft plummeted to earth. Bott's gallant actions were recognized with the Knight's Cross of the Iron Cross, a testament to his bravery and selfless service.[5]

Henfried Breinl

Henfried Breinl, a pilot who served in Sonderkommando Elbe during the closing months of World War II, was born on January 25, 1925, in Sankt Martin, part of the Rhineland in western Germany. Breinl joined the Luftwaffe and received training as a fighter pilot, in 1945 becoming part of Hans-Joachim Herrmann's special unit tasked with the ramming of Allied bomber formations.

On April 7, Breinl participated in the unit's only major operation. Alongside his fellow pilots, he took to the skies to intercept a formation of American B-17 bombers over northern Germany. He successfully executed a ramming maneuver against an American bomber, but as with many of these daring missions, this came at a great cost, resulting in the loss of his own aircraft and the sacrificing of his life. He was posthumously recognized for his bravery with the Knight's Cross of the Iron Cross.[6]

Hans Bröckelschen

While the details of Hans Bröckelschen's early life and early military endeavors remain unclear, it is known that he was recruited into Sonderkommando Elbe and took part in the unit's historic maiden mission on April 7, 1945.

Although he guided his Bf 109G-6 towards a stream of American bombers, he was unable to successfully complete a ramming maneuver. Amidst the swirling chaos of aerial combat, Bröckelschen was compelled to parachute from his aircraft over enemy-held territory. Captured by the Allied forces, he spent the waning days of the war in captivity. There are no confirmed details of Bröckelschen's postwar civilian life.[7]

Hans-Dieter Eitle

Eitle, born on September 7, 1924, in the vibrant German city of Stuttgart, joined the ranks of the Luftwaffe in 1942 as a teenager, being trained as a fighter pilot. His path converged with that of Sonderkommando Elbe, and in early 1945 found himself selected to become a member of this new unit.

On the day of the operation, April 7, Eitle's Bf 109G received heavy fire from enemy aircraft, which altered the path of its flight. He was forced to bail out from his stricken aircraft, but upon reaching the ground was captured by Allied forces. At the end of the war, Eitle transitioned back to civilian life, becoming an engineer and working for various German companies, including the illustrious IBM.

Eitle stayed in touch with fellow surviving members of Sonderkommando Elbe, taking part in several poignant reunions. He passed away, aged 89, on June 30, 2014, in his birthplace of Stuttgart.[8]

Herbert Frank

Herbert Frank became a pilot in the Luftwaffe and took part in Sonderkommando Elbe's sole mission on April 7, 1945. He took to the skies that day in his Focke-Wulf Fw 190, engaging headlong with a formation of American bombers.

Frank guided his fighter into the path of an American B-17 bomber, the two aircraft colliding violently. His Focke-Wulf was badly damaged, and he was forced to bail out, being taken prisoner by American troops after parachuting to earth.

After the war, he was prosecuted for his participation in the Sonderkommando Elbe operation but was ultimately acquitted. Thereafter, Frank returned to the skies as a test pilot for aircraft manufacturer Messerschmitt, later working for civilian airline company Lufthansa. He died in 1986 at the age of 66.[9]

Erich Funk

Born on June 17, 1921, in the picturesque town of Plauen, Erich Funk became a fighter pilot with the Luftwaffe. In 1945, Funk joined Sonderkommando Elbe, being handpicked for his skill and daring.

He took part in the unit's only mission on April 7, joining the orchestrated assault on a formation of American B-17 bombers. Amidst a fierce exchange of enemy fire, Funk steered his Bf 109G on a collision course with an American bomber, both planes hurtling to the ground after impact. Funk lost his life in this action and was posthumously bestowed with the Knight's Cross of the Iron Cross. He was subsequently laid to rest in a cemetery in his hometown of Plauen.[10]

Hans Fussinger

Hans Fussinger was born in Munich on March 22, 1924, joining the Luftwaffe in 1942 and training to become a fighter pilot. In early 1945, Fussinger was selected to join Sonderkommando Elbe.

On April 7, Fussinger took to the skies with his fellow pilots for Sonderkommando Elbe's solitary mission, a synchronized attack on a formation of U.S. B-17 bombers over northern Germany. His Messerschmitt Bf 109G faced a relentless barrage of enemy fire, but he pressed on, steering his aircraft into an American bomber. Fussinger was killed as both aircraft crashed to the ground. He was posthumously rewarded for his gallantry with the Knight's Cross of the Iron Cross and was buried in a Munich cemetery.[11]

Anton Grabinger

Anton Grabinger was born on August 24, 1921, in the Bavarian town of Tegernsee. He signed up with the Luftwaffe in 1941, honing his skills as a fighter pilot and being chosen to be a part of Sonderkommando Elbe in early 1945.

Grabinger took part in the unit's audacious mission on April 7, targeting a large formation of American B-17s flying over northern Germany. Grabinger's Bf 109G fighter withstood heavy enemy fire as he aimed his aircraft toward an enemy bomber. The collision destroyed both aircraft, Grabinger paying the ultimate price with the loss of his life. His brave effort that day earned him a posthumous Knight's Cross of the Iron Cross. His body was recovered, and he was buried in a cemetery in his hometown of Tegernsee.[12]

Karl-Heinz Greisert

Born in Berlin on December 4, 1924, Kurt Greisert joined the Luftwaffe in 1942, becoming a skilled fighter pilot. In 1945, Greisert was chosen to join the ranks of Sonderkommando Elbe, with which he was trained to execute a daring ramming attack against the surging tide of Allied bombers.

He took part in the unit's only mission on April 7 over northern Germany, aiming to bring down a U.S. heavy bomber. However, Greisert's fighter suffered serious damage, rendering his return to base impossible. He leapt to safety before his aircraft crashed to earth, but was subsequently captured by the Allies and ended up in a prisoner-of-war camp. When Greisert eventually emerged from captivity, he took back to the skies with a career as a commercial airline captain. He lived for many years after his retirement until his death on January 26, 2011, at the age of 86.[13]

Klaus Hahn

Klaus Hahn, born on August 4, 1924, in the city of Karlsruhe, joined the ranks of the Luftwaffe in 1942, becoming a proficient fighter pilot. In 1945 he was chosen to be part of the elite Sonderkommando Elbe.

Hahn joined his fellow Elbe pilots in the audacious assault on a massed formation of American B-17 bombers on 7 April. Hahn's Bf 109G fighter was badly damaged by enemy fire and he had to bail out, falling into the hands of Allied forces when he reached the ground. Spending the remaining weeks of the war in captivity, when peace came Hahn returned to civilian life, studying and working as an architect in his home city of Karlsruhe.

Hahn remained close with his surviving wartime comrades, attending Sonderkommando Elbe reunions until his death, aged 84, in Karlsruhe on October 15, 2008.[14]

Hugo Harms

Born in the bustling city of Hamburg on March 11, 1924, Hugo Harms joined the ranks of the Luftwaffe in 1942, becoming a fighter pilot. He faced the trials of the Eastern Front and the difficult terrain of Italy, where he honed his skills as a pilot.

In 1945 he joined Sonderkommando Elbe, training for its mission to shatter formations of Allied bombers through mid-air collisions. On April 7, the day of the mission, Harms witnessed a furious aerial engagement as he and his fellow pilots targeted a large formation of American bombers southwest of Schwarmstedt in Lower Saxony. Harms successfully executed his mission, ramming his Bf 109G into a bomber. Nevertheless, he found himself unable to bail out, trapped in his shattered aircraft.

Harms' body was found still in his mangled aircraft near Gilten. Posthumously, his valor was recognized with the Knight's Cross of the Iron Cross.[15]

Rudolf Heintz

Rudolf Heintz was born on February 12, 1924, in central Germany. He joined the Luftwaffe in 1942, becoming a fighter pilot. He embarked on intense training and refined his flying skills, to the extent that in early 1945 he was selected to join the ramming pilots of Sonderkommando Elbe, which was formed to launch suicidal attacks against Allied bombers over Germay.

On April 7, Heintz piloted an Me 262 jet aircraft in the elite unit's sole major operation in northern Germany. He courageously executed his mission, ramming into multiple Allied bombers, causing significant damage and compelling many others to scatter.

Heintz managed to survive and bail out of his battered aircraft but ended up in captivity after falling into the hands of Allied forces. With the cessation of hostilities, he was released from his prisoner of war camp and returned to his homeland to re-enter civilian life. Heintz passed away on September 7, 1996, aged 72.[16]

Walter Herbold

Born in the historic Thuringian city of Altenburg on August 8, 1920, Walter Herbold was enrolled into the Luftwaffe in 1940 and became a skilled fighter pilot. In the early days of 1945, Herbold's aerial prowess caught the eye of those forming Sonderkommando Elbe and joined the elite unit.

He embraced Elbe's ambition to launch a massed ramming attack on a formation of American B-17 bombers over northern Germany, and on April 7 took part in its sole mission. Amidst the tumult of aerial combat, his Bf 109G came under intense enemy fire but he still managed to maneuver his aircraft into an American bomber. Both planes hurtled toward the earth, Herbold sacrificing his life in the fiery collision. His determination earned him the posthumous accolade of the Knight's Cross of the Iron Cross, and he was buried in his hometown of Altenburg.[17]

Werner Husemann

Werner Husemann, who was born in the city of Rostock on August 18, 1922, joined the Luftwaffe in 1941, cultivating his skills as a fighter pilot. He was handpicked to be part of Sonderkommando Elbe as the war entered its final year, training intensely for the elite unit's audacious suicide ramming mission against Allied bombers.

On April 7, Husemann took to the skies over northern Germany for the unit's sole major operation. Husemann and his comrades executed daring ramming maneuvers, wreaking havoc upon the enemy formation and inducing it to splinter. He managed to bail out from his badly damaged fighter, but upon landing was captured by Allied forces and spent the remainder of the war as a prisoner of war. After his release at the end of the war, he carved a new path, achieving success as a businessman as Germany rose from the ashes of defeat. Husemann died on July 22, 2011, at the age of 88.[18]

Otto Köhnke

Otto Köhnke was born on September 26, 1923, in the city of Hamburg. He joined the ranks of the Luftwaffe in 1942, honing his skills as a fighter pilot over the front lines from the Eastern Front to Italy.

In the waning days of World War II, he was selected to join Sonderkommando Elbe, embracing its perilous mission to disrupt the formations of Allied bombers unleashing destruction on the Reich through mid-air ramming. He joined his fellow pilots on April 7 for Sonderkommando Elbe's only mission of the war. Köhnke executed a successful ramming maneuver, colliding his Bf 109G into an American bomber, an action in which he lost his life. Köhnke's ultimate sacrifice was posthumously honored with the Knight's Cross of the Iron Cross.[19]

Walter Körner

Born on November 23, 1921, in the town of Tostedt in Lower Saxony, Walter Körner signed up for the Luftwaffe in 1941. After becoming a skilled fighter pilot, he was chosen to be part of Sonderkommando Elbe in early 1945 and took part in its mission on April 7.

He took off in his Messerschmitt Bf 109G and joined in the coordinated assault on a vast fleet of American B-17 bombers over northern Germany. Despite coming under a hail of enemy fire, he showed unwavering resolve to execute a daring collision maneuver, sacrificing his own life to bring down an American bomber. For his unwavering dedication and ultimate sacrifice, Körner was posthumously bestowed with the Knight's Cross of the Iron Cross. His body was laid to rest in a cemetery in his hometown of Tostedt.[20]

Heinrich-Mathias Krüchem

Born on January 28, 1924, in the North Rhine-Westphalia town of Beuel, Heinrich-Mathias Krüchem enlisted in the Luftwaffe in 1942. He was trained as a fighter pilot, taking to the skies in defense of his homeland and joining the ranks of Sonderkommando Elbe in early 1945.

He trained with this elite unit for its solitary mission on April 7, engaging Allied bomber formations head-on with ramming maneuvers. Undeterred by a barrage of fire from enemy aircraft, Krüchem maintained control of his Bf 109G to successfully execute a collision maneuver which brought down an American bomber. Krüchem was killed in the impact, a sacrifice for which he was posthumously awarded the Knight's Cross of the Iron Cross. He was buried in a cemetery in Beuel, the town where he was born just over twenty-one years before.[21]

Hans-Ludwig Loscher

Born on November 7, 1924, in the town of Guben, in the state of Brandenburg, Hans-Ludwig Loscher enlisted in the Luftwaffe in 1943 while still a teenager. Loscher trained to become a skilled fighter pilot, serving on the Eastern Front.

He gained a position within Sonderkommando Elbe, with which he took part in the mission of April 7, 1945. Loscher successfully executed a maneuver to direct his Bf 109G to collide with an American bomber. Surviving the collision, Loscher bailed out of his stricken fighter but upon landing safely was taken into custody by the Allies, being held as a prisoner of war until Germany surrendered. After the war, Loscher embarked on a career as a businessman. He died on February 7, 2012, at the age of 87.[22]

Fritz Marktscheffel

Born on January 7, 1925, in the town of Breslau, Fritz Marktscheffel, answered his country's call of duty when he joined the Luftwaffe in 1943, training to become a fighter pilot.

In 1945, Marktscheffel was handpicked to join the ranks of Sonderkommando Elbe, with which he trained for the unit's mission to intercept and bring down American B-17 bombers through mid-air collisions. On April 7, 1945, Marktscheffel took to the skies alongside his fellow pilots in his Bf 109G fighter, coming under heavy enemy fire. Undeterred, he steered his Messerschmitt into the path of an American bomber, a collision that sent both planes hurtling to the ground. Marktscheffel paid for this with his life, an act for which he was posthumously awarded the Knight's Cross of the Iron Cross. He was buried in his hometown of Breslau, now known as Wroclaw, part of western Poland.[23]

Klaus Molly

Klaus Molly was born in Berlin on December 13, 1924, joining the Luftwaffe in 1943 and undergoing training to be a fighter pilot. Molly's life was intertwined with that of his uncle, the commander of the Luftwaffe, Reichsmarschall Hermann Göring.

Molly served on the Eastern Front and in the Italian theater, his courage and skill subsequently earning him a place among the ranks of Sonderkommando Elbe. On April 7, 1945, he embarked on Sonderkommando Elbe's sole mission, flying his Messerschmitt Bf 109G into an American bomber, causing a collision that destroyed both aircraft and cost him his life. Molly's bravery was posthumously recognized with the Knight's Cross of the Iron Cross.[24]

Heinz Müller

Born in the town of Teterow in northern Germany on September 8, 1923, Heinz Müller enlisted in the Luftwaffe in 1942. He became a skilled fighter pilot, serving on the Eastern Front and in Italy.

Müller joined Sonderkommando Elbe in 1945, taking part in the mission of April 7. He successfully crashed his Bf 109G fighter into an American bomber, and as Müller's damaged plane hurtled earthward, he was fired upon by a U.S. P-47 from the 56th Fighter Group. He managed to bail out of his stricken aircraft and somehow survived; days later, he reappeared in Stendal. Details of his later life are not known.[25]

Hugo Müller

Born in Regensburg in Bavaria on February 27, 1922, Hugo Müller joined the ranks of the Luftwaffe in 1941, honing his skills as a fighter pilot. Müller found himself handpicked to join Sonderkommando Elbe, taking part in its mission of April 7, 1945.

He and his comrades launched a daring massed attack on a formation of American B-17s over northern Germany. Müller's Bf 109G was badly damaged by enemy fire as he attempted to get into position for a ramming attack. U.S. escort fighters then bore down upon Müller, and he was shot down and killed.[26]

Hans Nagel

Hans Nagel was born on September 3, 1923, in the coastal city of Kiel, joining the Luftwaffe in 1942 and becoming a fighter pilot. He fought on the Eastern Front and in Italy, and in the final year of the war was recruited into Sonderkommando Elbe.

On April 7, 1945, Nagel and his comrades embarked on the unit's fateful mission against American bombers aiming for targets in northern Germany. Nagel executed a successful ramming maneuver with his Bf 109G into an American bomber, but his fighter suffered serious damage and he had to make an emergency landing in France, suffering fatal injuries. He was buried in the village of Berhof, his dedication to his task being honored with the posthumous award of the Knight's Cross of the Iron Cross.[27]

Novel Pesch

Born in the charming village of Nieder-Gemünden in Hesse on March 18, 1921, Novel Pesch enlisted in the Luftwaffe in 1939 and became a skilled fighter pilot. He served in both JG 26 and JG 27, earning a reputation as a formidable foe in aerial combat with a tally of more than thirty enemy aircraft shot down.

Pesch was selected to join Sonderkommando Elbe, training to perform high-risk mid-air rammings of enemy planes. On April 7, 1945, Pesch joined in the unit's massed attack on a formation of American B-17 bombers over northern Germany. Amid the chaos of the mission, enemy fire badly damaged Pesch's Bf 109G and he had to bail out. He suffered an injury to his leg and was nursed back to health in a French hospital near Cele. He was subsequently placed in the custody of advancing British forces, becoming a prisoner of war. Details of his later life are unknown.[28]

Heinrich Rosner

Born in Schwerin on December 14, 1924, Heinrich Rosner joined the ranks of the Luftwaffe in 1942, with whom he became a successful fighter pilot. He flew with renowned fighter units such as JG 27 and JG 3, downing over twenty enemy aircraft as he honed his skills.

Joining Sonderkommando Elbe in early 1945, Rosner took part in the daring mission of April 7, a massed attack against a large formation of American bombers over northern Germany. During the mission, Rosner was able to ram two B-24 Liberators. His own aircraft was destroyed in the ramming attack, and although injured Rosner was able to bail out and survive. There are no confirmed details of his postwar life.[29]

Ernst Rummel

Ernst Rummel hailed from the historic city of Dresden, where he was born on January 17, 1923. He joined the Luftwaffe in 1942, commencing his training as a fighter pilot. Serving with fighter units including JG 11 and JG 53, Rummel's marksmanship earned him an impressive tally of over fifty enemy aircraft shot down.

In 1945, Rummel was to take part in the audacious mission of Sonderkommando Elbe. On April 7, Rummel attempted to make ramming attacks in his Bf 109G-6, but canopy icing forced him to break off his ramming mission. He returned to base and survived the war.[30]

Georg Scholz

Scholz was born on December 1, 1921, in the city of Leipzig. He began his military service in 1940, training as a pilot and joining JG 27, a fighter squadron that operated primarily in North Africa. Scholz quickly established himself as a skilled pilot and was credited with shooting down several Allied aircraft.

In 1943, Scholz was transferred to the Eastern Front, where he continued to fly combat missions. In 1944, he was assigned to Sonderkommando Elbe and was among the pilots chosen for its mission on April 7, 1945, for which he underwent extensive training. He successfully rammed one American bomber but was unable to bail out of his aircraft before it crashed. Scholz was posthumously awarded the Knight's Cross of the Iron Cross for his actions.[31]

Franz-Josef Schmidt

Born on July 19, 1923, in the city of Essen, Franz-Josef Schmidt joined the Luftwaffe in 1942. He embarked on a path that would shape him into a skilled fighter pilot, serving on the Eastern Front.

In the waning months of the conflict, Schmidt was handpicked to join the ranks of Sonderkommando Elbe for its mission to disrupt enemy bomber formations through daring mid-air collisions. On April 7, he took off in an Fw 190 but was unable to make contact with the American bombers. Undeterred, he took to the skies once more, this time in a Bf 109G, only to be shot down by U.S. fighters near Weser. He managed to eject safely but became a prisoner of war under the watchful eyes of advancing American forces. Details of his later life are unknown.[32]

Karl-Heinz Schrader

Born on July 20, 1924, in Neustrelitz, northeast Germany, Karl-Heinz Schrader was recruited into the Luftwaffe in 1943, forging a path as a fighter pilot. Following service on the Eastern Front, he joined Sonderkommando Elbe in 1945.

On April 7, Schrader embarked on the only mission of Sonderkommando Elbe, but his Messerschmitt Bf 109G was shot down by an American P-47 Thunderbolt from the 56th Fighter Group. Schrader was trapped in the shattered cockpit of his fighter and killed as it fell to earth.[33]

Dietrich Schulz-Sembten

Dietrich Schulz-Sembten, who was born on October 9, 1923, in the Brandenburg village of Sembten, joined the ranks of the Luftwaffe in 1942. He became a skilled fighter pilot on the Eastern Front and in Italy.

In 1945, Schulz-Sembten was chosen to be a part of Sonderkommando Elbe, with which he trained for ramming attacks on Allied bomber formations. On April 7, he flew his Bf 109G towards an American bomber in a daring act of self-sacrifice. Killed in the subsequent collision, he was posthumously awarded the Knight's Cross of the Iron Cross for his valor.[34]

Horst Seidel

Horst Seidel was born on September 14, 1923, in the city of Frankfurt an der Oder, Germany. In 1941, Seidel joined the Luftwaffe as a pilot trainee, slowly mastering the art of aerial combat and earning his place in a fighter squadron on the Eastern Front.

In 1944, he was chosen to be part of Sonderkommando Elbe, tasked with bringing down Allied bombers through selfless acts of mid-air collision.

On April 7, 1945, he took part in the elite unit's only mission of the war. When Seidel's Bf 109G was skillfully and bravely rammed into an American bomber, he managed to bail out. However, Seidel's body was subsequently discovered in the embrace of Ostenholzen Moor, his parachute having failed to open. For his efforts that day, he was posthumously awarded the Knight's Cross of the Iron Cross.[35]

Ernst Sorge

Born on September 29, 1923, in Königsberg, Germany (now Kaliningrad, Russia), Ernst Sorge signed up with the Luftwaffe in 1942, determined to become a fighter pilot. He succeeded in doing so, serving on the Eastern Front and in Italy.

Sorge was selected to be part of Sonderkommando Elbe for its ramming attacks on Allied bomber formations.

He took part in the elite unit's sole mission on April 7, 1945. However, midway through the mission, a smoking engine on his Fw 189A forced him to make an emergency landing near Lüneburg. Nothing is known about his postwar fate.[36]

Ernst Tetzel

Born on September 14, 1921, in Rennertehausen, North Hesse, Ernst Tetzel enlisted in the Luftwaffe in 1940 to become a fighter pilot. He flew with various fighter units, including the illustrious JG 26 and JG 51, where he showcased his prowess by downing more than thirty enemy aircraft.

Picked to join the ranks of Sonderkommando Elbe in early 1945, he embarked on its solitary mission on April 7, a daring attack on a formation of American B-17 bombers over northern Germany. His Bf 109G came under a relentless barrage of gunfire, and Tetzel was forced into an emergency landing behind enemy lines. Captured by the Allies, he became a prisoner of war until Germany's surrender the following month.[37]

Armin Thiel

Armin Thiel, who joined the Luftwaffe in 1942, was born in the city of Wuppertal on December 27, 1923. He trained as a fighter pilot, honing his skills in battles on the Eastern Front and in the Italian theater.

In the closing months of the war, Thiel was recruited into Sonderkommando Elbe, taking part in its defining moment on April 7, 1945. Guiding his Bf 109K-2, Thiel and his fellow Elbe pilots were ordered to engage a massive formation of American bombers. Thiel's aircraft came under a barrage of American fire, being shot down by enemy fighters before he could launch a ramming attack.[38]

Georg Uhlich

Born on December 4, 1924, in the picturesque German town of Ottmachau—now Otmuchow in southern Poland—Georg Uhlich enlisted with the Luftwaffe in 1942, training to become a fighter pilot.

Uhlich was later assigned to Sonderkommando Elbe, with which he trained to execute suicide attacks against Allied aircraft. He took part in the unit's only mission on April 7, 1945. During the mission, Uhlich's Bf 109G came under intense enemy fire and he was forced to bail out. Captured by American forces, Uhlich spent years as a prisoner of war before being released. In peacetime he embarked on a new career as a commercial pilot for the airline Lufthansa. He passed away on January 27, 2013, at the age of 88.[39]

Manfred Wienkötter

Born in the North Rhine-Westphalia town of Lüdinghausen on September 20, 1925, Heinrich Wienkötter stepped into the ranks of the Luftwaffe in 1943, earning his coveted pilot's license the following year. While initially trained to fly transport planes, he soon transferred to training as a fighter pilot.

In November 1944, Wienkötter found himself in Sonderkommando Elbe, and on April 7, 1945, he took off in his Bf 109G on a mission to bring down a formation of U.S. B-17 bombers through ramming tactics. Amidst the chaos, Wienkötter managed to shoot down one of the enemy bombers, but he too was shot down. Miraculously surviving the crash, he nonetheless found himself a prisoner of war in the hands of the Allies. Released at the end of the war, he returned to Lüdinghausen and began a lengthy career in the construction industry. Wienkötter died aged 85 on October 19, 2010.[40]

Franz Winter

Franz Winter was born on June 6, 1921, in Schlesien (now part of Poland) and began his military career in 1940 when he joined the Luftwaffe as a trainee pilot. After completing his training, Winter was assigned to a fighter squadron and saw action on the Eastern Front. In 1944, he was selected to join Sonderkommando Elbe.

Winter flew his first and only mission with Sonderkommando Elbe on April 7, 1945, when he and his fellow pilots were ordered to attack a large formation of American bombers. Winter successfully rammed his Bf 109G into one of the enemy aircraft, managing to bail out and parachute to safety. He flew his final mission on April 20, when he again rammed an American bomber but was killed in the resulting crash. Winter was posthumously awarded the Knight's Cross of the Iron Cross.[41]

Jakob Zapp

Born on May 5, 1925, in the Rhineland town of Laubenheim, Hans Zapp joined the Luftwaffe in 1943. After training as a fighter pilot, Zapp's aerial combat skills were soon tested on the Eastern Front.

Zapp was conscripted into Sonderkommando Elbe in 1945, training to disrupt formations of Allied bombers through suicidal mid-air collisions. On April 7, he executed his mission flawlessly, colliding his Bf 109G into an American bomber. However, after parachuting from his wrecked fighter he was shot and killed by an enemy P-51. His gallantry was recognized with a posthumous Knight's Cross of the Iron Cross.[42]

Werner Zell

Born in Hamburg on August 15, 1924, Werner Zell joined the Luftwaffe in 1942 and trained as a fighter pilot. He was initially stationed in Italy and later saw action on the Eastern Front. In 1945, he was selected to join Sonderkommando Elbe.

On April 7, Zell flew his first and only mission with the elite unit. Ordered to attack a huge formation of American bombers, he successfully rammed his Bf 109K-4 into a B-17 but struggled to bail out because his canopy would not release. However, an attacking P-51 of 352 Fighter Group, 353 Fighter Squadron, piloted by Captain Harrison Tordoff, hit the canopy with 50cal fire and dislodged it, allowing Zell to parachute to safety as his aircraft crashed into a barn in Grindau. He was immediately taken prisoner by American forces and remained in captivity until the end of the war. After the war, Zell returned to Germany and worked as a businessman. He died in Kiel on November 11, 1988, at the age of 64.[43]

Franz Zens

Franz Zens was born in the quiet town of Neuss, near Düsseldorf, on May 19, 1924. He was enlisted into the Luftwaffe in 1942, embarked on a regime of rigorous pilot training, seeing action on the Eastern Front.

In 1945, he became a member of Sonderkommando Elbe, learning how to launch ramming attacks on Allied bomber formations. He took part in the unit's only mission on April 7, executing his task with precision as he flew his Fw 190A-4 into an American bomber. He was able to bail out and land safely, surviving the remaining weeks of the war.[44]

Other known pilots who participated in the mission, whose biographies could not be located, include Olaf Hansen, Reinhold Hedwig, Gerhard Jansen, Werner Linder, Fritz Meya, Eberhard Prock, Rudi Ringhofer, and Jurgen Thiel.

11

Allied Reports

Upon the return of American fighters and bombers to their bases on April 7, the customary post-combat reports were compiled. As was typical, the claims made by both fighter pilots and bomber gunners were overstated and inflated. This exaggeration primarily stemmed from the chaos of combat and, in some instances, wishful thinking. The escort fighters asserted that they had destroyed fifty-nine single-engine aircraft and an additional five jets. The well-known "gunner multiplication table"—where multiple gunners within a formation might have targeted the same fighter, each believing they had scored a hit and recording a claim—resulted in a total of thirty-three kills claimed by bomber crews; twenty-six from the 3rd Air Division and an additional seven from the 2nd Air Division.[1]

The frenetic sequence of engagements inherent in any battle does not provide an ideal context for examining and validating such claims. The formations utilized by the Eighth Air Force bombers undermine the reliability of gunners' claims, exacerbated by the absence of gun cameras to corroborate them. Meanwhile, fighter pilots frequently targeted the same enemy aircraft, leading to instances where even a pilotless and already doomed Luftwaffe fighter could be fired upon by another P-51, resulting in a second claim for the same "kill." An enemy fighter destroyed by a P-47 or P-51 might also have been targeted by bomber gunners, who could subsequently claim it as well. There is also the challenge that a few bullets finding their mark were often interpreted as conclusive evidence of a confirmed kill.[2]

While the exact numbers are difficult to determine, the official reports submitted by the fighter groups involved on April 7 have been scrutinized in an effort to clarify, to the best extent possible, the various claims made. The Luftwaffe lost 133 fighters on April 7. In total, III./JG 7 and I./(J) KG 54 together deployed sixty Me 262 jets, alongside 180 fighters from Sonderkommando Elbe and other fighter wings. The jets claimed eighteen kills, but over sixty of the Bf 109 force was destroyed in combat, along with twenty-seven Me 262s damaged, four destroyed (one by collision with a B-24). Nineteen pilots were killed or missing, with another five wounded. U.S. losses totaled nineteen bombers and eight escort fighters.[3]

Numerous claims made by the gunners aboard various bombers have been dismissed, primarily because these claims are largely impossible to substantiate, and many were duplicated in reports submitted by fighter pilots. The exceptionally close escort mission undertaken on April 7 increased the likelihood of fighters scavenging damaged German aircraft, a more frequent occurrence than usual. The only claims considered valid are instances where gunners believed their fire caused an Elbe fighter to collide with another bomber. While the Luftwaffe fighters were undoubtedly following their planned flight path, the defensive fire from the bombers had a detrimental impact on the precision of the young German pilots' attacks, leading to crashes, with often disastrous results. Out of the thirty-three claims made by gunners, only six can be attributed to enemy fighters that were destroyed before departing from the bomber formations due to defensive fire and collisions. However, it is worth noting that some of these German fighters may still be included in the overall listing of fighter claims. It is important to recognize the challenging nature of the air war fought by USAAF crews, especially given that most of these combats occurred over enemy territory, making verification of many claims difficult. Adrian Weir notes that previous operations have shown a USAAF claims-to-actual Luftwaffe losses ratio as high as three to one.[4]

An analysis of the operation reveals that many Sonderkommando Elbe fighters never came close to their target bomber formations. The inexperienced pilots faced difficulties in navigation, some grappled with severe freezing conditions for which they were unprepared, and others piloted aircraft ill-suited for combat operations. Additionally, the U.S. Eighth Air Force fighters remained prepared and in force to provide protection. Few of the pilots who encountered various Eighth Air Force fighter groups that day emerged unharmed. Many perished before their aircraft reached the intended targets, while others became trapped within their fighters during the crashes. Even those who managed to escape their damaged planes encountered further perils while parachuting to the ground. Nearly all those who survived the events of April 7 suffered injuries, often severe. Nonetheless, some of the young pilots managed to evade these dangers. Although precise figures are difficult to ascertain, Ulrich Saft's examination suggests that at most forty pilots died, with the figure potentially as low as twenty-five to thirty. Therefore, considering the 120 Sonderkommando Elbe pilots involved in combat, the highest estimated fatality rate would be around 33 percent.[5]

The 2nd Air Division lost three of its B-24s during the combat period, and a severely damaged bomber had to be abandoned by its crew while still over the European mainland. The 3rd Air Division endured the most concentrated series of attacks, resulting in the loss of fourteen B-17 bombers. Among these losses, one was attributed to flak, one to bombs falling from another aircraft, and possibly three to Me 262 units (although the jet units claimed six victories, only three could be confirmed). These statistics indicate that, for a maximum loss of thirty to forty pilots, the initial operation by the fledgling fighter force unit managed to claim as many as thirteen USAAF bombers destroyed. While the figures still favor the American forces, the balance had shifted somewhat back toward the German defenders.[6]

Apart from the bombers that were lost, the clashes in the final hours caused significant damage to those that managed to return to their bases. A total of 188 bombers reported varying degrees of damage, with fifty-four of them classified as "major." To contextualize these figures, one only needs to consider the pattern that had emerged by April 1945. Since the start of December 1944, despite nearly daily operations, USAAF bombers had experienced losses exceeding ten aircraft on just eight occasions, with many operations recording only one or two losses.[7]

If we consider that the Elbe operation was the sole significant initiative that the Luftwaffe could undertake on April 7 and was directed solely at the bombers of the 2nd and 3rd air divisions, the losses start to reveal their actual significance. The losses accounted for merely 2.18 percent of the bomber force. When the lost bombers are assessed as a portion of the entire Eighth Air Force mission, this figure drops to just 1.42 percent. By the close of 1944, American industry alone had manufactured 96,000 aircraft of various types. With such extensive resources, the USAAF could sustain operations even if greater losses were unavoidable. Considering that the combined Allied air forces conducted over 5,000 sorties on April 7, the loss of fewer than twenty aircraft equates to a mere 0.3 percent of the day's aircraft on operations.[8]

Eighth Air Force Combat Chronicle for April 7, 1945

STRATEGIC OPERATIONS (Eighth Air Force): Mission 931: 1,314 bombers and 898 fighters are dispatched to hit airfields, oil and munitions depots and explosive plants in Central and Northern Germany; all primary targets are bombed visually; they meet 100+ conventional fighters and 50+ jets; the German fighters attack fiercely and in the ensuing air battle down 15 heavy bombers; the Army Air Force claims 104-13-32 [destroyed, probably destroyed, and damaged] aircraft including a few jets:

1. 529 B-17s are sent to hit airfields at Kaltenkirchen (143) and Parchim (134), an oil depot at Büchen (36) and a munitions depot at Gustrow (104); secondary targets hit are the marshalling yards at Neumunster (37) and Schwerin (48); 1 other hit Salzwedel Airfield, a target of opportunity; they claim 26-10-10 aircraft; 14 B-17s are lost and 117 damaged; 1 airman is killed in action, 5 wounded in action and 117 missing in action. Escorting are 317 of 338 P-51s; they claim 31-1-8 aircraft; 3 P-51s are lost (pilots missing in action) and 1 damaged beyond repair.

2. 340 B-24s are dispatched to hit explosive plants at Krummel (128) and Düneburg (168); 26 others hit the marshalling yard at Neumünster; they claim 14-2-6 aircraft; 3 B-24s are lost, 1 damaged beyond repair and 44 damaged; 6 airmen are killed in action, 7 wounded in action and 25 missing in action. The escort is 252 P-47s and P-51s; they claim 30-0-7 aircraft; 2 P-51s are lost (pilots missing in action) and 1 damaged beyond repair.
3. 442 B-17s are sent to attack airfields at Wesendorf (107) and Kohlenbissen (93) and an oil depot at Hitzacker (115); 92 hit Lundeburg, the secondary; targets of opportunity are Fassberg Airfield (12) and the marshalling yard at Uelzen (13); they claim 0-0-1 aircraft; 27 B-17s are damaged; 1 airman is killed in action and 3 wounded in action. 209 of 222 P-51s escort without loss.
4. 3 of 4 B-17s and 29 P-51s fly scouting missions.
5. 23 of 25 P-51s escort 12 F-5s on photo reconnaissance missions over Germany.
6. The 374th and 376th Fighter Squadrons, 361st Fighter Group, move from Chèvres, Belgium to Little Walden, England with P-51s.[9]

390th Bomb Group, Mission 291, Neumünster, Germany: April 7, 1945

On April 7, 1945, the Eighth Air Force dispatched 529 B-17s to attack the airfields at Kaltenkirchen and Parchim, an oil depot at Büchen, and a munitions depot at Güstrow. Unforeseen circumstances forced thirty-seven planes (including those from the 390th Bomb Group) to divert to their secondary target: the marshaling yard at Neumünster.

The bombers landed hits across the southern part of the yard, with some bombs falling into the built-up area just east of the tracks. Additional hits were scored on a rail-over-road bridge just south of the train station and a number of industrial buildings located in the town.

The bombers dispatched by the 390th reported encountering at least ten enemy planes, three of which were Germany's new ME-262 jet fighters. One of the jets made a pass on the formation, single-handedly shooting down one B-17 before concentrated fire from the remaining bombers drove it off. Attacks such as these had become increasingly uncommon as the war drew to a close, primarily because the Luftwaffe did not have the resources necessary to retake control of the sky, let alone repel Allied bombers.

The one bomber from the 390th that was shot down was identified as the *Hard to Get*, Number 48225, which crashed near Celle, Germany. All ten members of the crew survived, but were subsequently taken prisoner by the Germans.[10]

452d Bombardment Distinguished Unit Citation

As authorized by Executive Order 9396 (Sec. I, WD Bui. 22, 1943), superseding Executive Order 9075 (Sec. 111, WD Bui. 11, 1942), citation of the following unit in the general orders indicated is confirmed under the provisions of Section IV, WD Circular 333, 1943, in the name of the President of the United States as public evidence of deserved honor and distinction. The citation reads as follows:

The 452d Bombardment Group (H) is cited for outstanding performance of duty in action against the enemy by accurately bombing the tactically important airfield at Kaltenkirchen, Germany, on 7 April 1945. A successful attack on this installation would ground a sizeable force of the enemy's jet-propelled fighters and reduce the effectiveness of his aerial efforts to harass Allied ground forces at a crucial time. Although under considerable pressure after having serviced 23 combat missions during the preceding 30-day period, the ground crews worked diligently and enthusiastically all night to insure mechanical perfection of their aircraft and the success of this tactically important mission.

On the morning of the attack, thirty-eight B-17 type aircraft carrying ninety-five and one-half tons of general-purpose bombs took off on this mission, involving a round trip of one thousand and one miles and of approximately seven and three-quarters hours duration. En-route to the target, harassing antiaircraft fire was encountered at Lauenburg, Germany. At 1242 hours in the Steinhuder Lake area, the group was subjected to sharp enemy fighter attacks. Approximately 40–50 mixed Me 109s, Fw 190s and Me 262s taking full advantage of cloud cover, contrails, and sun position, initiated a series of continuous, aggressive, and fanatical attacks upon the bombers. Desperation on the part of the enemy was evidenced by the closeness and utter abandon with which they pressed their attacks through a veritable wall of steel poured forth from the bomber formation.

Enemy tactics were thrown to the wind, and attacks were made from all clock positions. Two B-17s were rammed by F.W. 190s. This all-out effort to annihilate the group lasted 40 minutes and continued even while the group was on the bombing run. Three Fortresses were lost and thirteen suffered battle damage before the group reached the target. A fourth B-17 went down after the target as a result of damage inflicted during the attack. During the fierce aerial battle, the gallant crews maintained perfect formation under superior leadership and valiantly repulsed the aggressors, inflicting severe losses.

The gunners of the group accounted for 13 enemy aircraft destroyed, 2 probably destroyed, and 6 damaged. Without once wavering from its primary duty to destroy an enemy objective, the group made a highly successful bombing run over a five-tenths undercast. Thirty-five aircraft unleashed eighty-eight tons of bombs on the assigned target with devastating results. The officers and enlisted men of the 452d Bombardment Group (H) displayed extraordinary heroism, vigorous determination, and unwavering devotion to duty above and beyond that of all other units participating in the same operation. Their noteworthy accomplishments constitute an invaluable contribution to the war effort of the United States and reflect the highest credit on themselves and the Army Air Forces.[11]

401st Bomb Group, Mission No. 243, Luneburg, Germany, April 7, 1945

Briefing was again held at an early hour—0230 hours. Pilots were briefed for a crosswind takeoff. At 0440 hours all times were moved forward three hours, with Engines now scheduled for 0850, Taxi at 0900 and Takeoff at 0910 hours. Later, these scheduled times were delayed for still another hour, so it was not until 1047 hours that all operational aircraft were off on the mission. The two spares returned early as there were no aborts, and all operational aircraft had landed by 1859 hours—sixteen and a half hours after briefing. The 401st formed the 94th Combat Wing "C" Group on this mission, whose primary target was the airfield at Reinsehelsen. However, as the primary was not visible, the Group turned to the secondary target, the railroad marshalling yards at Luneberg. Bombing was carried out at 15,000 feet rather than the customary 25,000 feet. The Group history reports good results for the bombing and that much of the rolling stock in the railroad yards was damaged. The only opposition the 401st faced was meager flak, which caused no damage. However, other Groups were attacked by the Luftwaffe, which was met by violent resistance on the part of both American fighter escort aircraft and bomber crews. A large number of Luftwaffe aircraft were shot down in the fray.[12]

One B-17 Pilot's Story by W. Budd Wentz, 487th Bomb Group

It was my 28th mission for the 838th squadron but the third and last emergency landing my crew and I would fly in combat. Our combat missions would soon be over. The 487th Bomb Group had flown a total of 173 missions since May 1944 and would fly only 10 more missions by VE day May 8, 1945.

Saturday, April 7th 1945 started early like any other mission day, except today was my wife Bette's birthday. Nothing was normal, but the routine was well entrenched and rehearsed. Twenty-seven missions earlier our crew's first mission ended after we lost all four engines due to flak and I landed Fortress Number 43-38033 My Best Bette in a pasture in southeast Belgium behind enemy lines. After a tense encounter with local citizens, the local Belgian resistance group around Rienne arranged for us to hide in their homes for four days until American Troops entered the village. We were taken to a convent to stay for several days until we were flown back to England in an RAF C-47.

April 7, 1945 the European Theater of Operations mission #931 of the Eighth Air Force. Following the usual briefing we took off from Lavenham, England (station 137) flying the B-17G-105-BO (Number 43-39126) assigned to us in March in position #4 under the Group Leader's plane to bomb a ME-262 jet airfield at Parchim, Germany. Just to my left rear in position #6 flew Brudsey, my best friend since Flight School. The 838th Squadron was leading that day. The weather was excellent with only a few puffy clouds at about 20,000 feet. At approximately 1:10 p.m., I took the controls from the co-pilot while continuing to monitor the Group radio channel. The talk was relatively quiet with no calls announcing any German fighters or flak at that time.

Suddenly, while on route to the IP, we received a terrific jolt and bang. I tightened up on the wheel to prevent it from swerving. The waist gunner reported over the intercom that our plane had been hit in the tail by a Me-109 diving down from 4 o'clock high. The tail gunner, Sergeant Jewell, was shoved forward 4–5 feet but was only banged around. The plane was functioning okay, so I held position for a few moments. The crew reported pieces of the tail and rudder were falling off. Our Navigator, Boyer, reported we were over Donitz. The engineer in the top turret reported he could see that the vertical stabilizer was severely damaged. From the left side of the plane the crew observed that a Me-109 had severely damaged its right wing and was spinning down out of control. No parachute was seen while the crew could see the Me-109.

Not wanting to damage any other planes, I increased speed and planned to dive forward out of the formation. Unfortunately the plane didn't dive when I pushed the wheel forward. I flew ahead of the formation and then cut the throttles back and let down in a flat aspect. After leaving the formation, I found that kicking the rudder didn't turn the plane either. We couldn't climb, couldn't dive or turn; it was apparent that I had no rudder or elevator control. Keeping the airplane level, I let down and turned by cutting the throttle on the outboard engine on that side and skidded around.

To prepare for emergency landing we dropped our bomb load in an open area then headed westerly while making a large circle to keep a flat attitude. The crew continued to report pieces falling off. I felt I had better get the plane on the ground quickly; but not too quickly. The navigator and bombardier found an airfield to the north with a single light gray runway. It could have been worn asphalt or concrete. Low trees and cut grass surrounded the area. I approached in a northern direction and lightly touched down. It had been about 20 minutes since we were hit. Strange that we hadn't seen any other Luftwaffe fighters near our plane on the descent. We didn't know if any other B-17s were hit.

On the right side of the runway, in the southeast quadrant, there were one or two small one story low buildings. Several new looking Me-262s were lined up under the trees. It was definitely a small facility in a very rural location without much fanfare.

We were in Germany and expected to be in a Stalagluft as POWs in short order. At least we were on the ground unharmed. I came to a stop and taxied toward a building. To my surprise American soldiers came running and driving out to the plane. "What the hell are you doing? You aren't supposed to land here", shouted an American Army Major standing in his jeep. We learned that the Americans had just occupied the airfield only 2–3 hours earlier. In typical fashion I sarcastically told the Major what I thought of his demands and informed him of our predicament. He stormed off back to the buildings.

After exiting the plane and checking that the crew was unharmed, we inspected our plane and was shocked to see that the movable rudder was completely gone, and the vertical stabilizer was pretty extensively damaged. The right horizontal stabilizer was reduced to less than one-third its size while the left and right elevators were completely gone. The tail of the fuselage was crushed including the tail turret while [the] tip of a ME-109 wing was embedded in the fuselage. We pulled the tip of the Me-109 out and kept it as a souvenir.

Looking around we found a beat up B-17 under some trees at the edge of the runway. It was an old, camouflaged plane with no markings and no chin turret, probably a B17-E or F. It was in rough shape, but nonetheless there were no FLAK holes. The plane was pretty beat up, but after inspecting we decided to fuel it up and attempt to fly it out. From a jeep generator we started the decrepit B-17 and ran up the engines. Not wanting to waste any more time, we taxied to the end of the runway and commenced to take-off.

We headed west back to our airbase in England by flying slow and low at 3–4,000 feet keeping watch for airfields along the way just in case we needed to land again quickly. By now it was late in the day and starting to get dark. We landed at our home airbase in Lavenham several hours after the group had returned. Somewhat reminiscent of our earlier landing that day another American officer came racing out to our plane, "What the hell happened to my new 17? You were supposed to be here hours ago." I told the Major that we left his new plane back in Germany and traded it for this one instead.

We were driven to the mess hall but were never officially debriefed or interrogated. Later that evening I was taken to the Group Commander, Colonel William K. Martin, and gave him a short version of our events that day. He told me that we would not have to fly any further combat missions in the war, but he would not ground us. We had crash landed 2 times in 28 missions as well as returned 5 times on two engines. No doubt we were Lucky Bastards, and our war was over.[13]

12
Damage to Allied Bombers

Boeing B-17 Flying Fortresses

42-31366/*Old Outhouse—Never A Dry Run aka Snake Eyes* (452nd Bomb Group)
Missing in Action vicinity Kaltenkirchen Germany with Pilot: Dave Owens, Co-pilot: Jim Smouse, Navigator: Gene Ahrens, Bombardier: John Kennedy, Flight engineer/top turret gunner: Phil Ellis, Radio Operator: Frank Rudinsky, Ball turret gunner: Don Phelps, Waist gunner: Bill Auferoth, Tail gunner: Marion Rodgers (9 Killed in Action); mid-air collision with Me 109, crashed Stadthagen, Germany. Missing Air Crew Report 13886.[1]

42-97105/*Paper Doll* (388th Bomb Group)
Missing in Action vicinity Parchim Germany with Lew Hickman, Arnold Wolf, Cawthorn Perdue, Albert Vawter, Herman Meyer (5 Prisoner of War); John Hughes, Elwood Eisenhawer, Jim Martin, Bob Wetzel (4 Killed in Action); rammed by Bf109; crashed Luneburg, Germany.[2]

42-97071/*Andy's Dandy* (100th Bomb Group)
Missing in Action Parchim, Germany with Arthur R. Calder; rammed by Me 109, both exploded, and B-17 crashed close to Steinhuder Lake, near Hannover, Germany.[3]

42-37972/*Gold Brick* (100th Bomb Group)
Damaged in mid-air collision with 43-38514 but limped home and repaired.[4]

43-37985/*Mean Widdle* (487th Bomb Group)
Missing in Action Brandenburg 7/4/45 with Dick Althouse, Doug Coubram, Tom Eugene, Bill Bressler, Norman Garrison, Harry Gustine, Aaron Coon,

Lincoln Hudson (8 Prisoner of War); Clyde Oliver, Willis Peake (2 Killed in Action); flak and rammed, crashed Havelberg, Germany.[5]

43-38002/*Lady Helene* (490th Bomb Group)
Missing in Action Kaltenkirchen 7/4/45 with Dick Druhot, Bob Campbell, Edgar Plaeger, Ralph Hogan, Jim Kyser (5 Prisoner of War); Chas Bowers, Carmen Francis, Jim Bobo (3 evaded capture); Jack Knox (Killed in Action); rammed by enemy aircraft, crashed on continent.[6]

43-38058/*The Wish Bone* (379th Bomb Group)
Battle damage Parchim, Germany. Pilot: Cagle; midair collision with Me109 (by Sonderkommando Elbe rammer); returned to allied territory safely despite two engines out.[7]

43-38514/*E-Z Goin* (100th Bomb Group)
Pilot: Joe Martin. Rammed by enemy aircraft but limped home; in midair collision with 42-37972 (100 Bomb Group); badly damaging tail, but new one fitted.[8]

43-38868/*No Name* (452nd Bomb Group)
Missing in action Parchim, Germany. Pilot: Bill Richardson, Hjalmer Molner, Bob Renaud, Jack Kennedy, Jim Satterfield, John Loveless, Newell Snarr, Julius Albavich (8 KIA); Vance Urban, Stephen Kiss (2 Prisoner of War); rammed by Sonderkommando Elbe Me109, crashed Hamburg, Germany.[9]

43-38869/*Paula Sue* (388th Bomb Group)
Missing in Action Parchim, Germany with Bob Bares, Jim Westbrook, Bob Sonnenberg, George Shantz, Sam Hinstead, Vernon Hofmann, Andy Strable, Dave Becker, Jesse Rorie, Bob Pedersen (10 Killed in Action); rammed by enemy aircraft and hit by debris from aircraft above; crashed Steinhuden Meeres, Germany.[10]

43-39070/*No Name* (493rd Bomb Group)
Missing in Action Kaltenkirchen, Germany with Pilot: Warren Whitson, Co-pilot: Chas Morrow, Navigator: Dave Kames, Bombardier: Bob Flesher, Flight engineer/top turret gunner: Carmen Renaldi, Radio Operator: Bob Magee, Ball turret gunner: Jim Long, Waist gunner: Bob Belsinger, Tom Gardner, Jim Meyers (10 Prisoner of War); enemy aircraft, crashed Warin, Germany.[11]

43-39126/*My Best Bette* (486th Bomb Group)
Battle damaged during a mission to a Luftwaffe airfield at Parchim, Germany. Over Donitz, Germany, en route to the IP, it was struck by a suicide Bf 109 (Sonderkommando Elbe) flown by Klauz Hahn, ramming into the bomber against the tail, damaging the vertical stabilizer, rudder and tail turret.[12]

43-39163/*Happy Warrior* (486th Bomb Group)
MIA Parchim 7/4/45 Pilot: Walt Center, Giovanni Cirelli, Albert Harris, Wyatt Kerr, Sam Powell, Maj Bain Fulton (6 Prisoner of War); Doug Spath, George Lyford, Frank Pikula, Bob Frauenholtz (4 KIA); hit by incendiaries from above aircraft; crashed Parchim, Germany.[13]

44-8225/*Hard to Get* (390th Bomb Group)
Missing in Action Neumunster, Germany with Bill Kotta, Harvey Ainsworth, Carleton Gillmore, Jim Bowler, Chas Turner, Howard Johnson, Don Detwiler, Jim Whitling, Tom Walsh (9 Prisoner of War); shot down by Me 262 jet enemy aircraft, crashed Brunkensen, Germany.[14]

44-8528/*Flak Sack* (486th Bomb Group)
Missing in Action Parchim 7/4/45 with Carl Krenz (Knez), Ed Grenchus, Bill Murphy, Theo O'Neill, Dominic Wesolowski, John Wolff, Bob Crews, Edwin Morrell (8 Prisoner of War); Roland Fricault (evaded capture); Tom McMahon (Killed in Action); flak, crashed Seehausen, Germany.[15]

44-8531/*Miassis Dragon* (452nd Bomb Group)
Missing in action Parchim, Germany with Pilot: Bill Gill, Bill Barbean, Bill Lazzari, Hubert Smart, Sam Mock, Jim Perlonge, Leon Verrilli, Darwin Kusian (8 Prisoner of War); Bill Costley (KIA); Enemy aircraft, crashed Wandesbeck, Germany.[16]

44-8334/*No Name* (100th Bomb Group)
Delivered Hunter 13/8/44; Grenier 2/9/44; Assigned 349BS/100BG [XR-M/B] Thorpe Abbotts 9/9/44; Missing in Action Kaltenkirchen 7/4/45 with Bill Howard, Genaro Delgado, Doug Jones, Sam Lunsford, Ed Hall, Russ Bolding (6 Prisoner of War); Mike Maty, Lou Lehrman, George Thomas (3 Killed in Action); damaged by Me 262 jet, crashed Hannover, Germany.[17]

44-8634/*Ida Wanna* (452nd Bomb Group)
Missing in action Kaltenkirchen, Germany. Pilot: Dabney Sharp, Captain Doug Anderson, Carroll Gierde, Joe Stanfield, Jack Basor, Ellwood Fream, John Halbritter (7 Killed in Action); Arris Stephenson, Ralph DeCelle, Bob Pearce (3 Prisoner of War); Enemy aircraft, crashed Heide, Germany.[18]

44-8744 / *No Name* (385th Bomb Group)
Missing in Action Parchim, Germany with Pilot: George Burich, Co-pilot: Willard Huggins, Navigator: Elwood Randall, Bob Bayne, Flight engineer/top turret gunner: Wendel Rish, Radio Operator: Curtis Walker, Ball turret gunner: Jesse Clark, Paul Miller, Charles Stewart (9 Killed in Action); Rammed by Sonderkommando FW 190, crashed Gifhorn, Germany.[19]

Consolidated B-24 Liberators

42-94931/*Sacktime* (467th Bomb Group)
Pilot: R. M. Winger. Rammed near Krummel, Germany by Bf 109G-6 flown by Heinric Henkel of Sonderkommando Elbe. Able to fly to Belgium and crashed near St. Trond, Belgium. All 10 crew bailed out over Allied lines and were rescued.[20]

42-94870/*Axis Ex-Lax* (445th Bomb Group)
Rammed 15 miles south of Bremen. Aircraft exploded. Eighth Air Force Missing Air Crew Report 13894.[21]

44-49533/*Palace of Dallas* (389th Bomb Group)
Rammed Apr[il] by German Messerschmitt BF 109G-6 West of Soltau Germany while on a Mission on The Ammunition Factory at Düneburg Germany. Pilot: First Lieutenant Walter R Kunkel. Pilot of BF 109G-6 Flown By [sic] Heinrich Rosner of Sonderkommando Elbe. (11) Crew Were Killed. (2) Crew Bailed and Were Captured and Became Prisoners of War.[22]

44-49254/*No Name* (389th Bomb Group)
Rammed by German Messerschmitt BF 109G-6 West of Soltau Germany while on a Mission on The Ammunition Factory at Düneburg Germany. Pilot of BF 109G-6 Flown By [sic] Heinrich Rosner of Sonderkommando Elbe. (8) Crew Were Killed. (2) Crew Bailed and Were Captured and Became POWs.[23]

13

The Aftermath of the Sonderkommando Elbe Mission

Sonderkommando Elbe's mission was a desperate attempt by the German military to stem the tide of the Allied bombing campaign during the final days of World War II. The mission of April 7, 1945, involved ramming enemy bombers with fighter planes, a tactic that had been used sporadically by the Germans throughout the war. However, this mission was different in that it was a coordinated effort by a unit of specially trained pilots who were willing to sacrifice themselves in order to bring down as many Allied bombers as possible.[1]

Sonderkommando Elbe consisted of around 180 pilots who were trained to fly Focke-Wulf Fw 190 and Messerschmidt Bf 109 fighter planes. The pilots were divided into two groups: the attacking group and the decoy group. The attacking group was tasked with ramming into the enemy bombers, while the decoy group's task was to drawing enemy fighters away from the attacking group. The mission was a failure in terms of its strategic goals. The damage inflicted on the Allied bomber fleet was minimal, and the loss of the Elbe planes and pilots was a severe blow to the already weakened Luftwaffe. The failure of the mission was due to several factors.[2]

Firstly, the Allies had already achieved air superiority over Germany. The Luftwaffe was unable to prevent Allied planes from bombing German cities, and Colonel Hans-Joachim Herrmann's mission was unlikely to change that. Secondly, the mission was carried out without the knowledge or approval of Hitler, although Luftwaffe chief Göring authorized it. This lack of coordination and communication made the mission even more ineffective.[3]

The mission ended in tragedy for the pilots who participated. Many of them were either killed or captured by the Allies, while those who survived the mission were shot by German military police for disobeying orders or for their perceived cowardice. The families of the pilots were in many cases not informed of their fate, being left to wonder what had happened to their loved ones.[4]

The aftermath of the mission was also significant for the Wehrmacht as a whole. Sonderkommando Elbe's mission was a reflection of the desperate measures that the German military was willing to take in the final months of the war. It was also an indication of the disorganization and lack of coordination within the Wehrmacht at that time. The failure of the mission was a significant blow to the morale of the German armed forces and further eroded the confidence of the German people in their government and military leadership. The fate of the Elbe pilots after April 7, 1945, was varied. According to one source, "of the 200 pilots who participated in the mission, around 70 were killed, 30 were captured by the Allies, and the rest returned to their units."[5]

The bravery exhibited by Colonel Herrmann's pilots deeply moved him, prompting a strong commitment to their protection. However, for the men to be safeguarded, swift action was imperative. The remaining territory of the Reich was on the brink of being divided by the advancing Allies, necessitating a rapid repositioning. The once intricate structure of the Luftwaffe was now undergoing a significant simplification. All surviving forces were to be placed under the command of either Luftflotte Reich, situated in the remaining northern half of Germany, or Luftflotte 6 in the south.

As Colonel Herrmann tirelessly worked on organizing the next stage of his plan, an order arrived for the staff of IX Fliegerkorps (Aviation Corps) to transfer south. In the midst of his efforts, Major K. Köhnke, who had stayed with his men, promptly executed the move, ensuring its rapid implementation when the message reached Stendal. The safeguarding provided by the senior staff for the pilots and officers of the Elbe unit was essential due to another significant threat. While the Allies sought to seize Luftwaffe airfields or eliminate its remaining aircraft, elements within the leadership of the Luftwaffe itself appeared determined to dismantle the organization. Thousands of ground staff, technicians, and even air crews were already being labeled as surplus and organized into impromptu Luftwaffe field units, destined either for ground troop duty or manning flak units. Once again, the concern arose about losing young pilots to front-line demands. By the time preparations for relocation were completed, twenty-seven Elbe pilots who had taken off on the morning of April 7 had managed to return to Stendal, with each assured a place in the upcoming phase of Herrmann's plans. Alongside these individuals were the sixty pilots who had been compelled to return to their airfields, as well as some of the remaining volunteers who could not participate in the ramming mission.[6]

After covering a distance of over 300 miles, a journey that spanned three days and was carefully guided by Major Köhnke, the men finally arrived in Pocking, situated 14 miles southwest of Passau. Although this relocation was rooted in a tactical decision, it added another layer to the speculations circulating around the Elbe force. With the remaining German territory divided into north and south, forces faced two options for regrouping. Those, like Elbe, who moved south, found themselves in an area rumored to be the location of Festung Alpen (the Alpine Fortress), the redoubt where the continued defense of the Reich was supposedly coordinated. In reality, the forces that did move would have faced a grim fate regardless of the direction they chose. This is evident in the case of the IX Fliegerkorps staff, which seemingly ceased to exist while en route to its new base.[7]

The success of Herrmann and Köhnke in executing the move to Pocking can be seen as a testament to their resourcefulness and perhaps a stroke of luck. However, this move ultimately sealed the fate of Herrmann's plans for a second Elbe operation. The pre-existing confusion had now escalated into chaos. At airfields designated as collection points for the remaining Luftwaffe aircraft, fuel was scarce. Although aircraft arrived at their new locations, the vast majority were unable to take off again.[8]

In a final effort to seek clarification on his orders, Herrmann personally flew to meet with Reichsmarschall Göring, who had established a camp at Berchtesgaden since April 21. Herrmann was uncertain whether he was expected to carry out the large-scale Elbe operation, an endeavor he himself knew to be futile, or if there were alternative plans for his force within the framework of Festung Alpen. The very purpose for the existence of his force had already initiated the conclusion of its campaign. On April 20, Adolf Hitler's 56th birthday, the U.S. Eighth Air Force made its last return to Berlin. With the besieged city already trembling under Marshal Zhukov's Soviet artillery, B-17s and B-24s dropped their bombs on the remnants of the rail network. Remarkably, only one bomber was lost during this final raid. Herrmann, accompanied by one of his accomplished Sonderkommando Elbe pilots, encountered the SS upon landing at Salzburg, where they seemed to wield considerable power. Seeking an audience with his commander, Herrmann was informed that Göring no longer held any position within the Reich. Göring's final attempt to reclaim significance by assuming control from the besieged Hitler had immediately backfired. Those still influencing Hitler exploited Göring's telegram of April 23 to portray him as treacherous, revealing that the *Reichsmarschall* had unwittingly played into the hands of his own enemies.

On April 24, Generaloberst Robert Ritter von Greim, along with Hanna Reitsch, flew from Rechlin to Gatow Airfield in an Fw 190D9, escorted by twelve other Fw 190s from JG 26 led by Captain Hans Dortenmann. Then Reitsch and Greim changed planes and flew into Berlin in a Fieseler Fi 156 Storch, landing on an improvised airstrip in the Tiergarten near the Brandenburg Gate. Lieutenant General Hans Baur had made the strip by cutting down all the trees, in order to get Hitler and others out by air. Baur was there to greet them, as were SS Major General Wilhelm Mohnke, SS Lieutenant Colonel Otto Guensche, SS Sergeant Rochus Misch, Hitler's secretaries Traudl Junge and Gerda Christian, and others.

The uncomfortable and perilous journey into the Führer's last headquarters beneath the ruined Reich Chancellery was necessary for Greim to receive his new appointment to the rank of *Feldmarschall* and assume the role of Commander-in-Chief of the Luftwaffe. Considering that the individual who had endorsed the *Selbstopfermänner* ("self-sacrifice men") ramming mission proposals was now at the helm of the Luftwaffe, it seems prudent that Hajo Herrmann had maintained a certain distance between Berlin and his men.[9]

Although he later acknowledged that the news had convinced him that the end was imminent, Herrmann chose to persist with the original purpose of his visit. Consequently, he found himself in front of General Koller, the officer who had initially scaled down his original plans and subsequently rejected the idea of launching a second operation. However, before Herrmann could ascertain the fate of his force, Koller was summoned back to Berlin and the tumultuous environment of Hitler's bunker.

Unaware of the intended use of his force, Herrmann decided to make a final attempt to speak to Göring and drove to Berchtesgaden, only to have his perception of the chaos around him reinforced. Not only had the former *Reichsmarschall* been divested of all his titles and positions, but he was also under house arrest at Hitler's direct orders, awaiting a potential death sentence. Individuals he spoke to seemed to have formulated their own survival plans—a fight to the death in the mountains, surrender to the British or Americans, ongoing partisan warfare, or even a quiet relinquishment of arms and a return to civilian life. The primary remaining fear was the prospect of being captured by Soviet forces.[10]

In addition to his Elbe force, Herrmann had orchestrated a special commando unit called Sonderkommando Bienenstock (Beehive). Initially intended to complement Sonderkommando Elbe operations by targeting the airfields of USAAF bombers in Italy, from where they launched raids on crucial Luftwaffe jet bases in southern Germany, Herrmann received final orders from higher command. Surprisingly, these instructions directed the Bienenstock force to sabotage Soviet supply lines and impede the advance of their forces.

Between April 25 and 28, Herrmann's second force from Pocking carried out several successful raids, but their missions deviated from his original intent. Instead of executing a dramatic assault on a crowded Allied airfield, eliminating a significant number of bombers and ground facilities, the pilots were tasked with attempting to destroy various crossings over the River Donau. However, such efforts could not alter the course of the war for long. On April 29, any lingering hopes of German forces breaking through the encircling Soviet armor around Berlin were dashed. The following day, Hitler committed suicide and the Red Flag was raised atop the Reichstag. Thus, one man's aspirations for a lasting Third Reich came to a dramatic end.

While the British and American advances had come to a standstill at the River Elbe, the Soviet assault persisted. With each passing hour and day, the Red Army gained control of more and more of the debris-strewn landscape that covered Eastern and Central Europe. It was against this unstoppable Allied advance that the pilots gathered by Colonel Herrmann ultimately concluded their service in the Luftwaffe. Confronted by the breakdown of communications with the remaining elements of Oberkommando der Luftwaffe (OKL, the Luftwaffe High Command), and ultimately the complete loss of supplies by the beginning of

May, the remaining operational units ceased to exist. Even the overly optimistic on-paper strength of the Luftwaffe could no longer conceal the truth: the Luftwaffe, its fighter forces, and its pilots were finally relegated to history.[11] On April 10, the pinnacle of Luftwaffe jet operations had occurred when Fighter Wing 7 deployed fifty-five Me 262s. However, this achievement came at a significant cost. By the day's end, four of the fighters had been destroyed in the air. On May 3, at an airfield near Salzburg, fires were ignited using the last remnants of aviation fuel. The flames rapidly engulfed around sixty Me 262s, including the fighters of General Galland's Fighter Group 44, which had assembled over the preceding days. Symbolically, the final hopes of the Luftwaffe were being extinguished by fire. Even the revolutionary force that Herrmann had aimed to safeguard and the aircraft that many believed could rejuvenate the Luftwaffe were now reduced to burnt and twisted scrap by the hands of their own pilots.

While many of those around him managed to evade capture, Colonel Herrmann was compelled to surrender to Soviet forces in Budapest on May 11. He spent the next decade of his life as a prisoner. When he was eventually released, the events of 1945 had already started to fade with the passage of time. Many who had participated sought only to rebuild their lives and put the horrors of war behind them.

The families of the pilots who participated in the mission were often not informed of their fate. In some cases, families received letters stating that their loved ones were missing in action, while in other, families were not informed at all. The lack of information about the fate of the pilots caused great anguish and uncertainty for the families.[12]

The failure of Sonderkommando Elbe's mission had a significant impact on the morale of the German military. The mission was seen as a desperate measure that reflected the dire situation that the Wehrmacht was facing in the final months of the war. The failure of the operation was a stark reminder of the desperation and hopelessness that had permeated the German military by April 1945. It was a culmination of the strategic and tactical errors that had plagued the Luftwaffe since the beginning of the war. Despite having some of the most advanced aircraft and skilled pilots, the Luftwaffe had failed to adapt to the changing nature of air warfare and the overwhelming superiority of the Allied air forces.[14]

In the final months of the war, the German military leadership was grasping at straws to find any means of resistance against the advancing Allies. The Sonderkommando Elbe mission was just one of many desperate measures that were taken, including the formation of Volkssturm battalions composed of elderly men and teenage boys, the use of the Me 262 jet fighter as a bomber, and the deployment of human torpedoes to attack Allied shipping.[15]

The failure of Sonderkommando Elbe also highlights the moral and ethical issues surrounding the use of suicide tactics in warfare. The pilots who participated in the mission were essentially sacrificial lambs, sent to their deaths with no real chance of success. While their bravery and sacrifice cannot be denied, the use of such tactics raises questions about the value of human life and the ethics of sending soldiers on missions with little or no chance of survival.

In the decades since the end of World War II, Sonderkommando Elbe has been the subject of much historical debate and analysis. Some historians have praised the pilots for their courage and sacrifice, while others have criticized the mission as a senseless waste of life. Sonderkommando Elbe's mission has also been used as a cautionary tale about the dangers of desperation and the need for sound military planning and coordination.[16]

14

Epilogue

The Sonderkommando Elbe mission of April 7, 1945, was a desperate attempt by the Wehrmacht to turn the tide of the war in their favor. The mission was a reflection of the dire situation that Germany was facing in the final months of the war. The failure of the mission was a significant blow to the morale of the German military and further eroded the confidence of the German people in their government and military leadership. In this book, we have examined the Sonderkommando Elbe mission, undertaken to try to stem the tide of the Allied bombing campaign. We have looked at the strategic situation in late 1944 and early 1945, as well as the state of the Luftwaffe during this period. We have also examined the role of Colonel Hans-Joachim Herrmann, the man responsible for the formation of Sonderkommando Elbe, as well as the mission plans and preparation.

The strategic situation for Germany in late 1944 and early 1945 was dire. The Allied bombing campaign had devastated German cities, and Germany was losing ground on both the Eastern and Western fronts. The Wehrmacht was facing a severe shortage of resources, including fuel and ammunition, and its ability to mount an effective defense was severely compromised. The state of the Luftwaffe during this time was similarly dire. The Allied bombing campaign had severely weakened the Luftwaffe's ability to defend German airspace, and the Luftwaffe was struggling to replace the losses it had suffered. Meanwhile, its planes were often outdated and no match for the newer Allied aircraft.

"Hajo" Herrmann was a veteran Luftwaffe pilot who recognized the grim situation that the German military was facing. A man with a reputation for bravery and determination, he believed that the only way to turn the tide of the war was through desperate measures. Herrmann thus created Sonderkommando Elbe, a unit of pilots who were tasked with ramming their planes into Allied bomber formations.

The mission plans were drawn up in great secrecy. The pilots were trained to fly directly into Allied bombers, with the intention of destroying as many Allied planes as possible. The pilots were instructed to bail out at the last possible moment, in the hope that they would survive the crash. Pilot training for the Elbe mission was intense and focused on flying skills that were specific to the operation. The pilots were trained to fly in close formation and to maneuver their planes in such a way as to maximize the damage they could inflict on Allied aircraft. They also received instruction in the use of the new Focke-Wulf Fw 190 fighter, which was seen as the best plane for this type of mission.

The attack on April 7, 1945, was the only time that a Sonderkommando Elbe mission was carried out. The pilots took off from their base in Germany and flew towards the Allied bomber formations. The attack was chaotic and uncoordinated, with the fighter pilots flying in different directions and at different altitudes. The damage inflicted on the enemy bomber fleet was minimal, and the loss of planes and pilots was a severe blow to the already weakened Luftwaffe. The failure of the mission was also due to the fact that the Allies had already achieved air superiority over Germany. The Luftwaffe was unable to prevent Allied planes from bombing German cities, and Herrmann's mission was unlikely to change that. Furthermore, the mission was carried out without the knowledge or approval of Hitler or the German High Command, which made it even more ineffective.

Despite the failure of the mission, Herrmann remained committed to his belief that Sonderkommando Elbe's tactics could have been successful if properly executed. In the years following the war, Herrmann wrote extensively about his experiences as a fighter and bomber pilot and about the Sonderkommando Elbe mission. He argued that the German military leadership was too focused on technological superiority and failed to recognize the importance of innovative tactics and strategies. Herrmann believed that the Elbe's tactics could have been successful if more resources and support were given to the unit. Herrmann's views were not universally accepted, however. Some former Luftwaffe officers criticized him for his recklessness and for endangering the lives of his fellow pilots. Others argued that the Elbe mission was a reflection of the desperation and disorganization that characterized the Wehrmacht in the final months of the war.

In the decades following the war, the Sonderkommando Elbe mission has been studied extensively by military historians and analysts. It has been the subject of numerous books, articles, and documentaries, and has been analyzed in detail in military academies and war colleges around the world. On the one hand, the mission was a desperate and ultimately futile attempt to stop the Allied bombing campaign. The loss of the pilots who participated was a tragedy for their families and a blow to the already weakened Luftwaffe. On the other hand, it was a testament to the courage and determination of the pilots who participated, and to the innovative tactics and strategies that they developed.

In many ways, the Sonderkommando Elbe mission foreshadowed the changing nature of modern warfare. It demonstrated the importance of innovation and adaptability in the face of new military technologies and tactics. It also showed the potential for small, specialized units to have a significant impact on the outcome of a conflict. In the decades since 1945, militaries around the world have studied the mission and drawn lessons from it. The mission has been analyzed for its tactical and strategic implications, as well as for its psychological impact on the German military and civilian population.

The legacy of the Sonderkommando Elbe operation is a complex one, but it remains an important part of military history. The mission is a testament to the courage and determination of the German pilots who participated, and to the innovative tactics and strategies that they developed. It is also a reminder of the human cost of war and the importance of careful planning and coordination in military operations. The mission was a desperate and ultimately unsuccessful attempt to stop the Allied bombing campaign in the final months of the war. It reflected the terrible situation that the Wehrmacht was facing at that time, and the innovative tactics and strategies that some German pilots developed in response to changing military technologies. The aftermath of the mission was tragic for the pilots who participated and further eroded the confidence of the German people in the Nazi regime. However, the mission also had a lasting impact on military thinking and strategy and remains an important part of military history to this day.

Appendix A
Abbreviations and Definitions

Arado:	German aircraft manufacturer; produced trainers and reconnaissance aircraft
A.T.G.:	Allgemeine Transportgesellschaft (General Transportation Company), a German logistics and transport firm
Bf:	Bayerische Flugzeugwerke (Bavarian Aircraft Works), aircraft manufacturer later known as Messerschmitt
Bienenstock:	"Beehive"—a special commando unit intended to complement Sonderkommando Elbe
Blitzkrieg:	"Lightning war"—German military strategy emphasizing rapid, overwhelming attack
Blitzmädchen:	"Lightning girls"—female Luftwaffe auxiliaries performing communications and support roles
BM 1000 bomb:	Parachute mine/bomb used by the Luftwaffe
BMW:	Bayerische Motoren Werke (Bavarian Motor Works), aircraft engine and vehicle manufacturer
Bodenplatte:	"Base plate"; also the name of Operation Bodenplatte, the Luftwaffe's large-scale attack on Allied airfields (1 Jan. 1945)
CBW:	Combat Bomb Wing, a USAAF organizational unit controlling bomber groups
DFS:	Deutsche Forschungsanstalt für Segelflug (German Research Institute for Gliding), specializing in gliders and special aircraft
Do:	Dornier, German aircraft manufacturer
Elbe:	River Elbe in Germany, also referenced in Sonderkommando Elbe

Appendices 185

Festung Alpen:	"Alpine Fortress"—purported Nazi redoubt in the Alps at the end of the war
Fieseler Storch:	German liaison and observation aircraft (notable for short takeoff and landing)
FLAK:	*Fliegerabwehrkanone*, aircraft defense cannon fire (anti-aircraft artillery)
Flieger-HJ:	Flying section within the Hitler Youth (flight training for boys)
Fliegerkorps:	"Aviation Corps"—Luftwaffe operational formations
Fortress:	Allied name for the Boeing B-17 heavy bomber
Fw:	Focke-Wulf, German aircraft manufacturer
Gefechtsverband Helbig:	"Helbig Battle Group"—Luftwaffe strike formation commanded by Helbig
General der Jagdflieger:	"General of Fighters"—senior Luftwaffe officer in charge of fighter operations
Generaloberst:	Colonel General (four-star general rank)
Glitjager:	Glider fighter aircraft concept
Großer Schlag:	"Great Blow"—German air operation intended to strike Allied bombers
Grünherz:	"Green Heart"—emblem of JG 54, a fighter wing
(H):	After a bomb group designation, indicates "Heavy," referring to heavy bombers
Haus der Flieger:	"House of Aviators"—Luftwaffe headquarters building
He:	Heinkel, German aircraft manufacturer
HISMA:	Spanish-German/Spanish-Moroccan Transport Company; shipping firm collaborating with the Axis
Hs:	Henschel, German aircraft and armored vehicle manufacturer
IBM:	International Business Machines (American technology company)
IP:	Initial Point—designated location where bomber formations turn toward their targets
JG:	*Jagdgeschwader*, fighter wing.
JG 400:	Special Luftwaffe unit operating the Me 163 rocket fighter
Jinrai Butai:	"Godly Thunder Corps"—Japanese *Kamikaze* units
Kampfoper:	"Battle opera"—dramatic term used for propaganda or morale-building campaigns

Kikusui:	"Floating Chrysanthemum"—Japanese naval *Kamikaze* operation
Kriegstagebuch (KTB):	"War Diary"—combat log or unit diary
J1N1 Gekko:	Japanese twin-engine reconnaissance aircraft and night fighter ("Moonlight")
Ju:	Junkers, German aircraft manufacturer
Jungvolk:	"Young People"—Hitler Youth for boys aged 10–13
Kamikaze:	"Divine Wind"—suicide attacks by Japanese pilots
KG 200:	Kampfgeschwader 200—secret Luftwaffe unit for special missions
Liberator:	Allied name for the Consolidated B-24 heavy bomber
Luftgaue:	Administrative districts responsible for Luftwaffe air defense and logistics
Luftflotte Reich:	Air fleet responsible for defending German airspace
Luftflotten:	"Air fleets"—major Luftwaffe operational commands
Luftwaffe	German Air Force
Me	Messerschmitt, German aircraft manufacturer
Mistel:	"Mistletoe"—composite aircraft (bomber drone plus fighter controller) used as a giant flying bomb
MPI:	Mean Point of Impact (bombing accuracy term)
Mustang:	North American P-51 long-range escort fighter
Natter:	"Viper"—rocket-powered interceptor (Ba 349)
NSV:	Nationalsozialistische Volkswohlfahrt, Nazi social welfare organization
Oberst:	Colonel
OKL:	Oberkommando der Luftwaffe, Luftwaffe High Command
Pimpfen:	"Cubs"—Hitler Youth boys aged 6–10
RAF:	Royal Air Force (Britain)
Reichsjägerwelle:	"Imperial Hunting Wave"—radio frequency network for Luftwaffe fighters
Reichenberg:	Manned version of the V-1 flying bomb
RLM:	Reichsluftfahrtministerium, Reich Aviation Ministry
ROWAK:	Raw Materials and Goods Purchasing Company, Nazi economic entity

SS, Schutzstaffel:	"Protection Squad"—paramilitary organization of the Nazi Party
SS-Brigadeführer:	SS rank equivalent to brigadier general
SD:	Security service of the SS (intelligence agency)
SO:	"Self-sacrifice"—term for suicide attacks
Sonderkommando:	"Special Command"—designated special-purpose units
Sturm:	"Storm" or "assault"—term for attack formations
Schwarm:	"Swarm"—Luftwaffe tactical unit of four aircraft
Totenkopf-Jäger:	"Death's-head Fighters"—units using the skull insignia
UFA:	Universum Film Aktiengesellschaft, leading German film studio
USAAF:	United States Army Air Forces
V-1 Rocket:	Pulsejet-powered cruise missile ("buzz bomb")
V-2 Rocket:	Liquid-fueled ballistic missile
VE:	"Victory in Europe"—end of WWII in Europe
Volkssturm:	"People's Storm"—German militia formed in 1944
WAAF:	Women's Auxiliary Air Force (Britain)
Wehrmacht:	German armed forces (army, navy, air force)
Wfr. Gr. (Werfer-Granate 21):	Air-launched 21cm rocket
Wilde Sau:	"Wild Pig": night-fighter tactic using single-engine fighters
Zahme Sau:	"Tame Boar": controlled night-fighter interception method
Zerstörer:	"Destroyer": twin-engine heavy fighter aircraft
Zirkus Rosarius:	Luftwaffe unit testing captured Allied aircraft ("Circus Rosarius")

Appendix B

U.S. Eighth Air Force Aircraft Types Used on April 7, 1945 (Source: Eighth Air Force History)

On April 7, 1945, the U.S. Eighth Air Force flew a variety of aircraft types on various missions over Europe. The following are some of the types and their characteristics:

Boeing B-17 Flying Fortress

The B-17 was a four-engine heavy bomber used by the Eighth Air Force to conduct daylight bombing raids over Germany.

1. Performance:
    Maximum speed: Approximately 287–323mph (462–520km/h)
    Cruising speed: Around 182mph (293km/h)
    Range: Varied based on model and mission, but generally around 1,850–3,750 miles (2,977–6,035km)
2. Powerplant:
    Engines: Four Wright R-1820 Cyclone radial engines
    Horsepower: Each engine produced around 1,200hp
3. Armament:
    Guns: Heavily armed with defensive armaments, typically featuring thirteen .50-cal. (12.7mm) machine guns
    Bomb load: Typically around 4,000–8,000lb (1,814–3,629kg)
4. Dimensions:
    Wingspan: Approximately 103ft 9in. (31.62 meters)
    Length: Around 74ft 4in. (22.66 meters)
    Height: Approximately 19ft 1in. (5.82 meters)
5. Weight:
    Empty: Approximately 36,135lb (16,412kg)
    Loaded: Typically around 54,000–65,500lb (24,494–29,710kg)

6. Crew:
    Typically a crew of ten, including the pilot, co-pilot, navigator, bombardier/nose gunner, radio operator, flight engineer/top turret gunner, two waist gunners, ball turret gunner, and tail gunner
7. Service History:
    Introduction: Entered service in 1938
    Operational use: Played a crucial role in the European Theater of Operations, conducting strategic bombing missions against German targets; also used in the Pacific Theater
8. Notable Features:
    Known for its robust construction, which included extensive use of aluminum alloy, giving it a reputation for being able to withstand significant battle damage and return safely; "Flying Fortress" nickname came from its extensive defensive armament

The B-17 Flying Fortress became an iconic symbol of U.S. strategic bombing during World War II. It played a vital role in daylight precision bombing raids over Europe and contributed to the overall success of the Allied air campaign. The aircraft was celebrated for its durability and the ability of its crews to bring it back safely despite severe damage.

Consolidated B-24 Liberator

The B-24 was another heavy bomber used by the Eighth Air Force.

1. Performance:
    Maximum speed: Approximately 290–300mph (466–483 km/h)
    Cruising speed: Around 215mph (346 km/h)
    Range: Varied based on model and mission, but generally around 2,850–3,700 miles (4,586–5,955km)
2. Powerplant:
    Engines: Powered by four Pratt & Whitney R-1830 Twin Wasp radial engines.
    Horsepower: Each engine produced around 1,200hp
3. Armament:
    Guns: Equipped with various defensive armaments, including multiple .50-cal. (12.7mm) and .30-cal. (7.62mm) machine guns
    Bomb load: Typically around 8,800–12,800lb (3,992–5,806kg)
4. Dimensions:
    Wingspan: Approximately 110ft (33.53 meters)
    Length: Around 67ft 2in. (20.47 meters)
    Height: Approximately 18ft (5.49 meters)

5. Weight:
   Empty: Approximately 36,500–42,400lb (16,556–19,277kg)
   Loaded: Typically around 56,000–65,000lb (25,401–29,484kg)
6. Crew:
   Typically a crew of ten, including the pilot, co-pilot, bombardier, navigator, radio operator, flight engineer/top turret gunner, nose gunner, two waist gunners, and tail gunner
7. Service History:
   Introduction: Entered service in 1941
   Operational use: Extensive service in the European, Pacific, African, and Middle Eastern theaters of World War II; played a crucial role in long-range bombing missions
8. Notable Features:
   Distinctive twin-tail design, which contributed to its recognition, and a long-range capability, making it suitable for strategic bombing missions; was used by various Allied air forces, including the U.S. Army Air Forces and Royal Air Force

The B-24 Liberator was one of the most produced bombers of World War II and played a significant role in the Allied bombing campaign. Its long-range capabilities and substantial bomb load made it effective for strategic bombing missions against Axis targets. The B-24 contributed to the overall success of Allied air operations during the war.

North American P-51 Mustang

The P-51 was a single-engine fighter used by the U.S. Eighth Air Force to escort bombers and engage in air-to-air combat with German fighters.

1. Performance:
   Maximum speed: varied based on the model and configuration, but generally ranged from approximately 437–487mph (703–784km/h)
   Cruising speed: Around 275mph (442km/h)
   Range: Depending on the model and mission, the range could be around 1,650–2,300 miles (2,655–3,701km)
2. Powerplant:
   Engine: Powered by a Packard V-1650 Merlin engine (a license-built version of the Rolls-Royce Merlin); P-51A-C had the Allison 12-cylinder, many C types were converted, and Ds were all equipped with Merlin engines.
   Horsepower: The engine produced around 1,490–1,720hp.
3. Armament:
   Guns: Typically armed with six .50-cal. (12.7mm) M2 Browning machine guns, although some models had four guns.

Additional weapons: Could carry external ordnance, such as bombs and rockets, depending on the mission requirements
4. Dimensions:
Wingspan: Approximately 37ft (11.28 meters)
Length: Around 32ft 3in. (9.83 meters)
Height: Approximately 13ft 4½in. (4.08 meters)
5. Weight:
Empty: Approximately 7,125–7,635lb (3,229–3,466kg)
Loaded: Typically around 9,200–12,100lb (4,173–5,488kg)
6. Crew:
A single-seat fighter aircraft
7. Service History:
Introduction: Entered service in 1942
Operational use: Played a crucial role in the European Theater of Operations, particularly as a long-range escort for bombers, and also saw service in the Pacific Theater and later in the Korean War
8. Notable Features:
Excellent high-altitude performance and long-range capabilities, making it an effective escort for bomber formations, and its laminar flow wing design contributed to its speed and efficiency; introduction of the P-51D model with a bubble canopy improved visibility for the pilot

The P-51 Mustang is widely regarded as one of the best fighter aircraft of World War II. Its combination of speed, range, and firepower contributed significantly to the success of Allied air operations. The P-51 became an iconic aircraft, and its contributions extended ftrom World War II into the Korean War and beyond.

Republic P-47 Thunderbolt:

The P-47 was another single-engine fighter used by the U.S. Eighth Air Force.

1. Performance:
Maximum speed: Varied based on the model and configuration, but generally ranged from approximately 426–473mph (686–761km/h)
Cruising speed: Around 300mph (483km/h)
Range: Depending on the model and mission, the range could be around 800–1,900 miles (1,287–3,058km)
2. Powerplant:
Engine: Powered by a Pratt & Whitney R-2800 Double Wasp radial engine
Horsepower: The engine produced around 2,430–2,800hp
3. Armament:
Guns: Heavily armed with eight .50-cal. (12.7mm) M2 Browning machine guns, with different models featuring variations in the number of guns

Additional weapons: Could carry a variety of external ordnance, including bombs and rockets, as well as external fuel tanks
4. Dimensions:
   Wingspan: Approximately 40ft 9in. (12.42 meters)
   Length: Around 36ft 1¾in. (11.02 meters)
   Height: Approximately 14ft 3in. (4.34 meters)
5. Weight:
   Empty: Approximately 10,000–10,700lb (4,536–4,853kg)
   Loaded: Typically around 17,500–17,800lb (7,938–8,074kg)
6. Crew:
   A single-seat fighter aircraft
7. Service History:
   Introduction: Entered service in 1942
   Operational use: Utilized in various theaters of operation, including the European and Pacific; played a significant role in ground-attack missions, bomber escort, and air-to-air combat
8. Notable Features:
   Known for its robust construction, durability, and ability to absorb significant battle damage; had a distinctive bubble canopy that provided excellent visibility for the pilot; radial engine and large size contributed to its nickname "Jug" (short for "Juggernaut")

The P-47 Thunderbolt became one of the most successful and versatile fighter aircraft of World War II. Its rugged design, powerful engine, and heavy armament made it well-suited for a variety of roles, including air-to-air combat and ground-attack missions.

Martin B-26 Marauder

The B-26 was a twin-engine medium bomber used by the U.S. Eighth Air Force.

1. Performance:
   Maximum speed: Approximately 454mph (731km/h) for later models
   Cruising speed: Around 300mph (483km/h)
   Range: Varied based on the model and mission profile, but generally around 1,100–1,500 miles (1,770–2,414 km)
2. Powerplant:
   Engines: Early models powered by Pratt & Whitney R-2800 Double Wasp radial engines
   Horsepower: Each engine produced around 1,900–2,000hp

3. Armament:
    Guns: Equipped with various machine guns and cannons, including a combination of 12.7mm (.50-cal.) and 7.62mm (.30-cal.) machine guns.
    Bomb load: Capable of carrying up to 5,200lb (2,359kg) of bombs internally, and some versions had additional bomb racks for external stores
4. Dimensions:
    Wingspan: Approximately 65ft (19.81 meters)
    Length: Around 58ft (17.68 meters)
    Height: Approximately 21ft (6.4 meters)
5. Weight:
    Empty: Approximately 24,000lb (10,886kg)
    Loaded: Typically around 37,000–38,000lb (16,783–17,237kg)
6. Crew:
    Typically had a crew of six, including a pilot, co-pilot, bombardier, radio operator, and two gunners
7. Service History:
    Introduction: Entered service in 1941
    Operational use: Saw extensive use in the European and Pacific theaters during World War II, primarily employed in medium-altitude bombing missions
8. Notable Features:
    Known for its high speed and relatively short wings, which contributed to its nickname "The Widowmaker" during its early service due to handling challenges, although later modifications and improved training reduced the aircraft's reputation for being difficult to fly; played a crucial role in various bombing campaigns, including low-level attacks against strategic targets

The B-26 Marauder became an important asset in the U.S. Army Air Forces' bomber fleet during World War II, contributing to the Allied air campaign against Axis forces. It underwent several modifications and improvements during its service life to enhance its combat capabilities and address initial handling issues.

Appendix C

Aircraft Used by Sonderkommando Elbe on April 7, 1945 (Source: German Federal Archives)

Focke-Wulf Fw 190

The Focke-Wulf Fw 190 was a German single-seat, single-engine fighter aircraft used during World War II. It was designed by Kurt Tank in the late 1930s as a replacement for the Messerschmitt Bf 109.

1. Performance:
    Maximum speed: Varied depending on the model and configuration, but generally ranged from about 600–685km/h (373–426mph)
    Cruising speed: Typically around 590km/h (367mph)
    Range: Depending on the model, the range varied, but generally around 800–1,250km (497–777 miles)
2. Powerplant:
    Engines: Powered by various engines, including the BMW 801 radial engine in early models and the more powerful BMW 801D in later variants
    Horsepower: The BMW 801 engine produced around 1,700–2,100hp
3. Armament:
    Guns: Typically armed with a combination of machine guns and cannons, which varied but often included four 20mm MG 151/20 cannon and two 13mm MG 131 machine guns
    Additional weapons: Some versions could carry bombs or rockets for ground-attack missions

4. Dimensions:
   Wingspan: Approximately 10.51 meters (34ft 5in.)
   Length: Around 8.96 meters (29ft 5in.)
   Height: Approximately 3.95 meters (12ft 11in.)
5. Weight:
   Empty: Approximately 3,470kg (7,650lb)
   Loaded: Typically around 4,900–5,200kg (10,800–11,500lb)
6. Crew:
   Designed for a single pilot
7. Service History:
   Introduction: Entered service in 1941
   Operational use: Served on the Eastern and Western fronts and was used in various roles, including air superiority, ground-attack, and bomber escort
8. Notable Features:
   Known for its robust construction and excellent handling characteristics, with a wide track landing gear, providing stability during takeoff and landing; played a significant role in German air operations and was well-regarded by its pilots for its effectiveness in combat

Early 190A1 to A4 versions had cannons and two 7.92mm MGs, but later A5 and A6 models had cannons and two 13mm MGs. Many older models were retrofitted. The Fw 190D was a different bird, with a liquid-cooled BMW engine, not the air-cooled BMW. The Focke-Wulf Fw 190 was a key asset for the Luftwaffe and achieved notable success in various theaters of operation during World War II. Its adaptability and combat performance contributed to its reputation as one of the best German fighter aircraft of the war.

Messerschmitt Bf 109

The Messerschmitt Bf 109 fighter became one of the most produced and widely used fighters of the era. Different variants of the Bf 109 were produced throughout the war.
1. Production Numbers:
   Over 33,000 Bf 109s were built during its production run, making it one of the most mass-produced fighter aircraft in history
2. Performance:
   Maximum speed: Varied based on the specific variant, but generally ranged from around 560–700km/h (348–435mph)
   Range: Depending on the model and configuration, the range varied, but it was generally around 850–1,300km (528–808 miles)

3. Armament:
    Equipped with various weapons throughout its different models, including machine guns and cannons; the number and type varied, with configurations such as one or two 7.92mm MG 17 machine guns and one 20mm MG FF cannon being common
4. Powerplant:
    Also varied between different versions of the Bf 109, but was typically powered by a liquid-cooled, inverted-V12 aero engine, initially the Jumo 210 and later the Daimler-Benz DB 601
5. Service History:
    Saw extensive service throughout World War II on various fronts, including the Battle of Britain, the Eastern Front, and the Mediterranean; chiefly operated by the Luftwaffe but was also used by several Axis and postwar countries
6. Variants:
    Notable variants included the Bf 109E (Emil), known for its role in the Battle of Britain, the Bf 109F (Friedrich), and the Bf 109G (Gustav) Specific statistics can vary between different models and subvariants of the Messerschmitt Bf 109. The aircraft underwent continuous development and improvement throughout its operational history.

Messerschmitt Me 262

The Messerschmitt Me 262, also known as the *Schwalbe* ("Swallow") in German, was the world's first operational jet-powered fighter aircraft.

1. Performance:
    Maximum speed: Approximately 900km/h (560mph)
    Range: Around 1,050km (652 miles)
2. Powerplant:
    Engines: Initially equipped with two Junkers Jumo 004 axial-flow turbojet engines
    Thrust: Each Jumo 004 engine produced around 900kgf (1,984 lbf) of thrust
3. Armament:
    Guns: Typically armed with four MK 108 30mm cannon in the nose
    Additional weapons: Some variants had provisions for unguided rockets or air-to-air missiles
4. Dimensions:
    Wingspan: Approximately 12.5 meters (41ft)
    Length: Approximately 10.6 meters (34.9ft)
    Height: Approximately 3.8 meters (12½ft)

5. Weight:
   Empty: Around 4,980kg (10,980lb)
   Loaded: Approximately 7,130kg (15,720lbs)
6. Crew:
   Typically one pilot, although there were some two-seat trainer variants
7. Service History:
   Introduction: Entered service in mid-1944
   Operational use: Primarily used in the later stages of World War II for ground-attack and bomber interception
   Significance: The first operational jet-powered fighter aircraft, having a significant impact on the development of aviation technology
8. Notable Features:
   The Me 262 was known for its advanced design, featuring a sleek fuselage and swept wings; had a tricycle landing gear, which was uncommon for aircraft of its time

The Messerschmitt Me 262 played a crucial role in the evolution of jet-powered aircraft and represented a technological leap during World War II. Its introduction came relatively late in the conflict, and its impact on the overall outcome of the war was limited due to factors such as fuel shortages and production challenges.

Appendix D

Aircraft Used by the Wilde Sau (Source: German Federal Archives)

Messerschmitt Bf 110

The Messerschmitt Bf 110, often simply referred to as the Bf 110, was a twin-engine heavy fighter and fighter-bomber aircraft used by the Luftwaffe during World War II. Designed to serve various roles, the Bf 110 became one of the Luftwaffe's key aircraft in the early stages of the war.

1. Development and Design:
   Manufacturer: Bayerische Flugzeugwerke (later merged into Messerschmitt AG)
   Designer: Willy Messerschmitt
   First Flight: May 12, 1936
   Introduction into Service: 1937
2. Key Features:
   Twin-engine configuration: The Bf 110 was a twin-engine aircraft, powered by two Daimler-Benz DB 601 liquid-cooled inverted V12 engines, a configuration that provided the aircraft with enhanced speed and range
3. Crew:
   The Bf 110 typically had a crew of two—pilot and rear gunner/radio operator
4. Armament:
   Early versions were armed with machine guns and cannon armament for self-defense; later versions were equipped with a more powerful armament, including multiple 20mm MG FF/M or MG 151/20 cannon
5. Roles:
   Originally designed as a heavy fighter to provide air cover for bombers, but served as a fighter-bomber, ground-attack aircraft, and reconnaissance platform

6. Operational History:
    Saw combat during the Spanish Civil War, where it performed well in its intended role as a heavy fighter; during the early stages of World War II, the Bf 110 achieved notable successes, particularly during the invasion of Poland and the Battle of France
7. Limitations:
    Faced challenges when employed as a daylight fighter against more agile and maneuverable single-engine fighters, such as the British Supermarine Spitfire and Hawker Hurricane; suffered significant losses during the Battle of Britain, leading to a shift in its role to night fighting and ground-attack
8. Night-Fighter Role:
    Found success as a night fighter equipped with radar, targeting British bombers during nighttime raids, notable night-fighter variants including the Bf 110G-4 and Bf 110G-4/R3
9. Legacy:
    The Bf 110, while facing challenges in certain roles, contributed significantly to the early successes of the Luftwaffe. Its adaptation as a night fighter showcased its versatility, and it remains a notable aircraft in the history of aviation during World War II. Despite its limitations, the Bf 110 played a role in various operational theaters and operational contexts throughout the war.

Appendix E

United States Airborne Weapons (Source: U.S. Air Force Archives)

Colt-Browning M-2 Machine Gun

This excellent .50-caliber machine gun was the standard U.S. Army Air Forces machine gun, being mounted in the wings of the P-51 Mustang and the P-47, and flexibly mounted on various gun positions in the B-17. It could fire at a rate of 900 rounds per minute, and had a muzzle velocity of 2,900 feet per second and an effective range of 3,280 feet. It was possible for a single 2oz bullet from this machine gun to kill an enemy pilot from as far away as 4 miles. Each machine gun weighed 69lb (not counting the mounts, ammunition trays, or ammunition), and like all Colt-Browning machine guns, it had a reputation for reliability and ease of maintenance. The amount of ammunition carried for the M-2 varied with the aircraft, the mission, and the distance flown.

250/1,000lb Bombs

These were high-explosive, general-purpose bombs carried by the B-17, and by the fighter-bomber versions of the P-47 and the P-51. Occasionally, armor-piercing and incendiary bombs were carried by U.S. aircraft. The amount and the type of bombs carried varied, depending on the distance flown and the type of target.

Bazooka Rocket

These 4½-inch rockets were mounted in clusters of three under each wing of the P-47 and P-51, and were used for attacking ground targets.

Appendix F

German Airborne Weapons (Source: German Federal Archives)

Rheinmetall Borsig MG 131 Machine Gun

This powerful 13mm belt-fed machine gun was used on both the Focke-Wulf 190 and the Bf 109G and was originally installed as a machine gun that could do the work of a cannon if the latter jammed. The MG 131 fired up to 300 rounds at a rate of 930 rounds per minute, which was a higher rate of fire than the Colt-Browning M-2 .50-caliber machine guns carried by U.S. fighters. However, the MG 131 had a slightly lower muzzle velocity—2,560 feet per second—than the U.S. machine guns. (Muzzle velocity is the speed at which a bullet leaves the gun barrel; the higher the muzzle velocity, the less time it takes for the shells to reach the target.) Since it had large breech blocks, the installation of the MG 131 in the Bf 109G Gustav necessitated the redesign of the forward fuselage, and the subsequent fighter was appropriately nicknamed *die Beute* or "the Bump."

MG FF Cannon

At the time of the Battle of Britain, this was the standard 20mm cannon and was wing-mounted on early models of the Bf 109, as well as on the Fw 190A-5. It fired at a rate of 540 rounds per minute and had a relatively slow muzzle velocity of 1,920 feet per second. Though it was well liked by the German air ministry, the MG FF was eventually replaced by the superior MG 151 as standard equipment.

Mauser MG 151/20 Cannon

Both the Bf 109 and Fw 190 used this excellent 20mm belt-fed cannon, which could fire 750 rounds per minute and had a muzzle velocity of 2,310 feet per second. Although this reliable cannon was ideal for attacking sluggish U.S. bombers, its rate of fire was too slow against the .50-caliber machine guns carried by American fighters.

Rheinmetall Borsig MK 108 Cannon

This powerful 30mm belt-fed air-to-air weapon was used on the Bf 109, the Fw 190, the Me 262, and the Me 163. Designed as an anti-bomber weapon, it was rushed through development, and as a result it jammed easily at the rate of one stoppage for every hundred rounds fired. The MK 108 could fire sixty 11oz mine/tracer or incendiary shells at a rate of 660 per minute. It had an effective range of 1,300 feet, and with a relatively slow muzzle velocity of 1,705 feet per second, its shells would arc toward the target and could fall short if the pilot did not compensate. The MK 108 was nicknamed the "pneumatic hammer" by Allied aircrews because of the monotonous noise it made when fired. Usually, a few hits with this formidable cannon were enough to destroy any opposing fighter.

Rheinmetall Borsig MK 103 Cannon

An even deadlier anti-bomber weapon than the MK 108, this 30mm cannon was mounted in gondolas under the wings of several models of the Fw 190 and was intended to be installed in the wings of the jet-powered Ho 229. It had a greater effective range than the MK 108, at 2,000 feet, and a faster muzzle velocity, at 2,820 feet per second. It was also more reliable and less prone to jamming than the MK 108. However, at 420 rounds per minute, it fired its large, high-explosive shells at a slower rate than the MK 108.

R4M Air-to-Air Rocket

These 55mm missiles were the most formidable anti-bomber weapons in the Luftwaffe's arsenal. (The name "R4M" was an abbreviation for *Rakete,* or "rocket," 4 kilograms—the weight of each rocket—and *Minen Geschwss,* a thin-walled shell.) They were mounted on two wooden racks under the wings of the Me 262, with each rack holding twelve rockets. All twenty-four rockets could be launched in .03 seconds, and at 1,800 feet the missiles could scatter to cover the space occupied by a heavy bomber. One hit by these highly explosive rockets was sufficient to down a B-17.

SG 500 Jagdfaust Vertically Launched Rocket

This weapon was developed toward the end of the war for the Me 163 Komet in an effort to ensure that the pilots, most of whom were inexperienced at downing aircraft, would score a hit every time. The SC 500 Jagdfaust (SC being an abbreviation for *Sondergerdt*, or "special equipment") was a high-explosive 50mm rocket, and five of these were mounted in vertical tubes on each wing of the Komet. They were fired by a light-sensitive cell that was activated by the shadow of a bomber when the Me 163 flew underneath it.

Wfr. Gr. 21 Rocket-Fired Mortars

Two of these 21cm mortar shells were mounted beneath the wings of the Bf 109 and the Fw 190, one per wing. The Wfr. Gr. 21 (an abbreviation for *Werfer-Grarwite*, a rocket-propelled shell) was designed to be fired into tight bomber formations, to break them up so that individual bombers could then be attacked by other fighters. It was first used during the second U.S. bombing raid on Schweinfurt on October 14, 1943, and was launched from outside of the B-17s' field of fire. The Wfr. Gr. 21 had a slow muzzle velocity of 1,030 feet per second, and at a range of 3,280 feet it had a vertical deviation of 25 feet—which meant that it had to be fired above the bombers—and a horizontal deviation of 130 feet. It could also deviate depending on atmospheric conditions.

110/551/1,102/2,205lb Bombs

These were general-purpose bombs carried by various German fighter-bombers. The 110lb bomb was carried under the wings of the Bf 109 and the Fw 190. The 551lb bomb was a time-fused fragmentation bomb mounted under the wings of the Bf 109 and the Fw 190. It was dropped onto B-17 formations to break them up and had a three-second time delay before detonation. The 1,102lb and 2,205lb bombs were carried by the *Sturmvogel* fighter-bomber version of the Me 262.

Appendix G
Selected Biographies

Brigadier General Ira Eaker

Eaker, as commander of Strategic Forces for the U.S. Eighth Air Force, oversaw the buildup of American bombers in England during 1942 and 1943. He was a capable promoter of the doctrine of daylight strategic bombing at a time when many Allied leaders were doubting its effectiveness. However, his belief that this type of bombing could be accomplished without fighter escort proved disastrous when, in the first two raids on Schweinfurt, 120 U.S. bombers were lost. In 1944, Eaker became commander-in-chief of the Mediterranean Air Command, successfully directing air operations for the August 1944 invasion of southern France.

Feldmarschall Erhard Milch

A pilot in World War I, Milch became head of the German airline Lufthansa during the period between the wars. In this position, he secretly laid the groundwork for the future Luftwaffe and helped build it into a formidable force. In 1933, he became deputy air minister of the Luftwaffe and was second in command to Hermann Göring. A brilliant organizer and capable administrator, the ambitious Milch continually pushed for great numbers of existing models of aircraft to be produced, a move which hampered the development of newer models. However, Milch backed the Me 262 jet fighter once Adolf Galland convinced him of its worthiness. As the war progressed, Milch began losing influence with Hitler and Göring, and was removed from office after he argued with the Führer that the Me 262 should be used as a fighter instead of a bomber. After the war, Milch was sentenced to life imprisonment at the Nuremberg Trials, but was released after serving ten years.

U.S. Army Air Force General Curtis E. LeMay

A tactical innovator, proponent of strategic bombing, and ruthless taskmaster, LeMay was affectionately dubbed "Iron Ass" by the men who served under him in the Eighth Air Force's Fourth Bombardment Wing. Leading many raids himself, he developed the B-17 combat box formation, which gave the Fortresses better mutual firepower and protection. He also drilled his crews relentlessly on instrument flying, a skill that enabled them to take off on the historic August 17, 1943, raid on Regensburg, even though the English airfields were cloaked by fog. LeMay went on to direct B-29 bombing raids from the Marianas against Japan, and after the war became head of Strategic Air Command.

Luftwaffe Major Walter Nowotny

Nowotny, the first German pilot to reach the 250-victory mark, was considered to be the best young fighter ace of the Luftwaffe at only 24 years of age. Holder of the Knight's Cross with Oak Leaves, Swords, and Diamonds, he was given command of the first operational jet fighter unit, Kommando Nowotny, in the fall of 1944, and worked with Adolf Galland to develop jet fighter tactics. After downing a U.S. bomber on November 8, 1944, he was killed when his Me 262 was jumped by American fighters.

Luftwaffe General Adolf Galland

Galland first made his mark as one of the leading German aces in the Battle of Britain while commanding Jagdgeschwader 26. Later, he became general of the Luftwaffe's fighter arm at the age of 30, using the knowledge gained in combat to direct the fighter defense against Allied bombers. Wrongly blamed by Göring for the declining Luftwaffe fortunes, Galland was removed from his post but was later allowed to form his own Me 262 jet fighter squadron, Jagdverband 44. He finished the war as he began it, as a fighter pilot. An outstanding flier, leader, and tactician, Galland tallied 104 aerial victories.

U.S. Army Air Force Major General Carl Spaatz

The commanding general of the U.S. Eighth Air Force in 1942, he was temporarily assigned to oversee air operations for the North African theater and then commanded the Allied air forces for the invasion of Sicily and the Italian peninsula. Brought back to England in early 1944, Spaatz coordinated the overall bombing of Germany by the Eighth Air Force and the Fifteenth Air Force in Italy. On March 5, 1944, Spaatz issued the Oil Plan, which called for the bombing of Germany's vital oil installations before D-Day as a way to draw the Luftwaffe away from the invasion beaches. This was rejected in favor of the Transportation Plan, but he nevertheless ordered strikes on oil targets after D-Day, and these proved extremely successful in stifling the German war effort. Later, Spaatz directed the bombing of Japan by B-29 bombers, including the two that dropped atomic bombs on Hiroshima and Nagasaki.

Sir Arthur Travers Harris

Harris was made an air commodore in 1937, was named air vice marshal in 1939, rose to air marshal in 1941, and to commander-in-chief of RAF Bomber Command in February 1942. A firm believer in mass raids, Air Marshal Harris developed the saturation technique of mass bombing—concentrating clouds of bombers in a giant raid on a single city, with the object of completely demolishing its civilian quarters. Conducted in tandem with American precision bombing of specific military and industrial sites by day, saturation bombing was intended to break the will and ability of the German people to continue the war. Harris applied this method with great destructive effect in Germany—most notably in the firebombing of Hamburg and Dresden. During the preparations for the Normandy invasion in early 1944, Harris was subordinate to American commanders such as Dwight D. Eisenhower and Carl Spaatz and directed the destruction of transportation and communication centers in cities all across German-occupied France. Harris retired in September 1945, and the following year was made marshal of the RAF. Soon after, he wrote his story of Bomber Command's achievements in *Bomber Offensive*. The morality and even the efficacy of saturation bombing came under severe question after the war. Disappointed by such reappraisal of his war aims and methods, Harris lived for a time in South Africa, where between 1946 and 1953 he was managing director of the South African Marine Corporation.

Endnotes

Chapter 1
1. R. H. Bailey, *The Air War in Europe* (Alexandria, VA: Time-Life Books, 1979), p. 24.
2. Ibid., p. 52.
3. Ibid.
4. Ibid., p. 80.
5. Ibid., p. 93.
6. W. Daugherty, *The US Eighth Air Force in World War II: Ira Eaker, Hap Arnold, and Building American Air Power, 1942–1943* (Denton, TX: University of North Texas Press, 2024), p. 77.
7. Ibid.
8. Ibid.
9. Ibid.
10. R. Barker, *The Thousand Plan: The Story of the First Thousand Bomber Raid on Cologne* (London, UK: Chatto & Windus, 1965), p. 100.
11. L. Davis and D. Greer, *B-17 in Action* (Ellijay, GA: Squadron Signal Publications, 1984), p. 22.
12. Daugherty, p. 28.
13. Ibid.
14. Bailey, p. 35.
15. Ibid.
16. W. H. Morrison, *Fortress Without a Roof: The Allied Bombing of the Third Reich* (New York, NY: St. Martin's Press, 1982), p. 117.
17. Ibid.
18. B. Tillman, "Hard Targets," *Air Force Magazine*, February 2015.
19. "Churchill and Bombing Policy, Churchill Proceedings," *Finest Hour*, Issue 137, Winter 2007–08, p. 26.
20. Churchill.
21. Ibid.
22. "The Bomber Offensive from the United Kingdom," *Foreign Relations of the United States, 1941–1942, and Casablanca, 1943* (Washington: Government Printing Office, 2010), Document 412.
23. Morrison, p. 123.
24. Daugherty, p. 98.
25. Ibid.

26. R. M. Citino, *The Wehrmacht's Last Stand: The German Campaigns of 1944–1945* (Lawrence, KS: University Press of Kansas, 2020), p. 200.
27. Ibid.
28. Ibid.
29. J. Curatola, "Operation Gomorrah: The First of the Firestorms," *The War*, The National WWII Museum, July 10, 2023.
30. Bailey, p. 86.
31. Ibid., Curatola.
32. C. D. Heaton and A. Lewis, *Night Fighters: Luftwaffe and RAF Air Combat over Europe, 1939–1945* (Annapolis, MD: Naval Institute Press, 2008), p. 90.
33. "London: The Baby Blitz and V-Weapons, 1941–1945," *Blitz Stories*, Historic England Archive and Library.
34. V. Lupiano, *Operation Tidal Wave: The Bloodiest Air Battle in the History of War* (Guilford, CT: Lyons Press, 2020), p. 181.
35. Ibid.
36. Ibid.
37. R. Davis, *Bombing the European Axis Powers* (Maxwell Air Force Base, AL: Air University Press, 2006), p. 158.
38. Ibid.
39. C. D. Heaton and A. Lewis, *The German Aces Speak: World War II Through the Eyes of Four of the Luftwaffe's Most Important Commanders* (Minneapolis, MN: Zenith Press, 2011), p. 114.
40. Davis, p. 155.
41. H. Herrmann, Interview by Colin Heaton, 1999.
42. Davis, p. 160.
43. Morrison, p. 131.
44. Citino, p. 251.
45. Daugherty, p. 100.
46. Ibid., p. 276.
47. Ibid., p. 350.
48. C. D. Heaton and A. Lewis, *Above the Reich: Deadly Dogfights, Blistering Bombing Raids, and Other War Stories from the Greatest American Air Heroes of World War II, in Their Own Words* (Boston, MA: Dutton Caliber, 2021), p. 114.
49. Ibid., Curatola.
50. Ibid., p. 487.
51. F. Taylor, *Dresden: Tuesday, February 13, 1945* (New York, NY: HarperCollins Publishers, 2005), p. 383.

Chapter 2
1. D. Irving, *The War Between the Generals* (Laguna Hills, CA: Focal Point Publishing, 1981), p. 389.
2. J. Holland, *The Rise of Germany, 1939–1941* (New York, NY: Grove Press, 2015), p. 675.
3. Ibid.
4. I. Kershaw, *Hitler: 1936–1945* (New York, NY: W. W. Norton & Company, 2000), p. 710.
5. A. Beevor, *The Second World War* (New York, NY: Back Bay Books, 2012), p. 654.
6. Ibid.
7. Kershaw, p. 784.
8. Beevor, p. 462.
9. Ibid., p. 464.

10. A. Tooze, *The Wages of Destruction: The Making and Breaking of the Nazi Economy* (London, UK: Penguin Books, 2006), p. 418.
11. Ibid.
12. Beevor, p. 465.
13. R. Bessel, *Germany 1945: From War to Peace* (New York, NY: Harper, 2009), p. 93.
14. Ibid.
15. R. M. Citino, *The Wehrmacht's Last Stand: The German Campaigns of 1944–1945* (Lawrence, KS: University Press of Kansas, 2020), p. 446.
16. R. Goralski and R. Freeburg, *Oil and War: How the Deadly Struggle for Fuel in World War II Meant Victory or Defeat* (New York, NY: William Morrow and Company, 1987). p. 232.
17. Ibid.
18. Goralski, p. 261.
19. E. Beck, *Under the Bombs: The German Home Front, 1942–1945* (Lexington, KY: University Press of Kentucky, 1999), p. 172.
20. Ibid.
21. Ibid.
22. Bessel, p. 100.
23. Ibid.
24. Bessel, 112.
25. Ibid.
26. Citino, p. 451.
27. Ibid.
28. F. Huber, *Promise Me You'll Shoot Yourself: The Downfall of Ordinary Germans, 1945* (London, UK: Penguin Books, 2020), p. 227.
29. Ibid.
30. Ibid.
31. Ibid.

Chapter 3
1. W. Mahurin, *Hitler's Fall Guys* (Atglen, PA: Schiffer Military History, 1999), p. 14.
2. Ibid.
3. C. D. Heaton and A. Lewis, *The German Aces Speak: World War II Through the Eyes of Four of the Luftwaffe's Most Important Commanders* (Minneapolis, MN: Zenith Press, 2011), p. 76.
4. Ibid, p. 15.
5. Ibid.
6. Ibid, p. 17.
7. Ibid, p. 18.
8. Ibid.
9. Ibid.
10. J. Killen, *The Luftwaffe: A History* (Barnsley, UK: Pen & Sword Aviation, 2003), p. 47.
11. J. Keegan,, *The Second World War* (London, UK: Penguin Books, 2005), p. 357.
12. Ibid, p. 358.
13. M. Hastings, *Bomber Command* (New York, NY: Dial Press 1979), p. 388.
14. D. Irving, *The Rise and Fall of the Luftwaffe: The Life of Field Marshal Erhard Milch* (New York, NY: Little, Brown and Company, 1974), p. 103.
15. Ibid., p. 104.
16. R. Overy, *The Air War: 1939–45* (Lincoln, NE: Potomac Books, 2005), p. 155.
17. Ibid., p. 184.

18. Irving, p. 174.
19. Hastings, p. 391.
20. M. Bowman, *German Night Fighters Versus Bomber Command 1943–1945: The Second World War by Night* (Barnsley, UK: Pen & Sword Aviation, 2022), p. 57.
21. Heaton, p. 188.
22. D. Brown and K. Macksey, *The History of Air Warfare* (Bainbridge Island, WA: Barbarossa Books, 1976), p. 71.
23. Hastings, p. 400.
24. H. Herrmann, Interview by Colin Heaton, 1999.
25. H. Ihlefeld, Interview by Colin Heaton, 1984.
26. G. Roedel, Interview by Colin Heaton, 1984.
27. Hastings, p. 392.
28. C. Ryan, *The Longest Day: The Classic Epic of D-Day* (New York, NY: Simon & Schuster, 1994), p. 112.

Chapter 4
1. R. Overy, *Why the Allies Won* (New York, NY: W. W. Norton & Company, Inc., 1996), p. 324.
2. W. Murray, *Luftwaffe* (Boston, MA: Houghton Mifflin, 1983), p. 256.
3. Overy, p. 321.
4. H. Ihlefeld, Interview by Colin Heaton, 1984.
5. J. Corum, *The Luftwaffe: Creating the Operational Air War, 1918–1940* (Lawrence, KS: University Press of Kansas, 2007), p. 222.
6. Ibid., p. 221.
7. R. Overy, *The Bombers and The Bombed: Allied Air War over Europe 1940–1945* (New York, NY: Viking Press, 2014), p. 398.
8. E. R. Hooton, *The Luftwaffe: A Complete History 1933–1945* (Manchester, UK: Crecy Publishing, 2010), p. 255.
9. Ibid., p. 258.
10. Ibid.
11. A. Galland, *The First and the Last: The Rise and Fall of the German Fighter Forces 1938–1945* (New York, NY: Henry Holt and Company, 1954), p. 186.
12. W. Murray and A. Millet, *A War To Be Won: Fighting the Second World War* (Cambridge, MA: Belknap Press, 2001), p. 306.
13. J. Killen, *The Luftwaffe: A History* (London, UK: Frederick Muller Ltd, 1967), p. 196.
14. M. Cooper, *The German Air Force, 1933–1945: An Anatomy of Failure* (Croydon, UK: Jane's Information Group, 1981), p. 236.
15. J. Keegan, *The Second World War* (London, UK: Penguin Books, 2005), p. 271.
16. S. L. McFarland, *To Command The Sky* (Washington, DC: Smithsonian, 1991), p. 169.
17. Overy, p. 325.

Chapter 5
1. D. Irving, *The Rise and Fall of the Luftwaffe: The Life of Field Marshal Erhard Milch* (New York, NY: Little, Brown and Company, 1974), p. 279.
2. Ibid., p. 293.
3. W. H. Tantum IV and E. J. Hoffschmidt, *The Rise and Fall of the German Air Force, 1933 to 1945,* (Old Greenwich, CT: W. E. Publishing Company, 1969), p. 277.
4. C. D. Heaton and A. Lewis, *The German Aces Speak: World War II Through the Eyes of Four of the Luftwaffe's Most Important Commanders* (Minneapolis, MN: Zenith Press, 2011), p. 213.

5. W. Girbig, *Six Months to Oblivion: The Defeat of the Luftwaffe Fighter Force Over the Western Front 1944/1945* (Atglen, PA: Schiffer Publishing Ltd., 2004) p. 272.
6. Irving, p. 323.
7. Ibid.
8. Ibid.
9. Ibid.
10. H. Knoke, *I Flew for the Führer: The Memoirs of a Luftwaffe Fighter Pilot* (Barnsley, UK: Greenhill Books, 2020), p. 97.
11. H. Reitsch, *Flying is My Life* (New York, NY: G. P. Putnam's Sons, 1954), p. 214.
12. Ibid., p. 216.
13. Ibid., p. 218.
14. Ibid, p. 282.
15. Ibid.
16. O. Skorzeny, *Skorzeny's Secret Missions* (New York, NY: E. P. Dutton, 1950), p. 82.
17. A. Kesselring, *Thoughts on the Second World War* (Bonn: Athenäum-Verlag, 1955), p. 469.
18. R. T. Toliver and T. J. Constable, *Get Hartmann from Heaven!* (Stuttgart, Germany: Motorbuch Publisher, 1974), p. 7.
19. K. Bartz, *When the Sky Burned. The Route of the German Luftwaffe* (Hanover, Germany: Adolf Sponholtz Verlag, 1955), p. 235.
20. M. D. Miller and A. Schulz, *Gauleiter: The Regional Leaders of the Nazi Party and Their Deputies, 1925–1945, Volume 3* (Stroud, UK: Fonthill Media, 2021), p. 606.
21. R. Inoguchi, T. Nakajima, and R. Pineau, *The Divine Wind: Japan's Kamikaze Force in World War II* (London, UK: Hutchinson, 1959), p. 175.
22. Reitsch, p. 286.
23. "Irving Collection at the Air Force High Command," *War Diary, February 1–April 7, 1945*, National Archives and Record Services, Microfilm T-321, Roll 10.
24. A. Galland, *The First and the Last: The Rise and Fall of the German Fighter Forces 1938–1945* (New York, NY: Henry Holt and Company, 1954), p. 282.
25. Ibid.
26. Bartz, p. 254.
27. Knoke, p. 111.
28. W. Dahl, *Rammjäger, The Last Deployment* (Heusenstamm, Germany: Orion, 1961), p. 14.
29. Galland, p. 302.
30. Ibid.
31. Ibid.
32. Ibid., p. 28.
33. R. E. Freeman, *The Mighty Eighth: A History of the Units, Men and Machines of the US 8th Air Force* (London, UK: Arms & Armour, 2004), p. 6.
34. Galland, p. 282.
35. A. Price, *The Last Year of the Luftwaffe: May 1944–May 1945* (London, UK: Arms & Armour, 1995), p. 87.
36. Freeman, p. 60.
37. Ibid., p. 177.
38. Ibid.
39. Galland, p. 179.
40. Tantum, p. 294.
41. Freeman, p. 137.
42. Inoguchi, p. 17.
43. Ibid., p. 16.

44. Inoguchi, p. 55.
45. Susan C. Bartoletti, *Hitler Youth: Growing Up in Hitler's Shadow* (New York, NY: Scholastic Nonfiction, 2019), p. 114.

Chapter 6
1. J. Corum, *The Luftwaffe: Creating the Operational Air War, 1918–1940* (Lawrence, KS: University Press of Kansas, 1997), p. 79.
2. R. E. Bohn, "Not Flying by the Book: Slow Adoption of Checklists and Procedures in WW2 Aviation" (University of California, San Diego, July 2013).
3. D. Isby, *The Decisive Duel: Spitfire vs. 109* (Boston, MA: Little, Brown, 2012), p. 401.
4. E. Obermaier, *German Fighter Ace Werner Mölders: An Illustrated Biography* (Atglen, PA: Schiffer, 2006), p. 99.
5. E. Stilla, "The Air Force in the battle for air supremacy: Major influences in the defeat of the Luftwaffe in the defensive battle in West Germany in the Second World War, with particular emphasis on the factors of air defense, research and development and human resources," *PhD thesis* (Rheinische Friedrichs-Wilhelms-Universität, Bonn, 2005).
6. W. Murray, *Strategy for Defeat: The Luftwaffe 1933–1945* (Oxfordshire, UK: Routledge, 1983), p. 44.
7. Ibid.
8. C. Goss, "The *Luftwaffe's* Last Stand," *Aviation History*, 27(4), (2016), pp. 16–23.
9. J. Weal, *Luftwaffe Sturmgruppen* (Oxford, UK: Osprey Publishing, 2005), p. 103.
10. Gross.
11. Weal, p. 89.
12. A. Rose, *Radical Air Combat: The History of German Rammers* (Stuttgart, Germany: Motor Book Publisher, 1979), p. 223.
13. "Kamikaze Pilots, WWII Japan," Naval History and Heritage Command, *National Museum of the US Navy*.
14. Rose, p. 224.
15. Ibid.
16. Rose, p. 241.
17. Ibid.
18. T. E. J. de Witt, "The Economics and Politics of Welfare in the Third Reich," *Central European History*, vol. 11, no. 3, 1978, pp. 256–78.
19. Rose, p. 246.
20. Ibid.
21. M. Messerschmidt, *The Wehrmacht in the Nazi State. Time of Indoctrination* (Hamburg, Germany: Deeker, 1969), p. 278.
22. Ibid.
23. J. Weal, *Jagdgeschwader 2: Richthofen* (Oxford, UK: Osprey Publishing, 2012), p. 123.
24. Messerschmidt, p. 300.
25. Ibid.
26. Weal, p. 189.

Chapter 7
1. N. Ohler, *Blitzed: Drugs in the Third Reich* (Cologne, Germany: Kiepenheuer & Witsch GmbH, 2015), p. 233.

2. H. Herrmann, *Eagle's Wings: The Autobiography of a Luftwaffe Pilot* (Stuttgart, Germany: Motor Book Publisher, 1978), p. 89.
3. Ohler, p. 233
4. Ibid., p. 165.
5. Ibid., p. 161.

Chapter 8
1. W. Warlimont, *Inside Hitler's Headquarters, 1939–45*, trans. R. H. Barry (Novato, CA: Presidio Press, 1964), p. 239.
2. Mission 8AF 931 Narrative, *8th Air Force Operations Research Database*.
3. Eighth Air Force Intops Summary No. 342, Re: 7 April 1945, Paragraph C, Intelligence. National Archives, Record Group 18, Records of the Army Air Forces, 1941–1945.
4. Ibid.
5. Ibid.
6. Ibid.
7. Ibid.
8. Ibid.
9. Mission 8AF 931 Narrative, *8th Air Force Operations Research Database*.
10. 34th Bomb Group Mission Report, *8th Air Force Operations Research Database*.
11. Mission 8AF 931 Narrative.
12. 44th Bomb Group Mission Report, *8th Air Force Operations Research Database*.
13. Mission 8AF 931 Narrative.
14. Ibid.
15. Ibid.
16. Ibid.
17. Ibid.
18. 44th Bomb Group Mission Report, *8th Air Force Operations Research Database*.
19. Mission 8AF 931 Narrative.
20. Ibid.
21. 303rd Bomb Group Mission Report, *8th Air Force Operations Research Database*.
22. 91st Bomb Group/324th Bomb Squadron Mission Report, *8th Air Force Operations Research Database*.
23. 401st Bomb Group/614th Bomb Squadron Mission Report, *8th Air Force Operations Research Database*.
24. Mission 8AF 931 Narrative.
25. Ibid.

Chapter 9
1. J. Schultz, The last thirty days: From the war diary of the OKW April to May 1945 documents on contemporary history. Edited by Jürgen Thorwald (Stuttgart, Germany: Steingrüben, 1951), p. 22.
2. Ibid., p. 333.
3. F. C. Wesley, *The Army Air Forces in World War II* (Washington, DC: Office of Air Force History1983), p. 752.
4. R. E. Freeman, *The Mighty Eighth: A History of the Units, Men and Machines of the US 8th Air Force* (London, UK: Arms & Armour, 2004), p. 176.
5. Ibid.

6. D. Caldwell, *Day Fighters in Defence of the Reich: A War Diary, 1942–45* (Barnsley, UK: Frontline Books, 2012), p. 300.
7. Ibid., p. 324.
8. Freeman, p. 189.
9. Ibid.
10. Ibid., p. 314.
11. H. Herrmann, *Eagle's Wings: The Autobiography of a Luftwaffe Pilot* (Stuttgart, Germany: Motor Book Publisher, 1978), p. 203.
12. Ibid.
13. Ibid.
14. Ibid.
15. A. Weir, *The Last Flight of the Luftwaffe* (London, UK: Arms & Armour, 1997), p. 87.
16. Ibid., p. 93.
17. Ibid.
18. A. Rose, *Radical Air Combat: The History of German Rammers* (Stuttgart, Germany: Motor Book Publisher, 1979), p. 267.
19. Ibid.
20. Ibid.
21. Ibid.
22. Rose, p. 289.
23. Ibid.
24. Rose, p. 301.
25. Freeman, p. 299.
26. "Missing Air Crew Report 13888," *National Archives and Records Administration*, Washington DC, 2005.
27. Rose, p. 304.
28. Ibid.
29. Freeman, p. 307.
30. "Missing Air Crew Report 13723," *National Archives and Records Administration*, Washington DC, 2005.
31. "Missing Air Crew Report 13724," *National Archives and Records Administration*, Washington DC, 2005.
32. Freeman, p. 310.
33. Ibid.
34. Herboth, John B., Colonel B-24 Number 44-49524, *American Air Museum in Britain*.
35. H. Trevor-Roper, *The Last Days of Hitler* (London, UK: Pan Macmillan, 2013), p. 255.
36. "Missing Air Crew Report 13894," *National Archives and Records Administration*, Washington DC, 2005.
37. Freeman, p. 315.
38. Ibid.
39. Ibid.
40. Ibid.
41. Rose, p. 321.
42. Freeman, p. 316.
43. Rose, p. 323.
44. Ibid.
45. "Missing Air Crew Report 13891," *National Archives and Records Administration*, Washington DC, 2005.
46. Freeman, p. 299.

47. "Missing Air Crew Report 13716," *National Archives and Records Administration*, Washington DC, 2005.
48. "Missing Air Crew Report 13721," *National Archives and Records Administration*, Washington DC, 2005.
49. Rose, p. 335.
50. Ibid.
51. Freeman, p. 224.
52. Rose, p. 336.
53. "Missing Air Crew Report 13890," *National Archives and Records Administration*, Washington DC, 2005.
54. Rose, p. 337.

Chapter 10

1. Hans-Joachim Herrman. Personnel records of members of the Reichswehr and Wehrmacht, Personnel File Number: PA/20671. Bundesarchiv, Freiburg.
2. Karl-Heinz Anton. Personnel records of members of the Reichswehr and Wehrmacht, Personnel File Number: LP/58612. Bundesarchiv, Freiburg.
3. Joachim-Wolfgang Böhm. *Berlin Document Center* (BDC) Collection: Personal documents, Personal File Number: VBS 284/6202003993. Berlin-Lichterfelde.
4. Gerhard Böhnke. Personnel records of members of the Reichswehr and Wehrmacht, Personnel File Number: LP/3555. Bundesarchiv, Freiburg.
5. Hans Bott. Personnel records of members of the Reichswehr and Wehrmacht, Personnel File Number: LP/71889. Bundesarchiv, Freiburg.
6. Henfried Breinl. Personnel records of members of the Reichswehr and Wehrmacht, Personnel File Number: PA/5104. Bundesarchiv, Freiburg.
7. Hans, Bröckelschen. *Berlin Document Center* (BDC) Collection: Personal documents, Personal File Number: SA/4000000396. Berlin-Lichterfelde.
8. Hans-Dieter Eitle. *Berlin Document Center* (BDC) Collection: Personal documents, Personal File Number: VBS 3/3330002426. Berlin-Lichterfelde.
9. Herbert Frank. Personnel records of members of the Reichswehr and Wehrmacht, Personnel File Number: LP/8361. Bundesarchiv, Freiburg.
10. Erich Funk. Personnel records of members of the Reichswehr and Wehrmacht, Personnel File Number: LP/67852. Bundesarchiv, Freiburg.
11. Hans Fussinger. Personnel records of members of the Reichswehr and Wehrmacht, Personnel File Number: unknown. Bundesarchiv, Freiburg.
12. Anton Grabinger. Personnel records of members of the Reichswehr and Wehrmacht, Personnel File Number: LP/10147. Bundesarchiv, Freiburg.
13. Karl-Heinz Greisert. Personnel records of members of the Reichswehr and Wehrmacht, Personnel File Number: LP/45292. Bundesarchiv, Freiburg.
14. Klaus Hahn. *Berlin Document Center* (BDC) Collection: Personal documents, Personal File Number: VBS 283/6015015240. Berlin-Lichterfelde.
15. Hugo Harms. *Berlin Document Center* (BDC) Collection: Personal documents, Personal File Number: unknown. Berlin-Lichterfelde.
16. Rudolf Heintz. *Berlin Document Center* (BDC) Collection: Personal documents, Personal File Number: VBS 1/1040020775. Berlin-Lichterfelde.
17. Walter Herbold. Personnel records of members of the Reichswehr and Wehrmacht, Personnel File Number: LP/74533. Bundesarchiv, Freiburg.
18. Werner Husemann. Personnel records of members of the Reichswehr and Wehrmacht, Personnel File Number: LP/14175. Bundesarchiv, Freiburg.
19. Otto Köhnke. Personnel records of members of the Reichswehr and Wehrmacht, Personnel File Number: LP/17208. Bundesarchiv, Freiburg.

20. Walter Körner. Personnel records of members of the Reichswehr and Wehrmacht, Personnel File Number: unknown. Bundesarchiv, Freiburg.
21. Heinrich-Mathias Krüchem. Personnel records of members of the Reichswehr and Wehrmacht, Personnel File Number: unknown. Bundesarchiv, Freiburg.
22. Hans-Ludwig Loscher. *Berlin Document Center* (BDC) Collection: Personal documents, Personal File Number: VBS 1/1070044793. Berlin-Lichterfelde.
23. Fritz Marktscheffel. *Berlin Document Center* (BDC) Collection: Personal documents, Personal File Number: VBS 1/1070078001. Berlin-Lichterfelde.
24. Klaus Molly. Personnel records of members of the Reichswehr and Wehrmacht, Personnel File Number: H2/25425. Bundesarchiv, Freiburg.
25. Heinz Müller. Personnel records of members of the Reichswehr and Wehrmacht, Personnel File Number: LP/22710. Bundesarchiv, Freiburg.
26. Hugo Müller. Personnel records of members of the Reichswehr and Wehrmacht, Personnel File Number: H2/10805. Bundesarchiv, Freiburg.
27. Hans Nagel. Personnel records of members of the Reichswehr and Wehrmacht, Personnel File Number: LP/77830. Bundesarchiv, Freiburg.
28. Novel Pesch. Personnel records of members of the Reichswehr and Wehrmacht, Personnel File Number: LP/79461. Bundesarchiv, Freiburg.
29. Heinrich Rosner. *Berlin Document Center* (BDC) Collection: Personal documents, Personal File Number: VBS 271/5204012263. Berlin-Lichterfelde.
30. Ernst Rummel. Personnel records of members of the Reichswehr and Wehrmacht, Personnel File Number: LP/83045. Bundesarchiv, Freiburg.
31. Georg Scholz. Personnel records of members of the Reichswehr and Wehrmacht, Personnel File Number: 49823. Bundesarchiv, Freiburg.
32. Franz-Josef Schmidt. Personnel records of members of the Reichswehr and Wehrmacht, Personnel File Number: NRW/169448. Bundesarchiv, Freiburg.
33. Karl-Heinz Schrader. Personnel records of members of the Reichswehr and Wehrmacht, Personnel File Number: LP/45466. Bundesarchiv, Freiburg.
34. Dietrich Schulz-Sembten. *Berlin Document Center* (BDC) Collection: Personal documents, Personal File Number: VBS 264/4001006346. Berlin-Lichterfelde.
35. Horst Seidel. *Berlin Document Center* (BDC) Collection: Personal documents, Personal File Number: VBS 283/6055007413. Berlin-Lichterfelde.
36. Ernst Sorge. Personnel records of members of the Reichswehr and Wehrmacht, Personnel File Number: LP/83951. Bundesarchiv, Freiburg.
37. Ernst Tetzel. Personnel records of members of the Reichswehr and Wehrmacht, Personnel File Number: LP/33841. Bundesarchiv, Freiburg.
38. Armin Thiel. *Berlin Document Center* (BDC) Collection: Personal documents, Personal File Number: VBS 284/6219011501. Berlin-Lichterfelde.
39. Georg Uhlich. *Berlin Document Center* (BDC) Collection: Personal documents, Personal File Number: VBS 1/1180020196. Berlin-Lichterfelde.
40. Manfred Wienkötter. *Berlin Document Center* (BDC) Collection: Personal documents, Personal File Number: VBS 284/6221002156. Berlin-Lichterfelde.
41. Franz Winter. Personnel records of members of the Reichswehr and Wehrmacht, Personnel File Number: unknown. Bundesarchiv, Freiburg.
42. Jacob Zapp. Personnel records of members of the Reichswehr and Wehrmacht, Personnel File Number: unknown. Bundesarchiv, Freiburg.
43. Werner Zell. Personnel records of members of the Reichswehr and Wehrmacht, Personnel File Number: unknown. Bundesarchiv, Freiburg.
44. Franz Zens. Personnel records of members of the Reichswehr and Wehrmacht, Personnel File Number: LP/94502. Bundesarchiv, Freiburg.

Chapter 11
1. A. Weir, *The Last Flight of the Luftwaffe* (London, UK: Arms & Armour, 1997), p. 172.
2. Ibid.
3. Ibid., p. 169.
4. Ibid., p. 171.
5. U. Saft, *An Eclipse Without A Future: The Battles for North Germany 1945* (Winnipeg, Manitoba: J. J. Fedorowicz Publishing Inc., 2015), p. 435.
6. Weir, p. 168.
7. Ibid., p. 170.
8. Ibid., p. 171.
9. K. Carter and R. Mueller, *Combat Chronology, 1941–1945, U. S. Army Air Forces in World War II* (Washington, DC: Center for Air Force History, 1991), p. 668.
10. "Mission Number 291, April 7, 1945," *390th Bomb Group* (Tucson, AZ: 390th Memorial Museum Foundation).
11. "452nd Bombardment Group," *Distinguished Unit Citation for Action on April 7, 1945* (Irving, TX: Army Air Corps Library and Museum).
12. "401st Bomb Group, Mission No. 243, Luneburg, Germany, April 7, 1945," *401st Bomb Group (H) Association*, Gig Harbor, Washington.
13. W. Budd Wentz, "Rammed Over Germany, One B-17 Pilot's Story," *487th Bomb Group*, https://wbuddwentz.com/lastmission/.

Chapter 12
1. Eighth Air Force Missing Air Crew Report 13886.
2. Eighth Air Force Missing Air Crew Report 13724.
3. Eighth Air Force Missing Air Crew Report 13718.
4. Dave Osborne, B-17 Fortress Master Log.
5. Eighth Air Force Missing Air Crew Report 13883.
6. Eighth Air Force Missing Air Crew Report 14294.
7. Dave Osborne, B-17 Fortress Master Log.
8. Dave Osborne, B-17 Fortress Master Log.
9. Eighth Air Force Missing Air Crew Report 13888.
10. Eighth Air Force Missing Air Crew Report 13723.
11. Eighth Air Force Missing Air Crew Report 13890.
12. Dave Osborne, B-17 Fortress Master Log.
13. Eighth Air Force Missing Air Crew Report 13889.
14. Eighth Air Force Missing Air Crew Report 13891.
15. Eighth Air Force Missing Air Crew Report 11487.
16. Eighth Air Force Missing Air Crew Report 13893.
17. Eighth Air Force Missing Air Crew Report 13716.
18. Eighth Air Force Missing Air Crew Report 14184.
19. Eighth Air Force Missing Air Crew Report 13721.
20. 467th Bombardment Group (H) research site.
21. American Air Museum in Britain.
22. Eighth Air Force Missing Air Crew Report 13892.
23. Eighth Air Force Missing Air Crew Report 14113.

Chapter 13
1. A. Price, *The Last Year of the Luftwaffe: May 1944–May 1945* (London, UK: Greenhill Books, 1995), p. 89.

2. Ibid.
3. Ibid.
4. A. Weir, *The Last Flight of the Luftwaffe* (London, UK: Arms & Armour, 1997), p. 173.
5. I. Kershaw, *Hitler: 1936–1945* (New York, NY: W. W. Norton & Company, 2000), p. 175.
6. Ibid.
7. Ibid.
8. A. Rose, *Radical Air Combat: The History of German Rammers* (Stuttgart, Germany: Motor Book Publisher, 1979), p. 338.
9. Ibid.
10. Ibid.
11. Ibid.
12. Ibid.
13. H. Sprekelmeyer,, *Special Commandos of the Luftwaffe, 1938 to 1945* (Stuttgart, Germany: Motorbuch Publisher, 1993), p. 275.
14. Ibid.

Bibliography

34th Bomb Group Mission Report. *8th Air Force Operations Research Database*
44th Bomb Group Mission Report. *8th Air Force Operations Research Database*
303rd Bomb Group Mission Report. *8th Air Force Operations Research Database*
91st Bomb Group/324th Bomb Squadron Mission Report. *8th Air Force Operations Research Database*
401st Bomb Group/614th Bomb Squadron Mission Report. *8th Air Force Operations Research Database*
"401st Bomb Group, Mission No. 243, Luneburg, Germany, April 7, 1945," *401st Bomb Group (H) Association* (Gig Harbor, Washington)
"452nd Bombardment Group," *Distinguished Unit Citation for Action on April 7, 1945* (Irving, TX: Army Air Corps Library and Museum)
Anton, Karl-Heinz. Personnel records of members of the Reichswehr and Wehrmacht, Personnel File Number: LP/58612 (Bundesarchiv, Freiburg)
Bailey, Ronald H., *The Air War in Europe* (Alexandria, VA: Time-Life Books, 1979)
Barker, Ralph, *The Thousand Plan: The Story of the First Thousand Bomber Raid on Cologne* (London, UK: Chatto & Windus, 1965)
Bartoletti, Susan C., *Hitler Youth: Growing Up in Hitler's Shadow* (New York, NY: Scholastic Nonfiction, 2019)
Bartz, Karl, *When the Sky Burned. The Route of the German Luftwaffe* (Hanover, Germany: Adolf Sponholtz Verlag, 1955)
Beck, Earl, *Under the Bombs: The German Home Front, 1942–1945* (Lexington, KY: University Press of Kentucky, 1999)
Beevor, Antony, *The Second World War* (New York, NY: Back Bay Books, 2012)
Bessel, Richard, *Germany 1945: From War to Peace* (New York, NY: Harper, 2009)
Bohn, Roger E., "Not Flying by the Book: Slow Adoption of Checklists and Procedures in WW2 Aviation" (San Diego, CA: University of California, July 2013)
Böhm, Joachim-Wolfgang. *Berlin Document Center* (BDC) Collection: Personal documents, Personal File Number: VBS 284/6202003993 (Berlin-Lichterfelde)
Böhnke, Gerhard. Personnel records of members of the Reichswehr and Wehrmacht, Personnel File Number: LP/3555 (Bundesarchiv, Freiburg)
Bott, Hans. Personnel records of members of the Reichswehr and Wehrmacht, Personnel File Number: LP/71889 (Bundesarchiv, Freiburg)
Bowman, M., *German Night Fighters Versus Bomber Command 1943–1945: The Second World War by Night* (Barnsley, UK: Pen & Sword Aviation, 2022)
Brown, David, and Kenneth Macksey, *The History of Air Warfare* (Bainbridge Island, WA: Barbarossa Books, 1976)

Breinl, Henfried. Personnel records of members of the Reichswehr and Wehrmacht, Personnel File Number: PA/5104 (Bundesarchiv, Freiburg)

Bröckelschen, Hans. *Berlin Document Center* (BDC) Collection: Personal documents, Personal File Number: SA/4000000396 (Berlin-Lichterfelde)

Caldwell, Donald, *Day Fighters in Defence of the Reich: A War Diary, 1942–45* (Barnsley, UK: Frontline Books, 2012)

Carter, Kit, and Robert Mueller, *Combat Chronology, 1941–1945, U. S. Army Air Forces in World War II* (Washington, DC: Center for Air Force History, 1991)

"Churchill and Bombing Policy, Churchill Proceedings," in *Finest Hour*, Issue 137 (Winter 2007–08), p. 26

Citino, Robert M., *The Wehrmacht's Last Stand: The German Campaigns of 1944–1945* (Lawrence, KS: University Press of Kansas, 2020)

Cooper, Mathew, *The German Air Force, 1933–1945: An Anatomy of Failure* (Croydon, UK: Jane's Information Group, 1981)

Corum, James S., *The Luftwaffe: Creating the Operational Air War, 1918–1940* (Lawrence, KS: University Press of Kansas, 2007)

Curatola, John, "Operation Gomorrah: The First of the Firestorms," *The War*, The National WWII Museum (July 10, 2023)

Dahl, Walther, *Rammjäger, The Last Deployment* (Heusenstamm, Germany: Orion, 1961)

Davis, Richard G., *Bombing the European Axis Powers* (Maxwell Air Force Base, AL: Air University Press, 2006)

Davis, Larry, and Don Greer, *B-17 in Action* (Ellijay, GA: Squadron Signal Publications, 1984)

Daugherty, William J., *The US Eighth Air Force in World War II: Ira Eaker, Hap Arnold, and Building American Air Power, 1942–1943* (Denton, TX: University of North Texas Press, 2024)

de Witt, Thomas E. J., "The Economics and Politics of Welfare in the Third Reich" in *Central European History*, vol. 11, no. 3 (1978), pp. 256–78

Eighth Air Force Intops Summary No. 342, Re: 7 April 1945, Paragraph C, Intelligence. *National Archives*, Record Group 18, Records of the Army Air Forces, 1941–1945

Eitle, Hans-Dieter. *Berlin Document Center* (BDC) Collection: Personal documents, Personal File Number: VBS 3/3330002426 (Berlin-Lichterfelde)

Frank, Herbert. Personnel records of members of the Reichswehr and Wehrmacht, Personnel File Number: LP/8361(Bundesarchiv, Freiburg)

Freeman, Roger E., *The Mighty Eighth: A History of the Units, Men and Machines of the US 8th Air Force* (London, UK: Arms & Armour, 2004)

Funk, Erich. Personnel records of members of the Reichswehr and Wehrmacht, Personnel File Number: LP/67852 (Bundesarchiv, Freiburg)

Fussinger, Hans. Personnel records of members of the Reichswehr and Wehrmacht, Personnel File Number: unknown (Bundesarchiv, Freiburg)

Girbig, Werner, *Six Months to Oblivion: The Defeat of the Luftwaffe Fighter Force Over the Western Front 1944/1945* (Atglen, PA: Schiffer Publishing Ltd, 2004)

Goralski, Robert, and Russell W. Freeburg, *Oil and War: How the Deadly Struggle for Fuel in World War II Meant Victory or Defeat* (New York, NY: William Morrow and Company, 1987)

Goss, Chris, "The *Luftwaffe's* last stand," in *Aviation History*, 27(4) (2016), pp. 16–23

Grabinger, Anton. Personnel records of members of the Reichswehr and Wehrmacht, Personnel File Number: LP/10147. (Bundesarchiv, Freiburg)

Greisert, Karl-Heinz. Personnel records of members of the Reichswehr and Wehrmacht, Personnel File Number: LP/45292 (Bundesarchiv, Freiburg)

Hahn, Klaus. *Berlin Document Center* (BDC) Collection: Personal documents, Personal File Number: VBS 283/6015015240 (Berlin-Lichterfelde)
Harms, Hugo. *Berlin Document Center* (BDC) Collection: Personal documents, Personal File Number: unknown (Berlin-Lichterfelde)
Heaton, Colin D., and Ann-Maria Lewis, *Above the Reich: Deadly Dogfights, Blistering Bombing Raids, and Other War Stories from the Greatest American Air Heroes of World War II, in Their Own Words* (Boston, MA: Dutton Caliber, 2021)
Heaton, Colin D., and Ann-Maria Lewis, *Night Fighters: Luftwaffe and RAF Air Combat over Europe, 1939–1945* (Annapolis, MD: Naval Institute Press, 2008)
Heaton, Colin D., and Ann-Maria Lewis, *The German Aces Speak: World War II Through the Eyes of Four of the Luftwaffe's Most Important Commanders* (Minneapolis, MN: Zenith Press, 2011)
Heintz, Rudolf. *Berlin Document Center* (BDC) Collection: Personal documents, Personal File Number: VBS 1/1040020775 (Berlin-Lichterfelde)
Herbold, Walter. Personnel records of members of the Reichswehr and Wehrmacht, Personnel File Number: LP/74533 (Bundesarchiv, Freiburg)
Herboth, John B., Colonel, B-24 Number 44-49524, *American Air Museum in Britain*
Herrmann, Hans-Joachim, *Eagle's Wings: The Autobiography of a Luftwaffe Pilot* (Stuttgart, Germany: Motor Book Publisher, 1978)
Herrman, Hans-Joachim. Personnel records of members of the Reichswehr and Wehrmacht, Personnel File Number: PA/20671 (Bundesarchiv, Freiburg)
Herrmann, H., interview by Colin Heaton (1999)
Holland, James, *The Rise of Germany, 1939–1941* (New York, NY: Grove Press, 2015)
Hooton, Eric R., *The Luftwaffe: A Complete History 1933–1945* (Manchester, UK: Crecy Publishing, 2010)
Huber, Florian, *Promise Me You'll Shoot Yourself: The Downfall of Ordinary Germans, 1945* (London, UK: Penguin Books, 2020)
Husemann, Werner. Personnel records of members of the Reichswehr and Wehrmacht, Personnel File Number: LP/14175 (Bundesarchiv, Freiburg)
Ihlefeld, H., interview by Colin Heaton (1984)
Inoguchi, Rikihei, Tadashi Nakajima, and Roger Pineau, *The Divine Wind: Japan's Kamikaze Force in World War II* (London, UK: Hutchinson, 1959)
Irving, David, *The Rise and Fall of the Luftwaffe: The Life of Field Marshal Erhard Milch* (New York, NY: Little, Brown and Company, 1974)
Irving, David, *The War Between the Generals* (Laguna Hills, CA: Focal Point Publishing, 1981)
Isby, David, *The Decisive Duel: Spitfire vs. 109* (Boston, MA: Little, Brown, 2012)
"Kamikaze Pilots, WWII Japan," Naval History and Heritage Command, *National Museum of the US Navy*
Keegan, John, *The Second World War* (London, UK: Penguin Books, 2005)
Kershaw, Ian, *Hitler: 1936–1945* (New York, NY: W. W. Norton & Company, 2000)
Kesselring, Albert, *Thoughts on the Second World War* (Bonn, Germany: Athenäum-Verlag, 1955)
Knoke, Heinz, *I Flew for the Führer: The Memoirs of a Luftwaffe Fighter Pilot* (Barnsley, UK: Greenhill Books, 2020)
Köhnke, Otto. Personnel records of members of the Reichswehr and Wehrmacht, Personnel File Number: LP/17208 (Bundesarchiv, Freiburg)
Körner, Walter. Personnel records of members of the Reichswehr and Wehrmacht, Personnel File Number: unknown (Bundesarchiv, Freiburg)
Krüchem, Heinrich-Mathias. Personnel records of members of the Reichswehr and Wehrmacht, Personnel File Number: unknown (Bundesarchiv, Freiburg)

Loscher, Hans-Ludwig. *Berlin Document Center* (BDC) Collection: Personal documents, Personal File Number: VBS 1/1070044793 (Berlin-Lichterfelde)

"London: The Baby Blitz and V-Weapons, 1941–1945," *Blitz Stories*, Historic England Archive and Library

Lupiano, V., *Operation Tidal Wave: The Bloodiest Air Battle in the History of War* (Guilford, CT: Lyons Press, 2020)

Marktscheffel, Fritz. *Berlin Document Center* (BDC) Collection: Personal documents, Personal File Number: VBS 1/1070078001 (Berlin-Lichterfelde)

Mahurin, Walker, *Hitler's Fall Guys* (Atglen, PA: Schiffer Military History, 1999)

Messerschmidt, Manfred, *The Wehrmacht in the Nazi state. Time of Indoctrination* (Hamburg, Germany: Deeker, 1969)

Miller, Michael D., and Andreas Schulz, *Gauleiter: The Regional Leaders of the Nazi Party and Their Deputies, 1925–1945*, Volume 3 (Stroud, UK: Fonthill Media, 2021)

"Missing Air Crew Report 13716," National Archives and Records Administration, Washington DC (2005)

"Missing Air Crew Report 13721," National Archives and Records Administration, Washington DC (2005)

"Missing Air Crew Report 13723," National Archives and Records Administration, Washington DC (2005)

"Missing Air Crew Report 13724," National Archives and Records Administration, Washington DC (2005)

"Missing Air Crew Report 13888," National Archives and Records Administration, Washington DC (2005)

"Missing Air Crew Report 13890," National Archives and Records Administration, Washington DC (2005)

"Missing Air Crew Report 13891," National Archives and Records Administration, Washington DC (2005)

"Missing Air Crew Report 13894," National Archives and Records Administration, Washington DC (2005)

"Mission Number 291, April 7, 1945," *390th Bomb Group* (Tucson, AZ: 390th Memorial Museum Foundation)

Mission 8AF 931 Narrative. *8th Air Force Operations Research Database.*

Molly, Klaus. Personnel records of members of the Reichswehr and Wehrmacht, Personnel File Number: H2/25425 (Bundesarchiv, Freiburg)

Morrison, William H., *Fortress Without a Roof: The Allied Bombing of the Third Reich* (New York, NY: St. Martin's Press, 1982)

Müller, Heinz. Personnel records of members of the Reichswehr and Wehrmacht, Personnel File Number: LP/22710 (Bundesarchiv, Freiburg)

Müller, Hugo. Personnel records of members of the Reichswehr and Wehrmacht, Personnel File Number: H2/10805 (Bundesarchiv, Freiburg)

Murray, Williamson, and Allan Millet, *A War To Be Won: Fighting the Second World War* (Cambridge, MA: Belknap Press, 2001)

Murray, Williamson, *Strategy for Defeat: The Luftwaffe 1933–1945* (Oxfordshire, UK: Routledge, 1983)

Nagel, Hans. Personnel records of members of the Reichswehr and Wehrmacht, Personnel File Number: LP/77830 (Bundesarchiv, Freiburg)

Roedel, G., interview by Colin Heaton (1984)

Obermaier, Ernest, *German Fighter Ace Werner Mölders: An Illustrated Biography* (Atglen, PA: Schiffer, 2006)

Ohler, Norman, *Blitzed: Drugs in the Third Reich* (Cologne, Germany: Kiepenheuer & Witsch GmbH, 2015)

Overy, Richard, *The Air War: 1939–45* (Lincoln, NE: Potomac Books, 2005)
Overy, Richard, *The Bombers and The Bombed: Allied Air War over Europe 1940–1945* (New York, NY: Viking Press, 2014)
Overy, Richard, *Why the Allies Won* (New York, NY: W. W. Norton & Company, Inc., 1996)
Pesch, Novel. Personnel records of members of the Reichswehr and Wehrmacht, Personnel File Number: LP/79461 (Bundesarchiv, Freiburg)
Price, Alfred, *The Last Year of the Luftwaffe: May 1944–May 1945* (London, UK: Arms & Armour, 1995)
Reitsch, Hanna, *Flying is My Life* (New York, NY: G. P. Putnam's Sons, 1954)
Rose, Arno, *Radical Air Combat: The History of German Rammers* (Stuttgart, Germany: Motor Book Publisher, 1979)
Rosner, Heinrich. *Berlin Document Center* (BDC) Collection: Personal documents, Personal File Number: VBS 271/5204012263 (Berlin-Lichterfelde)
Rummel, Ernst. Personnel records of members of the Reichswehr and Wehrmacht, Personnel File Number: LP/83045 (Bundesarchiv, Freiburg)
Ryan, Cornelius, *The Longest Day: The Classic Epic of D-Day* (New York, NY: Simon & Schuster, 1994)
Saft, Ulrich, *An Eclipse Without A Future: The Battles for North Germany 1945* (Winnipeg, Manitoba: J. J. Fedorowicz Publishing Inc., 2015)
Schultz, Joachim, *The last thirty days: From the war diary of the OKW April to May 1945 documents on contemporary history*, edited by Jürgen Thorwald (Stuttgart, Germany: Steingrüben, 1951)
Scholz, Georg. Personnel records of members of the Reichswehr and Wehrmacht, Personnel File Number: 49823 (Bundesarchiv, Freiburg)
Schmidt, Franz-Josef. Personnel records of members of the Reichswehr and Wehrmacht, Personnel File Number: NRW/169448 (Bundesarchiv, Freiburg)
Schrader, Karl-Heinz. Personnel records of members of the Reichswehr and Wehrmacht, Personnel File Number: LP/45466 (Bundesarchiv, Freiburg)
Schulz-Sembten, Dietrich. *Berlin Document Center* (BDC) Collection: Personal documents, Personal File Number: VBS 264/4001006346 (Berlin-Lichterfelde)
Seidel, Horst. *Berlin Document Center* (BDC) Collection: Personal documents, Personal File Number: VBS 283/6055007413 (Berlin-Lichterfelde)
Skorzeny, Otto, *Skorzeny's Secret Missions* (New York, NY: E. P. Dutton, 1950)
Sorge, Ernst. Personnel records of members of the Reichswehr and Wehrmacht, Personnel File Number: LP/83951 (Bundesarchiv, Freiburg)
Stilla, Ernst, *The Air Force in the battle for air supremacy: Major influences in the defeat of the Luftwaffe in the defensive battle in West Germany in the Second World War, with particular emphasis on the factors of air defense, research and development and human resources*, PhD thesis (Bonn: Rheinische Friedrichs-Wilhelms-Universität, 2005)
Tantum, W. H. IV, and E. J. Hoffschmidt, *The Rise and Fall of the German Air Force, 1933 to 1945* (Old Greenwich, CT: W. E. Publishing Company, 1969)
Taylor, Frederick, *Dresden: Tuesday, February 13, 1945* (New York, NY: HarperCollins Publishers, 2005)
Tetzel, Ernst. Personnel records of members of the Reichswehr and Wehrmacht, Personnel File Number: LP/33841 (Bundesarchiv, Freiburg)
"The Bomber Offensive from the United Kingdom," *Foreign Relations of the United States, 1941–1942, and Casablanca, 1943* (Washington, DC: Government Printing Office, 2010), Document 412
Thiel, Armin. *Berlin Document Center* (BDC) Collection: Personal documents, Personal File Number: VBS 284/6219011501 (Berlin-Lichterfelde)

Tillman, Barrett, "Hard Targets," *Air Force Magazine* (February 2015)
Toliver, Raymond F., and Trevor J. Constable, *Get Hartmann from Heaven!* (Stuttgart, Germany: Motorbuch Publisher, 1974)
Tooze, Adam, *The Wages of Destruction: The Making and Breaking of the Nazi Economy* (London, UK: Penguin Books, 2006)
Trevor-Roper, Hugh, *The Last Days of Hitler* (London, UK: Pan Macmillan, 2013)
Uhlich, Georg. *Berlin Document Center* (BDC) Collection: Personal documents, Personal File Number: VBS 1/1180020196 (Berlin-Lichterfelde)
Warlimont, W., *Inside Hitler's Headquarters, 1939–45*, trans. R. H. Barry (Novato, CA: Presidio Press, 1964)
Wienkötter, Manfred. *Berlin Document Center* (BDC) Collection: Personal documents, Personal File Number: VBS 284/6221002156 (Berlin-Lichterfelde)
Winter, Franz. Personnel records of members of the Reichswehr and Wehrmacht, Personnel File Number: unknown (Bundesarchiv, Freiburg)
Weal, John, *Jagdgeschwader 2: Richthofen* (Oxford, UK: Osprey Publishing, 2012)
Weal, John, *Luftwaffe Sturmgruppen* (Oxford, UK: Osprey Publishing, 2005)
Wentz, W. Budd, "Rammed Over Germany, One B-17 Pilot's Story," *487th Bomb Group*, https://wbuddwentz.com/lastmission/
Wesley, Frank C., *The Army Air Forces in World War II* (Washington, DC: Office of Air Force History, 1983)
Zapp, Jacob. Personnel records of members of the Reichswehr and Wehrmacht, Personnel File Number: unknown (Bundesarchiv, Freiburg)
Zell, Werner. Personnel records of members of the Reichswehr and Wehrmacht, Personnel File Number: unknown (Bundesarchiv, Freiburg)
Zens, Franz. Personnel records of members of the Reichswehr and Wehrmacht, Personnel File Number: LP/94502 (Bundesarchiv, Freiburg)